COLLEGE AND UNIVERSITY CURRICULUM

PAUL L. DRESSEL
Michigan State University

McCutchan Publishing Corporation
2526 Grove Street
Berkeley, California 94704

PREFACE

For many years I have been concerned with research and evaluation in higher education. Repeatedly, I have become involved in evaluation of programs—courses and curriculums—in which there was difficulty in agreeing upon relevant data and methodology and in which the results were ambiguous, inconsequential—and ignored. A program which is not well planned initially in relation to major educational goals is not worth the effort of evaluation.

It is difficult to get college and university faculty to focus on the curriculum in the sense discussed in this volume. In constructing a major edifice, detailed plans are made, and materials are selected and brought together in orderly fashion to achieve a well delineated result. In the university (and the college, too) the curriculum may be likened to sundry and assorted bricks, blocks, and stones. An uncoordinated professoriate and confused students pile these bricks, blocks, and stones in assorted patterns to construct the walls of an edifice which no one envisions clearly. No unified structure ever becomes apparent because between lack of mortar (although there are mortar boards) and lack of coordination (although there are deans) what is reared one year falls or is torn down the next. It is a tribute to the intellect and resiliency of youth that, in some fashion, they still acquire the rudiments of an education, but it is even more of a tribute to their insight that many of them are beginning to reject a pattern of education based on disciplines, vocations, and professorial convenience rather than on acceptance of the responsibility for the education of individuals.

There are signs in the many recent reports of innovations that a significant segment of faculty recognizes the delinquency of their kind and is ready to confront their responsibility. Yet, even the efforts of these conscientious individuals seem too frequently to attempt to achieve a new pattern by hanging a few worn strands of educational practice on a few weak pegs, thus constructing a ladder too fragile even to carry the burden of the eulogies lavished on the effort.

The curriculum is a result of gradual cumulative actions, and it involves so many and uncorrelated, if not conflicting, interests that it is not easily replaced. When there is a readiness to confront the higher education curriculum task *de novo,* there is very little available in the way of principles or of structure to provide guidance. And thus, even in new institutions, the curriculum may be but dimly revealed by courses and gimmicks rather than seen clearly as a path by which students move from what they are to what they should become to be recognized as graduates.

In an age of increasing specialization and technology in which the virus of research and graduate education has infected nearly every college and faculty member, the production of such a volume as this may only be, in the vulgar phrase, "spitting in the wind." Yet it could be that those who too readily move with the wind may pause at the sight of such obstinancy and reflect that fleeing before the wind is good only if it blows whither one wishes to go. And if one lacks the courage to head into the wind, he can take another tack. Perhaps this volume will help him to do so.

In writing this volume, I have drawn heavily on experiences and conversations with many persons in many colleges. I have freely used ideas from the writings of others, most often in paraphrase, for I abhor long quotations. Even so, acknowledgements appear in some form so that the sensitive reader should recognize them. In fact, I make no claim for any originality of idea, and I detect little of originality in curriculum writings generally. Like the well considered curriculum, this volume, if it possesses any originality, attains this by its useful organization of ideas rather than from the ideas themselves.

The efforts of one individual require explicit acknowledgement. Miss Ruth Frye, my secretary and co-worker, has been invaluable, as always, in preparation of bibliography and in overseeing the several typings and proofings needed to bring the manuscript to publication.

Paul L. Dressel

CONTENTS

INTRODUCTION

Most colleges and universities offer an impressive but bewildering variety of courses. In 1965 eight major universities listed from 2,469 to 5,975 courses. Undergraduate courses alone ranged from 1,757 to 3,111. Total undergraduate semester credit hours numbered from 4,779 to 9,333. Of course, these are large universities with enrollments of 25,000 to 40,000 and a great variety of programs. The offerings are as impressive in content as in number. Such titles as Quantitative Endocrinology, Stochastic Processes and Technological Applications, and Macromolecules and Surface Chemistry are awesome. But are university credit courses in carpentry, welding, wiring, food preservation, bowling, paddle ball, and social dancing also valid?

The universities, particularly public institutions, enthusiastically accept the challenge to provide instruction in every field. The liberal arts colleges, while covering fewer fields, offer an even greater variety of courses. McGrath's 1958–59 data on fourteen liberal arts colleges showed credit hours ranging from 773.5 to 1,387 in colleges with enrollments of 620 to 1,591.* The ratio of credit hours to enrollment varied from .71 to 1.80. One college I visited had more courses than students.

On the departmental level, undergraduate courses in English in the eight universities ranged from 52 to 133 courses and from 121 to 386 semester credit hours. Literature is offered by author, period, literary form (drama, novel, poetry), type (romantic, realistic, naturalistic), and national origin (English, American, Canadian). Courses in linguistics and various forms of writing also appear. The situation is similar in other departments and, despite the efforts of administrators, courses multiply each year. The faculty member who stated that curriculum expansion is essential because able faculty members can be hired only if

---

*Earl J. McGrath, *Memo to a College Faculty Member,* Bureau of Publications, Teachers College, Columbia University, New York, 1961.

they are permitted to teach courses in their special interests was at least honest. The usual plea that students demand the new course or must have it for graduate school savors of duplicity.

Such a variety of courses makes it difficult for undergraduates to achieve any sense of unity and coherence in their programs. Even in institutions which have emphasized planning, one frequently finds an over-reliance on traditional practices, such as majors and distribution requirements, or on "gimmicks" (usually inaccurately labeled as innovations), such as independent study, service projects, study abroad, elimination of grades, seminars, and larger course blocks. These programs have educational possibilities but they are often so completely unrelated to the student's overall experience that they confuse rather than edify.

Unfortunately, most of the extensive writing about curriculum is irrelevant to the college level. Much of the literature is either unconstructive criticism or unfounded enthusiasm. Few writers objectively present the problems of curriculum development and suggest solutions to those problems.

This volume is directed toward faculty members and administrators concerned with curriculum review and development and toward students interested in higher education curriculum problems. It is not a philosophical analysis, such as Philip Phenix's *Realms of Meaning*. It is not limited to liberal education, nor does it propose a definite solution for a particular type of institution, such as Daniel Bell's *The Reforming of General Education*. It is not a review of programs, actual or planned, such as Samuel Baskin's *Higher Education: Some Newer Developments*. These volumes, excellent as they are, do not speak meaningfully to the average faculty member.

Phenix's volume relies too heavily on an esoteric classification of knowledge. It solves few problems, and to apply it would require a revolution in faculty thinking. Bell is provincial in an elitist sort of way, and ignores the large publicly-supported universities. Baskin's volume excellently presents a wide variety of ideas, but tends to glorify the means of education without relating them to its ends.

Too much writing about higher education has been either a catalog of what is being done where, or a glorification of some particular institutional program. In this volume I have not identified particular institutions, although I recognize that this may be an irritation to some and a major omission to others. My reasons for so doing are:

(1) Any statement of institutional practices ought to be cleared with the institution to assure an accurate reflection of what is

being done. Such clearance is tedious and often requires an expanded statement to satisfy insitutional ego.

(2) Practices are subject to change so that any catalog of institutional practices is soon outdated.

(3) The prestige of an institution or the number of institutions
using a given practice is irrelevant to an appraisal of the worth
of that practice.

(4) The emphasis in this volume is on a total program rather than
on individual practices.

This volume is also limited in its use of quotations and of specific
recognition of the writings of others. There is little that is new in curriculum, and even less that is documented by research. I have drawn
widely on the writing of many persons, and have tried to indicate this
by the chapter bibliographies. Where an idea, conception, or forceful
phraseology of another person has been consciously used, I have assigned credit for it. Otherwise, I have felt that the ideas should be
examined on their own merit.

To achieve a coherent undergraduate program, the faculty must
understand, accept, and interpret it to the students. Daily learning
must relate to the full curriculum. Yet colleges and universities are de-
partmentalized, and faculties are specialists. The content-based, highly-
organized sequences of the sciences are irrelevant to the social sciences
and the humanities. The concern of the latter with values, eternal
verities, and centrality of the humanities in a liberal education fails to
impress the science faculty. Unless the entire faculty of an institution
is concerned with the nature and quality of the total program of undergraduate education, no solution will emerge which is more than a
patchwork of compromises, a reluctant agreement by diverse and competing interests to experiment with new ideas as long as they involve
minimal interference with vested interests.

Some faculties have risen above their individual and departmental
concerns to develop well-conceived programs. To do so, many hours of
discussion and self-education are necessary, but the lack of adequate and
relevant material has hampered this education. This volume grows out
of consultation with such groups. It attempts to confront the problems
of curriculum in a language readily understood by faculty members
who are not adept in educational, psychological, or philosophical jar-
gon and who are concerned with arriving at practical solutions rather
than idealizing about what the curriculum *ought* to be in the best of all
possible worlds. This volume attempts to provide a structure for the
study of curriculum, and a pattern for the solution of problems. Per-

haps the curriculum itself should be a series of experiences which develop competency in identifying problems and searching for answers rather than providing them. Obviously this implies as much about instruction as it does about curriculum. This is why the development of an abstract curriculum without the active involvement and consensus of the faculty is foredoomed.

Effective and even inspired instruction in isolated courses does not constitute good education. A faculty member must see his role as one of a team composed of an entire faculty dedicated to developing a series of interrelated and coherent educational experiences which stimulate and assist the student to become a self-educating individual. Unfortunately, little in the formal training of the faculty fosters this conception. Indeed, much in the graduate school experience implies that the faculty member has no responsibility beyond effective presentation of his own courses. Nevertheless, there are many faculty members who accept some responsibility for the total education of students, but are so bewildered by their own deficiencies and by the limitations of departmental organizations that they cannot take constructive action. If this volume is in some manner helpful to such persons, it will have fulfilled its purpose.

1

Issues and Problems

Because of the wide variety of institutions of higher education in the United States, it is difficult to make many statements about curriculum which are universally true. The curriculum often appears to be one of the most stable features of an institution. Some courses have existed unchanged for years; some continue to be listed in the catalog although not offered for years. Yet, almost every institution in the country has either added new courses or changed existing courses in the last ten years. The dissatisfaction of those interested in curriculum re-examination and reform is not that there is no change but that the change too often is merely the addition of new courses or the repackaging of old materials. In the absence of a larger vision, the factors which influence the faculty to recommend changes are likely to be self-interest, advances in the field, or redefinitions of specialties. Faculties often resist curriculum examination and change, although many institutions, as a result of intensive faculty effort, have made major changes in the program.

Although faculty members resist change, the history of American higher education reveals that social and economic pressures have had major impact over the years. The early Colonial colleges offered only the classical curriculum: grammar, rhetoric, logic, arithmetic, geometry, and astronomy. Faculty members were expected to master all subjects taught, and a class might complete its full four years under the same teacher. Harvard College did not introduce specialized teaching until 130 years after its founding. Specialization was necessary because the curriculum was already changing. Philosophy had been divided into such fields as history, government, commerce, and natural science, and modern foreign languages and mathematics were becoming more important. The teacher ceased to be a master of all fields, although the students were still expected to cover the entire curriculum.

These changes demonstrated that higher education would respond to social and economic needs. In the nineteenth century, in spite of the

1

temporarily restraining effect of the Yale Report of 1829, which emphasized the sanctity of the classical curriculum and decried all modern or optional offerings, major curriculum changes occurred. The state universities, land-grant colleges, and graduate schools came into being largely because existing institutions refused to alter their programs to meet these pressures. Butts categorizes the major developments in higher education during the nineteenth century:

1. A *broad elective* curriculum replaced a narrow prescribed curriculum.
2. *Modern subjects*—languages, sciences, social sciences—were included in liberal arts.
3. *Motor and manual skills* were introduced.
4. The *university* began to replace the college, and the lecture and the laboratory began to replace the recitation.
5. *Specialization* for the professions began to encroach upon the cultural subjects of the undergraduate curriculum.
6. *Individually designed programs* of study began to replace the required disciplines of the classical curriculum.
7. *Provision for individual differences* among students eliminated the practice of expecting the same courses and the same performance of all students.
8. *Secular preparation* for citizenship and for occupation began to replace religious preparation.
9. *Greater freedom* for students in universities led to the relaxing of the rigid controls that had characterized the colleges.
10. *All classes of society* began to aspire to higher education, forcing a revision of its aristocratic purposes (10, p. 203).

Most of these changes have continued into the twentieth century. At the same time, new forces and pressures are bringing about major changes in contemporary institutions of higher education, changes welcomed by some and deplored by others. This chapter examines some of the major factors currently influencing higher education and defines some of the issues and problems which arise from these pressures.

SOCIAL AND ECONOMIC PRESSURES

International Developments. The international opposition of two competing and seemingly incompatible ideologies and the improvement in communication and travel have caused colleges and universities to concern themselves with international, as well as local and national affairs. The expansion of studies dealing with Asia, Africa, and the Soviet Union, the increasing number of students from these areas on the campus, and the establishment of overseas campuses all reflect this new preoccupation. Faculty members are involved in travel, research, and consultation in all parts of the globe. Language instruction is more significant to many students and vocational possibilities are seen in international rather than purely national or local terms. The Committee on University and World affairs has recommended that all American institutions of higher learning make the study of world affairs an important and permanent dimension of their undergraduate programs (48, p. 4).

Struggle for Equality. In our own country, the struggle for economic, social and political equality has excited the sympathies of students and faculties. Institutions of higher education have been forced to re-examine their admission, recruitment, and hiring policies. Except for a few institutions in the Deep South, every university and college has wished to demonstrate its non-discriminatory practices by accepting some Negro students and professors. The government has provided resources to make education more readily available to those who have been denied the privilege or have been antagonized by educational experiences. As a result, colleges and universities have set up special educational opportunities and programs for minority groups. These programs reveal that the assumptions, values, and instructional methodology upon which higher education has been based are not always compatible with the way students from less privileged backgrounds are accustomed to think and learn.

Technology and Specialization. Technology has disorganized man's thinking, values, and patterns of living. The complexity of technology tends to make the individual insignificant and insecure. It narrows his range of decisions and actions, even though it offers him material benefits. Technology leads to increased specialization and to new job possibilities, but, at the same time, it often completely changes or eliminates existing jobs. Even in the college classroom, technological developments promise an improved education for the student but also constitute a threat to the professor who must master new developments or fall hopelessly behind in his field.

Because improved diet, sanitation, medical treatment, and economic productivity permit the support of large families, the population of the United States and of the world increases rapidly. But, at the same time, this technology pollutes the air and water and threatens depletion of natural resources. And always lurking in the background is the concern that the concentrations of energy made possible by fission and fusion may be unleashed to yield complete destruction.

Increasing Demand for Higher Education. Current studies predict that in a few years, half of the high school graduates will seek further schooling. In addition, the number of adults returning to college is growing. Many of these people demand a practical education which does not rely on texts and lectures.

Rising Educational Costs and Demands for Efficiency. Although most citizens in this country value higher education, not all of them are willing to bear the cost. Universities and colleges are accused of inefficiency in curriculum, staffing, and use of space. Since faculties and administrators appear unwilling or unable to answer these criticisms, central coordinating agencies are often given the authority particularly in publicly supported institutions, to approve or veto all new programs and budgetary increases. In the extreme, such control practically determines curriculum and instructional organization. However, even with restricted budgets, institutions introduce new curricula and higher levels of education unless specifically forbidden.

Federal Support of Higher Education. Extensive Federal support of higher education is a recent development resulting from the growth in enrollments and costs. Inevitably, government support of both private and public institutions will continue to increase until this distinction, already obscure in many instances, will be of little significance. Federally supported contract research has already affected the large universities. Each of the numerous Federal agencies tends to regard only its own interests and to view the university as a means to accomplish its particular mission rather than as an institution essential to the general welfare of the nation. Also, government concentration on scientific research and on graduate programs often diverts faculty attention from undergraduate curriculum and instruction.

Federal grants for special programs in foreign languages, counseling, and science have caused some institutions to expand their curriculum in ways which are inappropriate to their character. Because Federal support is earmarked for particular purposes and because negotiations are usually between individual Federal agencies and individual institutions, little consideration is given to total higher education requirements.

INCREASING KNOWLEDGE

The rapid expansion in knowledge is documented by the increasing number of books, articles, and new disciplines, and by the many new university courses, curricula, departments, and degrees. Interdisciplinary institutes and centers of research and service also tend to formulate courses, curricula, and ultimately graduate or professional specialities. Nuclear research, space exploration, and computer development all give rise to new specialities, which may be subdivisions of existing fields or amalgamations of several previously distinct fields. The National Register of Scientific and Technical Personnel lists nearly 1,000 distinct specializations in the natural sciences. Twenty years ago, the number was approximately 50. Physics presently is divided into over 80 specialties, and the life sciences into approximately 200. Biochemistry and biophysics, new fields only a few years ago, are now departments in many universities and each already has nearly a score of subspecialties.

The problem of data processing and evaluation has let to many new fields, most of which require the use of a computer. These fields, all of which draw heavily on mathematics and statistics, include operations research, linear programing, game theory, and systems analysis. The effect of these new fields on traditional disciplines and on university operation has not been fully assessed.

Non-Western Studies. Interest in non-western studies has increased the range of knowledge considered relevant to the curriculum. A profusion of new courses in non-western culture, and the expansion of comparative courses in art, literature, philosophy, religion are the initial results. Gradually, some courses are being developed from a world rather than a western point of view.

Structure of the Disciplines. The multiplication of disciplines and the amount of material covered in each field pose serious problems of organization and classification. The number and relationship of disciplines constitute one problem; their substance and structure present another. Disciplines differ in subject matter (object of investigation), in patterns of investigation or inquiry (mode of investigation), in purposes (types of outcomes desired), and in prerequisites (training of investigators). Since the content and the organization of disciplines are continually changing, one must understand the structure of the disciplines to master the results of investigations. Otherwise, one fails to anticipate or grasp new developments.

Changing Conceptions of Learning. The existence of recognized disciplines suggests that learning experiences should be compartmentalized and pursued in diverse ways, each of which corresponds to the logic of the particular discipline. However, the logic or the structure of a discipline may not correspond to the way in which the discipline was developed or to the way in which it should be learned. Learning is worthwhile only if it can be put to use, transferred to a situation different from the original one. Transfer depends not only on *what* a person learns but also on *how* he learns it. Effective learning results not from memorization and drill, but from mastery of broad concepts and principles and from experiences which encourage adaptation, generalization, and application. The phrase, *learning how to learn,* is still an apt description of an effective approach to education.

CHANGES IN STUDENTS

Preparation. Contemporary college students are quite different from those of a few years ago. More students demand an education relevant not only to their future ambitions but also to their current concerns. The college preparation of many students has deviated from established norms in both content and approach. Even though a student may be able, his lack of preparation and atypical pattern of motivation may require individual attention at the very time when increasing numbers threaten to mechanize much of education.

Students in Action. Disturbed by the chaos of the national and international situation and by the inability or unwillingness of leaders, particularly professors and administrators, to take action to relieve injustice and resolve tensions, small groups of activist students threaten to take matters into their own hands. Many students also reject the paternalistic policies of institutions which, though justified as essential to student health, safety, and morality, often are enforced solely to avoid parental and public criticism. Regarding professors and administrators as irresponsible and not altogether frank, such students do not hesitate to complain and act against further attempts to curb their freedom. Generally student activism has a beneficial effect, for it demonstrates to the faculty and administration that students will think for themselves when properly stimulated. What is disconcerting is that the behavior of these activist students does not appear to have been affected by their educational experiences. They are irrational, irresponsible, and unrealistic.

Student Movement. Ours is a mobile population. Families and individuals move about the country for new jobs; they travel extensively for recreation and for family reunion; and they travel to other countries on other continents. Thus, it is not surprising that many students think nothing of traveling across the country to college or of using portions of their college years to travel and study elsewhere within or outside the country. Such travel, coupled with variations in college costs and offerings, and marriages between students attending different institutions, encourages undergraduates to transfer from one college to another. Furthermore, colleges themselves encourage discontinuities in campus living for service activities or study elsewhere in this country or abroad.

Over half the college students in the United States live at home and commute. Although some of the large urban universities and community colleges have a core of resident students, many consist almost entirely of commuters. As Peter Drucker has suggested, the trend toward urban living, the cost of room and board on campus, and the improvements in transportation may eliminate resident campuses in another generation (26, p. 88). In recent years, Columbia College has reported that half its graduates are residents of New York City and Johns Hopkins reports that three-quarters of its freshmen are from Baltimore.

Many commuter students could not or would not attend college otherwise. Many view higher education as a means to prepare for a vocation, to kill time or to avoid the draft, rather than as an end in itself. They often retain high school attitudes and practices and fail to assume personal responsibility because their environment remains static. To be sure, cultural and educational opportunities are available, but many commuter students have full-time or part-time jobs, and many are married with family responsibilities. Such students are only partially involved with college, and their education consists primarily of class attendance and credit accumulation. Yet many colleges are urging or requiring the resident student to give up the campus for an experience remarkably similar to that of the commuter student.

Graduate Education. Just as a larger percentage of high school graduates are seeking higher education, a larger percentage of college graduates are entering graduate and professional schools. Business, industry, and government often demand advanced degrees. In many states, teachers are required to take post-baccalaureate study. In the sciences, expanded research grants both require and support graduate students. In addition, the rapid growth of colleges and universities provides employment opportunities for graduate degree recipients. In many universities, the number of professional students equals or exceeds that of undergraduates. Faculty interests and activities correspond more closely to those of graduate students than to those of undergraduates. Inevitably, then, resources originally assigned for undergraduate education are diverted to graduate study. The university undergraduate may justifiably feel neglected, although research and productive scholars generate the excitement of the university.

Scholarship Programs. Presumably, the purpose of scholarship programs is to enable students to attend college who otherwise could not afford to do so. Actually, scholarships awarded on the basis of need are dependent on information submitted by the family, which is not beyond suspicion. In many cases, scholarship recipients only attend more expensive institutions farther away from home. Competition for able students continues, and many scholarships are used primarily for recruiting.

Some forms of scholarship awards indirectly subsidize private institutions and enable them to raise their fees. Perhaps the most important achievement of scholarship programs has been to suggest that scholarship is at least as important as athletic prowess. Indirectly, scholarship grants have generated interest in honors programs in colleges and in secondary schools. For the able student, too much of secondary school and college work has been repetitive and boring, and has failed to provide cumulative and sequential learning experiences. The honors programs tend to utilize a wider range of media, and to emphasize inductive teaching and specialized modes of inquiry.

CHANGES IN FACULTY ORIENTATION

Status. College and university faculty are not venerated in the United States as they are in many European countries. Colleges are more numerous, college attendance is commonplace and curricula include many purely vocational courses. Nevertheless, the professor's ego has been well nourished in recent years. Salaries have increased and, since the days of Roosevelt's "Brain Trust," professors have been in demand as consultants and government officials. Government, industry, and universities compete for the privilege of employing the competent researcher. A professor can usually find opportunities for travel, consultation, or research support. Naturally, then, he expects to define his own role in the institution and to participate in the administration of the institution. He demands academic freedom and salary, promotion, and tenure policies which are generous and explicit. As the student rejects the *in loco parentis* conception of college control, so the faculty rejects the paternalistic dean or president, however reasonable and generous he may be.

The faculty member who has not made a permanent commitment to teaching tends to be totally involved in his discipline, his professional societies, and his department. Since many undergraduates lack enthusiasm for his discipline, he gives little attention to undergraduate instruction.

Professors do face serious problems as a result of technological development and the rapid increase in knowledge. The conscientious professor must devote much of his time to keeping up with new developments in his field. To understand new research in many fields requires familiarity with quantitative research methodology and with the computer. The scholar must be concerned with more than classroom instruction and cannot teach 15 or 16 hours per week which once was the norm and still is accepted in some institutions.

CHANGES IN CHARACTER OF INSTITUTIONS

Size, Number, and Type. The pattern of multiple campuses operating as a single institution confuses discussions of size, for institutional
size to most persons, still connotes enrollment on a single campus. Even
the latter figure is questionable when applied indiscriminately to both
institutions with a large part-time student enrollment and institutions
with primarily a full-time enrollment. Despite such problems, it is clear
that institutions have grown and are still growing. In 1950, there were 9
institutions with fall enrollments of over 20,000, and 37 with over 10,000
(17). In 1965, the corresponding figures were 39 and 135 (34). The number of institutions has also increased in 1950, 1,888 and in 1965, 2,238.
Some of this increase is due to the community college movement, but
there are also new technical institutes, four-year colleges, and universities. The latter are largely state supported, and many ultimately will
enroll 20,000 or more students. In the next twenty years, the proportion
of students enrolled in publicly supported institutions will rise from the
present two-thirds to four-fifths or more. The percentage of students who
commute to college will also rise. Evidently, undergraduate liberal education as a four-year experience on a small college campus will soon be
replaced by an experience analogous to secondary school attendance.
Thus, it is essential that college curricula and instructional practices
be truly *higher* education.

Governance. The demands of students and of faculty for a role in
governance have already been noted. Governing boards concerned with
rapidly increasing budgets, public criticism of the university and indications of unrest among students and faculty are taking a more active role
in governance than in the past. Super-boards, state budget agencies, and
legislatures, equally concerned with costs and program expansion demand more detailed information and make decisions which interfere
with or destroy institutional autonomy. Cooperation among private
institutions is effective only if individual institutions willingly give up a
degree of local autonomy. All these pressures severely curtail the administrator's area of action. He must spend much of his time explaining,
pleading, discussing, and arbitrating. The policy-making dean or president is rapidly being replaced by administrators who must manipulate
people and events to reach sensible and acceptable conclusions.

Finance, Facilities, and Efficiency. As operating costs increase, all
institutions intensify their fund raising efforts. State universities report
that less than half their income comes from the state. Gifts from individuals, foundations, business, and industry, student fees, and federal support account for the rest. Private institutions profit indirectly from

state scholarships, and a few have direct state support for portions of their programs. Private institutions compete with public ones for facilities grants and loans, research and service grants and contracts, and grants for instructional and research equipment. The cost of certain equipment (computers, cyclotrons, and information disseminating and retrieval systems) is such that private and public institutions will have to cooperate. Though public funds do not change private institutions, the struggle to obtain them does. Likewise, the securing of significant sums from private sources changes public institutions. Hence, the distinctions in purpose, character, and quality between private and public education may become relatively insignificant. The overt and often bitter competition of the past may be replaced by cooperation and supplementation in seeking faculty, students, new educational programs, and research projects.

Conceptions and Functions of Education. Institutions of higher education exist to preserve, organize, transmit, and to augment, the cultural heritage. Although emphases may differ, most universities and colleges accept these fundamental purposes. The technical institute, community college, and liberal arts college certainly do not try as hard as the university to augment the cultural heritage. However, institutions should have more specific purposes. Graduate professional programs for example, have highly specific goals which differ from both those of the liberal arts college and those of the arts and science graduate school.

A pseudo-hierarchy of excellence exists in higher education. The best institutions in this hierarchy are those which (a) obtain most of their support from private rather than public sources; (b) have large endowments; (c) charge high tuition; (d) pay high salaries; (e) offer primarily a liberal education at the undergraduate level; (f) have graduate schools; (g) have some graduate professional schools, particularly law and medicine. However, true excellence results from meeting educational goals essential in our society. In the United States, most people expect that every young person will have an opportunity for the education which will most fully develop his potential. The education which most effectively accomplishes this, whether it is based on intellectual abilities and books or on physical skills and machines, is excellent. A major difficulty has been that few institutions are content to be what they are. The technical institute aspires to community college, the community college to the four-year college, and four-year college to the university status. The university in turn, tries to add a full roster of graduate professional programs and to rank among the first ten universities in its graduate and research programs. This pattern is not in the national interest because it denigrates certain kinds of education and applauds mediocrity in others.

This hierarchical pattern is based largely on a parallel pattern of vocational hierarchy, with professional positions at the top and unskilled manual labor at the bottom. However, institutions do accept goals which are not purely vocational. Education for civic responsibility is such a goal, although many institutions reject this responsibility on the grounds that intellectual skill and independent judgment are the most important qualities of a citizen in a democratic society. Character development is another goal which college presidents frequently cite but which faculties largely ignore. The only values for which higher education takes full responsibility are those which relate directly to the worth, attainment, and application of knowledge.

Specialization and Vocation.   Catalogs of colleges and universities usually present many pages of courses grouped under departmental headings. In addition, they present many pages showing various groups of courses which will prepare a student for a given field. If students and their parents are not already convinced that a specific vocational choice is essential for college success, the catalog will do so. It is not even enough to know that one wants to be a teacher, engineer, veterinarian, home economist, nurse, dentist, librarian, minister, physician, journalist, lawyer, artist, musician, laboratory technician, or occupational therapist; in many institutions, he must know whether his prospective major in mathematics is leading to graduate school, secondary school teaching, computer science, or to applications in business, physical science, or social science. Statistics is often a separate major from mathematics and, in some universities, is a distinctive major in as many as a half dozen different departments.

Many pressures, aid or force this proliferation of courses and curricula. The faculty member who establishes a new course or curriculum or a different organization of existing courses is regarded as an innovator and accorded respect and responsibility. Admissions personnel like to find in the catalog a course corresponding to every interest of a prospective student. Presidents take pride in recounting their range of offerings and especially the unique ones (for example, Sanskrit). Business, industry, and vocational or professional organizations also like to find college programs in their specialty, particularly when this becomes a means of attaining recognition, respectability, or professional status.

Impact on Curriculum.   The preceding review has briefly indicated the impact on curriculum of the various pressures, issues, and problems in higher education. Subsequent chapters will explore this in greater detail. Such pressures often cause institutions to make decisions and add programs on the basis of expediency rather than sound judgment. Administrative officers who are able to grasp the total curriculum and to evaluate it in relation to the individual student and to pervasive educational goals are often unwilling to face the unpopularity of a ruthless review of curriculum and curriculum development practices. In effect, central administration has lost control over curriculum. Thus, the curriculum is dominated by departments and by graduate and professional schools. The result is profusion, confusion, and waste. The ensuing pressure on the student to choose a vocation early threatens to destroy liberal and general education.

These developments might be acceptable if they were a result of deliberation rather than circumstance. However, current education of the undergraduate demonstrates a failure to confront issues. Curriculum improvement requires wrestling with and providing at least an institutional answer to such crucial issues as : (a) What students shall we educate? (b) To what ends shall they be educated? (c) What shall constitute the materials and means of instruction? (d) How much diversity in program and goals shall be encouraged and permitted? (e) How can the quality of higher education be evaluated and improved? (f) How is higher education to be financed?

REFERENCES

1. Academic Senate, *Education at Berkeley,* University of California Press, 1966.
2. Herman R. Allen, *Open Door to Learning,* University of Illinois Press, 1963.
3. George Z. F. Bereday and Joseph A. Lauwerys, eds. *The Education Explosion,* Harcourt, Brace and World, New York, 1965.
4. Clyde E. Blocker, *The Two Year College,* Prentice Hall, Inc., Englewood Cliffs, N. J., 1965.
5. Theodore Brameld, *Education for the Emerging Age,* Holt, Rinehart and Winston, Inc., New York, 1965.
6. Theodore Brameld and Stanley Elam, eds., *Values in American Education,* Phi Delta Kappa, Bloomington, Ind., 1964.
7. Hugh S. Brown and Lewis B. Mayhew, *American Higher Education,* The Center for Applied Research in Education, Inc., Washington, D. C., 1965.
8. John S. Brubacher, *Bases for Policy in Higher Education,* McGraw-Hill Book Company, Inc., New York, 1965.
9. John S. Brubacher and Willis Rudy, *Higher Education in Transition: An American History, 1636–1956,* Harper and Brothers, New York, 1958.
10. R. Freeman Butts, *The College Charts Its Course,* McGraw-Hill Book Company, Inc., New York, 1939.

11. Oliver C. Carmichael, *Universities: Commonwealth and American,* Harper and Brothers, New York, 1959.
12. Margaret Clapp, ed., *The Modern University,* Cornell University Press, 1950.
13. Burton R. Clark, *Educating the Expert Society,* Chandler Publishing Co., San Francisco, 1962.
14. _____, *The Open Door College,* McGraw-Hill Book Company, Inc., 1960.
15. Lawrence E. Dennis and Joseph F. Kauffman, eds., *The College and the Student,* American Council on Education, Washington, D. C., 1966.
16. William C. DeVane, *The American University in the Twentieth Century,* Louisiana State University Press, 1957.
17. *Fall Enrollment in Higher Education Institutions,* Office of Education, C-281, Federal Security Agency, Washington, D. C., 1950.
18. Charles Frankel, *Issues in University Education,* Harper and Brothers, New York, 1959.
19. John W. Gardner, *Self-Renewal,* Harper and Row, Publishers, New York, 1964.
20. *General Education in a Free Society,* Report of the Harvard Committee, Harvard University Press, 1945.
21. *Goals for Americans,* The Report of the President's Commission on National Goals, The American Assembly, Columbia University, 1960.
22. Seymour E. Harris, et al, eds., *Challenge and Change in American Education,* McCutchan Publishing Corporation, Berkeley, 1965.
23. Seymour E. Harris, ed., *Education and Public Policy,* McCutchan Publishing Corporation, Berkeley, 1965.
24. Everett H. Hopkins, ed., "Innovation in Higher Education: Developments, Research, and Priorities," *New Dimensions in Higher Education* No. 19, Office of Education, U. S. Department of Health, Education, and Welfare, April, 1967.
25. Kenneth Keniston, *The Uncommitted: Alienated Youth in American Society,* Harcourt, Brace and World, Inc., New York, 1965.
26. J. Martin Klotsche, *The Urban University: And the Future of Our Cities,* Harper and Row, Publishers, New York, 1966.
27. Fritz Machlup, *The Production and Distribution of Knowledge in the United States,* Princeton University Press, 1962.
28. David Mallery, *Ferment on the Campus,* Harper and Row, Publishers, New York, 1966.
29. Leland L. Medsker, *The Junior College,* McGraw-Hill Book Company, Inc., New York, 1960.
30. L. Richard Meeth, ed., *Selected Issues in Higher Education,* Teachers College Press, Columbia University, 1965.
31. Matthew B. Miles, ed., *Innovation in Education,* Teachers College Press, Columbia University, 1964.
32. W. R. Niblett, *The Expanding University,* Faber and Faber, London, 1962.

33. John K. Norton, *Critical Issues in American Public Education,* University of Pittsburgh Press, 1965.

34. *Opening (Fall) Enrollment in Higher Education, 1965,* Office of Education, C-796, OE-54003-65, U. S. Department of Health, Education, and Welfare, Washington, D. C., 1965.

35. Manning Pattillo, Jr. and Donald Mackenzie, *Church-Supported Higher Education in the United States,* American Council on Education, Washington, D. C., 1966.

36. James A. Perkins, *The University in Transition,* Princeton University Press, 1966.

37. F. B. Pinion, *Educational Values in an Age of Technology,* Pergamon Press, Inc., New York, 1964.

38. Murray G. Ross, *New Universities in the Modern World,* St. Martin's Press, New York, 1966.

39. James E. Russell, *Change and Challenge in American Education,* Houghton Mifflin Company, Boston, 1965.

40. Nevitt Sanford, ed., *The American College: A Psychological and Social Interpretation of the Higher Learning,* John Wiley and Sons, Inc., New York, 1962.

41. L. F. Snow, *The College Curriculum in the United States,* Teachers College Press, Columbia University, 1907.

42. W. Hugh Stickler and Milton W. Carothers, "The Year-Round Calender in Operation: Status, Trends, Problems," *SREB Research Monograph* No. 7, Southern Regional Education Board, Atlanta, Ga., 1963.

43. Francis Sweeney, S. J., ed., *The Knowledge Explosion,* Farrar, Straus and Giroux, Inc., New York, 1966.

44. Russell Thomas, *The Search for a Common Learning,* McGraw-Hill Book Company, Inc., 1962.

45. James W. Thornton, Jr., *The Community Junior College,* Second Edition, John Wiley and Sons, Inc., New York, 1966.

46. Elton Trueblood, *The Idea of a College,* Harper and Brothers, New York, 1959.

47. Robert Ulich, *The Education of Nations,* Harvard University Press, 1961.

48. *The University and World Affairs,* Report of the Committee on University and World Affairs, The Ford Foundation, New York, 1960.

49. *The University Calendar,* Committee on the University Calendar, American Association of Collegiate Registrars and Admissions Officers, American Council on Education, Washington, D. C., 1961.

50. Edward W. Weidner, *The World Role of Universities,* McGraw-Hill Book Company, Inc., New York, 1962.

51. S. P. Wiggins, *The Desegregation Era in Higher Education,* McCutchan Publishing Corporation Berkeley, 1966.

52. E. G. Williamson and John Cowan, *The American Student's Freedom of Expression,* University of Minnesota Press, 1966.

2

Basic Considerations in Curriculum Development

Discussions of curriculum too often are preoccupied with means rather than ends, with details rather than structure, and with courses rather than learning. Although many hours may be spent developing a statement of objectives, the statement hardly provides practical guidance for curriculum planning. Faculty members usually recognize that the college exists to educate students. Driven by the administration to restudy curriculum, they feel obligated to state (or restate) objectives. Bewildered, disturbed, and exhausted by the time and energy expended in reaching an agreement, the faculty finally issues a statement of pious hopes and exhortations rather than a program of curriculum review. The statement contains some reference to each of the disciplines to please the various segments of the faculty, some expression of concern for citizenship and social participation to satisfy the personnel staff and some allusion to religion or values to satisfy the president, trustees, and parents. The objectives are so inclusive, vague, and inconsistent that they satisfy no one, and no one expects they will be met. Moreover, faculty members think primarily in terms of their own courses, and most of the objectives do not define the conduct of a single course.

There are many ways to approach curriculum development. Three distinctive approaches will be developed here. The first is especially adapted to college and university problems. The second, which involves considerations of educational philosophy, is instructive but unsuitable to pluralistic institutions. The third defines objectives, selects and organizes appropriate educational experiences, then evaluates their effectiveness. This third pattern is commendable, but it does not describe what goes on in actual curriculum development.

15

A STRUCTURE FOR CURRICULUM ANALYSIS (APPROACH NO. 1)

The preceding remarks are perhaps superfluous because the circumstances depicted are so common. However, this fact raises several significant questions. First, is it wise to initiate curriculum study by looking at objectives? This step seems essential and logical, but is often unproductive. Second, what is meant by curriculum? If the college curriculum is no more than structured courses in the accepted disciplines, then curriculum reform can be little more than a reshuffling of courses and requirements. In this view, the faculty is concerned only with the student's knowledge and mastery of his field of concentration. If, in contrast, curriculum is the total college experience, then curriculum reform involves the collective planning of a coherent, cumulative program. Colleges can provide very different patterns of educational experience. Although these different patterns imply different objectives, it is surprising how similar the stated objectives are for institutions which are at opposite poles in other respects. This chapter introduces several continuums based on these polarities. It also considers some essential elements involved in planning a curriculum and some of the characteristics which place colleges at various points on the continuum.

Four Continuums. Figure 1 exhibits four continuums. The *first* contrasts concern for the individual student with concern for the disci-

1. Individual student	Disciplines
Personal development	Mastery of content
Behavioral orientation	Structure and methodology of disciplines
Affective concerns	Scholarly objectivity
2. Problems, policies, actions	Abstractions, ideas, theories
Competencies	Verbal facility
Present and future oriented	Past oriented
3. Flexibility, autonomy	Rigidity, conformity
Adaptation to individual's needs and interests	Prescribed program and standards based on demands of disciplines and/or "average" student or ideal scholar
Democratic	Authoritarian
4. Integration, coherence, and unity in and from learning experiences	Compartmentalization, inconsistency, and discord in learning experiences

Figure 1. Continuums Suggestive of Possible Curricular Emphases.

pline. If concern for the individual dominates program development, then objectives emphasize the growth and development of the individual in a wide range of areas and roles. Affective and psychomotor goals are as important as cognitive ones. The disciplines represent arbitrary but potentially useful organizations of knowledge. At the other extreme of this continuum, the disciplines represent the accumulated wisdom of mankind and are more important than the individual who merely assimilates them.

Although some faculty members' views lie at these extremes, few institutions adhere to these radical positions. Most institutions fall somewhere between the extremes, but the majority are far closer to the discipline than to the individual approach. Only a few experimental colleges approach the left-hand extreme. In some institutions in which the faculty is strongly oriented toward disciplines, the left-hand end of the continuum is represented only by special courses in "Personal Development."* Alternatively, concern for the individual and his development may be relegated to the student personnel staff.

The *second* continuum contrasts a practical with an "ivory tower" conception of education. On one side, the curriculum focuses on problems and on the policies, actions, and competencies required to deal effectively with them. Such a program tends to be oriented toward the present and the future because it deals with current and continuing problems. The other extreme of this continuum emphasizes knowledge and understanding of abstractions, ideas, and theories. Verbal facility in discussing and analyzing these replaces practical ability to use them. The orientation is to the past rather than to the present or future. On this continuum, disciplines differ as much as professors and colleges. The social sciences are more likely to concentrate on problems, policies, and actions than are the humanities or the sciences. However, a problem-oriented course in any discipline may be restricted to problems intrinsically related to that discipline. Since most of the major issues and problems of society are interdisciplinary in nature, the problem orientation is not readily attainable in a curriculum which maintains rigid distinctions among disciplines.

The *third* continuum contrasts highly flexible, adaptable programs with rigid, uniformly imposed patterns. At the left extreme, the student is free to plan his program, state his goals, and perhaps even set his standards for attainment of them. At the right, the student conforms to

---

*Such courses are no longer in favor, and most of those developed fifteen or twenty years ago have disappeared from the curriculum.

prescribed programs and standards. Again, examples of the extremes are rare. Only a few experimental institutions aim at the left extreme. Fully prescribed liberal arts college programs are unusual, although combinations of college and departmental requirements sometimes approximate this. Vocational and professional programs, however, are often quite rigid, even to the point of specifying required electives.

The *fourth* continuum contrasts programs which seek integration, coherence, and unity with those which ignore these qualities. Since integration is ultimately an individual act, a completely integrated program is both undesirable and impossible. What is needed is a program which encourages and assists the student to organize his knowledge and experience in meaningful ways. The program must cross disciplinary boundaries and relate abstractions and theories to the world of action. At the right extreme, program integration is either considered irrelevant to this age of specialization or regarded as a completely personal and subjective matter. Extreme departmentalization, competition for majors, overt criticism of one department by another, and complete separation of student personnel services from instruction characterize this not uncommon extreme.

Despite obvious relationships among the four continuums, they are largely independent of each other. Concern for the individual student does not necessarily lead to a problem-oriented curriculum. Some programs of personal adjustment consist primarily of courses, principles, and requirements. Religious concern is frequently accompanied by required courses, required daily chapel attendance, and required church attendance. Flexibility and autonomy in a program do not necessarily result in integration, coherence, and unity. Thus, it is possible in planning a curriculum to consciously seek the extreme of each of these four continuums. Whether these extremes are desirable will be discussed later.

Essential Elements. In planning a curriculum, several essential elements must be considered. These fundamental and recurrent concerns require attention regardless of the desired position on the four continuums. This discussion will consider five of the most important elements:

1. Liberal and vocational education.
2. Breadth and depth.
3. Continuity and sequence.
4. Conception of learning and teaching.
5. Continuing planning and evaluation.

Liberal and vocational education are often contrasted and might be regarded as extremes on a fifth continuum. However, the problem is one of balance rather than of incompatibility. A liberal education which results in (1) knowledge of basic cultural heritage, (2) competency in utilizing the modes of thought characteristic of the major areas of human knowledge, (3) competency in communicating, and (4) conscious commitment to a set of values, is excellent preparation for almost any vocation. Any vocation which requires post-secondary school education will, to some extent, require these results. Furthermore, in a rapidly changing technology all vocational training is soon outdated. The vocational student must be taught to exercise independent judgment and to educate himself. Thus, to some extent, vocational education can and must be liberal.

One's definitions of liberal and vocational education are relevant to attaining balance. A liberal education may be defined by objectives, content, problems, or ideas, and the definition may be flexible and variable or rigid and universal. A vocational education may also be defined by objectives, content, problems, or ideas. It, too, may be defined flexibly for each individual or rigidly for all. In addition, vocational education may be defined as training for a specific job or, more generally, for a group of related jobs. The latter approach has much more in common with liberal education.

Breadth and *depth*, like liberal and vocational education, are sometimes regarded as antithetical. In its simplest form, breadth is the modern version of the early classical curriculum. In practice, breadth is equated, in most colleges, with a distribution requirement specifying minimal credits in each of several disciplines. The introductory interdisciplinary course is another characteristic approach to breadth. Neither the introductory departmental course nor the interdisciplinary general education course is a satisfactory solution to the problem. The first is too concerned with providing facts and skills essential for majors in the field. Some departments (mathematics, chemistry, art, music) simply refuse students lacking a strong background in the discipline. The required interdisciplinary course too often becomes a survey course in which the student covers much but understands little. Moreover, students react negatively to the requirement, and the large classes are difficult to staff with enthusiastic instructors.

Breadth includes such diverse interpretations as:

1. Knowledge of some of the essential facts and concepts in all major areas of knowledge.

2. Understanding of the structure, basic concepts, and modes of thought of the various disciplines.
3. Awareness and understanding of those ideas and values which have had a marked impact on the development of western culture.
4. Understanding of the values and modes of thought of one or more non-western cultures.
5. Awareness of the interrelationships of disciplines.
6. Insight into and active concern with the major problems of our society.
7. Commitment to a set of values and conscious attempt to reinforce them by thought and action.

Departmental offerings satisfying distribution requirements seldom go beyond the first interpretation, although they could and should contribute to the second and third. Introductory interdisciplinary courses vary and are difficult to type. The majority are most effective in the first and third interpretations, but a few have been quite effective in the second, fifth, and sixth. Courses in non-western cultures are a relatively recent development, and some are specifically designed to meet the fourth interpretation. The real weakness of the required course approach to breadth is that none of the concepts of breadth can be attained in isolated freshman and sophomore courses. Some sequence of courses is required to deal effectively with values or the relation of the disciplines. Significant concepts of breadth must be pursued over a period of years rather than consigned to a single course. There must be depth in breadth.

Depth is usually interpreted as a departmental or divisional major, although broader conceptions implied by the term "concentration" are also used. The term, depth, is unfortunate. Its opposite, height, would be more appropriate, for it implies both an increased level of competency in a special area and a comprehensive view of the total range of knowledge. Depth can mean any of the following:

1. Detailed knowledge of the facts and terminology of a discipline.
2. Knowledge of the language, culture, politics, economics, and geography of a country or region.
3. Sufficient mastery of the structure and methods of scholarly investigation to engage in independent study in a discipline.
4. Thorough investigation of a problem, of the information and methods of attack required to deal with it, and the implications of various possible solutions to it.
5. Study of all aspects of the culture of a designated place and period.

6. Mastery of some methodology or technique (e.g., statistics, laboratory analysis, musical instrument, art medium, computer).

The departmental major, composed of a recommended series of courses, is too broad for some of these conceptions of depth and too specialized for others. The question arises as to how much specialization is appropriate, particularly at the undergraduate level. It becomes important to consider the relevance of breadth *in* depth. Many departments which offer several specialties still require certain basic courses of all majors, as do many business, engineering, and vocational programs. Clearly, depth and breadth are not antithetical; they are counterbalancing elements in the development of a sound program.

Continuity and *sequence* are closely related terms. Continuity implies that terms, ideas, and skills introduced early in a program should continue to be used. Sequence implies that learning experiences should relate to preceding and succeeding experiences. In mathematics and the sciences, this is inevitable, as the nature of these disciplines is sequential and cumulative. In the social sciences and the humanities, courses tend to have minimal prerequisites. Their emphasis is primarily on acquisition of isolated knowledge rather than on more complex skills and insights which require time and sequential experiences for their development. In spite of the many programs of independent study, few institutions or departments offer programs which effectively develop this ability. Long-term objectives also receive limited attention. Writing is a good example; every graduate should write well, but few receive any formal training after their freshman year.

If education is to be a connected, developmental experience, continuous use of fundamental knowledge, skills, abilities, and values is essential. The experiences must be organized so that later experiences relate to and extend earlier ones. Even in non-cumulative fields, concepts of sequence may be introduced to assist the student in mastering fundamental ideas and grasping various relationships. Sequence may be based on such concepts as simple-complex, near-remote, familiar-unfamiliar, inductive-deductive, and concrete-abstract. Sequence often results from the intrinsic nature of the field of study in that the student must acquire certain skills before he can progress to the next level. Sequence may be contrived by presenting a course in American Colonial history, for example, in such a way that a detailed knowledge of European history is required. Thus, the student realizes that courses are not isolated entities, and he seeks to understand and use their relationships.

The concept of integration, introduced in the fourth continuum, is a natural extension of continuity and sequence. Integration may result from an organized program in which students grasp the constructs developed by their teachers. An integrated program may also encourage and assist the student to develop his own organization of various fields of study, and of his academic study and personal, social, and world problems. The latter seems more fundamental, for it encourages the student to seek relations between new and old experiences and to develop greater insight and unity in his life.

Every curriculum study must develop some conception of the relation of *learning* to *teaching*. Since Chapter 8 considers this duality in detail, the comments will be very brief. Professors tend to concentrate on the content of a course and on their own responsibility in presenting it. They view student inadequacy as lack of motivation and application rather than as lack of stimulation. The professor seldom sees beyond his course and hence accepts little responsibility for long-term educational goals. A good curriculum provides a structure both for learning and for instruction. A sound education rarely results from excellent teachers who operate in complete isolation from one another. A curriculum must be based on some concept of human learning and on some formulation of the obligations of teachers to this concept.

All curricula change, but few of these changes are based on *continuing planning and evaluation*. Most curriculum planning is a series of compromises to vested interests and emotional reactions rather than a comprehensive, rational attempt to achieve certain goals. A new curriculum is evaluated only after it is fully developed and then evaluation is more likely to be regarded as a threat than as a means of improvement. Chapter 9 will deal with this problem in greater depth. Perhaps the use of a structure for curriculum study will help faculty members to regard any program as merely one possible approach to certain desired ends. Such a view makes continuing evaluation and planning natural and inevitable. However, unless a curriculum reform explicitly includes plans for future revision, any attempt at evaluation and further modification of the program will meet with resistance.

Every curriculum study must consider liberal and vocational education, breadth and depth, and continuity. Every curriculum must also be based on some concept of learning and teaching. Since every curriculum will change, the curriculum must include policies and procedures for continuing planning and evaluation. Ideally, the curriculum will emphasize some of these concerns and minimize others in response to conscious commitment to certain objectives.

Facilitating Agents. Facilitating agents should give to a curriculum the character implied by the choices made in regard to continuums and essential elements. However, too often decisions are made first in regard to agents, and the character of the program emerges hazily out of these decisions. The agents include:

1. Requirements, recommendations, electives.
2. Various modes of organizing learning and teaching:
    (a) structured courses requiring regular class attendance;
    (b) relatively unstructured seminar experiences;
    (c) tutorials, individualized instruction;
    (d) independent study.
3. Non-course experiences:
    (a) on campus (work, student activities, community government);
    (b) off campus (work, travel, service, independent study).
4. Daily and weekly schedules developed to enforce certain standard practices or to permit and encourage various combinations of learning and instruction.
5. Annual calendars which require or permit marked variation in the organization of learning and instruction at various times of the year.
6. Examinations, grades, records of student achievement.
7. Numbers of different courses (or other learning experiences) taken by students or taught by the faculty.
8. Selection, initial orientation, and advising of students.
9. Selection, initial orientation, in-service education and evaluation of the faculty.
10. Administrative organization, financial and budgeting practices.

The choices and combinations of these alternatives give structure and character to the curriculum. On the basis of these, students, new faculty members, and outside observers judge the institution's philosophy of education and specific objectives. What is implicit in these decisions speaks more effectively than the explicit objectives, concerns, and rationale of a program. For example, a required program comprised of several general education courses may be introduced on the assumption that almost every student needs and would benefit from such a program. However, instructors may develop these courses to suit their own conception of what is important. Soon the students and those faculty members not involved in the courses come to regard them as unreasonable requirements that interfere with other more interesting educational experiences. Continuing orientation of students and faculty, on one hand, and continuing evaluation and modification of the program on the other, are essential if the program is to continue to fulfill the ends for which it was designed.

A few comments on the relation of facilitating agents to essentials and continuums will suffice. Requirements, for example, can have significantly different implications. The imposition of a course requirement is essentially different from the specification of a proficiency requirement. Foreign students in colleges with a foreign language course requirement have often been required to study a third language. Proficiency in a second language is a different and more significant educational requirement. Likewise, the requirement of specific general education courses, or a distribution requirement, is different from the requirement of demonstrated proficiency on a comprehensive examination.

Colleges impressed with the virtues of study abroad, off-campus work experience, or community service have added these agents without considering continuity and sequence. Newer programs of independent study, library research programs, and ungraded courses often result in total incoherence for both faculty and students. Structure need not be provided by traditional methods, but it must be provided.

Some curriculum studies have viewed seminars, tutorials, or independent study as the primary ingredient for rehabilitating undergraduate education. The worth of these is undeniable, but only if they are integrated into a coherent program. A few small private colleges, such as Sarah Lawrence, may base their entire program on tutorials, small group seminars, conferences, and independent study. However, most institutions cannot afford this, and many feel that such a program isolates and limits the student. In some cases, tutorials and independent study are introduced as antidotes to structured courses rather than as complements to them. Some independent study programs have failed because the student's ability to carry on independent study was assumed rather than developed. Faculties occasionally reject independent study because they prefer to lecture and fail to see the necessity of such a program when courses on every conceivable topic are available. Faculty commitments to courses, requirements, and lectures too often result from personal predilection rather than from concern with student learning. In many institutions, facilitating agents are accepted as essential determinants of the learning experience rather than as alternative methods of effecting a predetermined pattern of experience.

Flexible weekly or daily schedules and variant annual calendars permit combinations of learning experiences not possible in the traditional fifty-minute period and two-semester or three-quarter calendar. Yet, such innovations cannot be successful if the course-credit requirements remain rigid.

Examinations and grades have been discarded in some programs because it is feared that they interfere with learning. Students, however, often require certain pressures and restraints for motivation. If only highly motivated students are admitted, and if only inspiring faculty members are hired, formal structures and checks may be unnecessary. Socrates, Plato, and Aristotle *may* have attained this ideal, but that pattern of completely voluntary education has limited relevance today. In most institutions, motivation and continuing appraisal are essential. Even in Great Britain, where the final paper has always been the basis for the award of degree and honors status, the new universities accept this necessity.

There is little evidence to support the reasonable contention that a lighter course load is more conducive to intensive study. There is no adequate test, for such concentrated load patterns pose problems of sequence and may require extensive reorganization of content. Composition, mathematics, science, and foreign language present valid arguments for attention in the freshman year which often forces postponement of social science, history, religion and other less sequential but more popular fields. For some students, a concentrated dose of a discipline they dislike may be fatal. Thus, a three-course or a four-course program is unlikely to be successful and permanent unless other factors are adjusted to it.

Major curricular reorganization often requires a new administrative agency to insure the viability of the change. The University College general education programs at Michigan State University and at the University of Florida outlasted many programs based on the existing departmental structure simply because they were granted an independent administration and budget. Current attempts at small, experimental liberal arts colleges within large universities often fail because the university faculty denies the college a separate staff. Such a program cannot succeed with a part-time and continually changing faculty.

Our proposal for a structure of curriculum analysis and development is twofold: first, that a neutral structure based on the fundamental educational concept of the institution, be used to analyze and describe the curriculum; second, that the desired learning environment be determined in detail before methods are selected to achieve it. No profound reconstruction of curriculum emerges from leaping from vague objectives to decisions about facilitating agents.

PHILOSOPHIES OF EDUCATION (APPROACH NO. 2)

The nature of the curriculum in any institution depends on the educational philosophies of the faculty, the administration, and, to some extent, the constituency supporting the institution. The plural "philosophies" suggests the existence in most institutions of differing and conflicting theories of education, few of which provide a consistent, formally stated basis for educational planning. Nevertheless, these opinions, beliefs, attitudes, judgments and prejudices give the institution its educational philosophy.

No attempt to describe the educational philosophy of an individual or an institution will be authentic or accepted. No attempt to distinguish a few educational philosophies will meet with general approval by philosophers, for the number of distinctive philosophies and their interrelationships defy classification. Taylor has presented a useful discussion of rationalist, neo-humanist, and instrumentalist philosophies in discussing various approaches to general education (8). However, the names chosen for these categories have so many different definitions that the discussion is often confusing and over simplified.

Modifying Taylor's analysis with my own observation of and consultation with faculties, I shall present briefly three contrasting patterns of thought about education: traditionalism, eclecticism, and relativism.*
Although some faculty members and colleges might be classified in each of these patterns, most colleges have representatives of all three philosophies. Educational and evaluation practices usually result from interaction and compromise among these views, and it is this time-consuming process which makes unified program so difficult to achieve.

The *traditionalist* believes that the great minds of the past have isolated and communicated all significant truth and value. Education consists, then, of bringing the student in contact with these ideas through a curriculum of a limited number of required subjects. The subjects are chosen because they discipline the mind, develop the reason, and inculcate an absolute and monolithic set of values which prescribe modes of action. They are logically organized and contain a definite body of knowledge, broad and general in nature. An elite group of students serve a novitiate under a faculty characteristic of a priesthood or of Plato's philosopher-kings. The government of the institution is essentially a theocracy or an oligarchy.

An institution operating according to this pattern is necessarily small, for it must be composed of an elite group. Any attempt to expand such a college beyond a few hundred students would create a heterogeneity of students and faculty which would destroy the ideal and endanger the discussion group, seminar, and individual conference pattern essential to the program.

---

*Adapted from Paul L. Dressel and Associates, *Evaluation in Higher Education,* Houghton Mifflin Company, Boston, 1961, pp. 20–24.

Evaluation, in such a program, is highly subjective, emphasizing oral and written procedures which are cumulative and comprehensive in nature. Evaluation, as a basis for determination of educational policy, is unlikely to utilize data collection or other empirical procedures. If traditional educational practice does not directly supply an answer to a problem, rational analysis and discourse by well-informed scholars will. The traditionalist sees issues and courses of action in black and white. Shades of gray suggest compromise and expediency not to be tolerated by free men who know the truth. Although such individuals must be respected, one always suspects that they, like some of the early Sophists, too easily justify any means which will attain their ends.

Since the traditionalist position is extreme and not in accord with prevalent modes of thought, colleges which fully exemplify it are difficult to find. St. John's College at Annapolis and a few selective, sectarian liberal arts colleges very nearly exemplify this view. In the larger universities, certain departments, particularly in the humanities, are clearly traditionalist in their offerings, objectives, and departmental operations. The conflict between this group and others is one aspect of the humanistic-scientific schism which makes unity in the university so difficult of achievement.

The *eclectic* recognizes that our society is pluralistic and that many disciplines and professions are just beginning to be defined. Education, then, must bring the student into brief contact with a wide range of courses and into extended contact with a particular body of knowledge. The curriculum is composed partly of required courses, both specific and general, and partly of electives. The intellectual abilities required by each discipline differ as do the value systems. Pluralism in values tends to make scholarly objectivity the supreme value. Since no agreement is possible on a general body of knowledge, emphasis is often on specific facts, and on concepts and principles which differentiate one discipline from another. Integration of knowledge is regarded either as the responsibility of the individual student, or as a state reached only when pursuit of a particular discipline impinges on other disciplines. The wide range of courses and curricula, from physical education to atomic physics and from secretarial science to philosophy, results in a heterogeneous body taught by professors who are authorities in their own specialty and who profess ignorance in others. The government of an eclectic institution vacillates between monarchy in matters determined by the administration and anarchy in those determined by the faculty. Although individual faculty members may be traditional or relativist in orientation, their views are hardly free of elements of eclecticism. Complete commitment to a traditional or relativistic viewpoint would hardly be consistent with continued residence in an eclectic environment.

Evaluation in such a program tends to focus on mastery of a body of factual knowledge and of the intellectual skills needed to deal with it. Cumulative, comprehensive evaluation is of little worth, since courses and disciplines are isolated and unrelated. Credits and grades constitute the major evaluation of learning. If comprehensive examinations are required of seniors, the department, or occasionally the division, is the responsible agency. Although intangible values may accompany the student's contact with the scholar, there is no interest in making them explicit. Perhaps the main reason for hypothesizing these intangibles is to provide a basis for rejecting systematic attempts at evaluation of instruction. Administrators often desire justification for policy decisions which inevitably appear to benefit one department or college more than another. Thus, evaluation studies become administration-oriented and are viewed with doubt and distrust by the faculty.

Because of the pluralistic nature of our society and of our college and universities, most institutions operate on an eclectic basis. The range of positions within this compromise is suggested by the great variation in commitment to educational experimentation and evaluation.

The *relativist* believes that each individual and society must seek its own truths and values, which are always relative to the times and conditions. He views education as an instrument for progress and improvement. Education is primarily concerned with the development of the total person, in whom intellect and emotion are inextricably mingled. The curriculum develops habits of thinking in each individual and encourages him to interpret his experiences in more meaningful ways. Integration is a conscious concern but, since it is a continuing process rather than a final achievement, previous methods of integration serve only as models. Each individual must search for satisfying organizations of his own experience.

Educational experiences for the relativist are not limited to academic courses and programs. To fully develop the individual, courses and experiences must be adapted to his abilities and interests. Professors serve as motivators, counselors, and democratic leaders rather than as authoritarian directors of the educational program. The government of the relativist institution is democratic, with faculty, administration, and students participating in all decisions.

Relativist programs are empirically oriented. The most effective education is that which produces the greatest personal and social responsibility, and knowledge and self-direction in individuals. Hence, evaluation must furnish evidence of change in individuals and relate the change to the educational program. Since all facets of the institution are a part of the educational environment, they are all subject to continuing study. Evaluation is not simply a basis for decisions; it is a significant and necessary educational experience which teaches students and faculty the habits, attitudes, and skills necessary to make such decisions. Only in the relativist pattern is evaluation fully accepted as a vital phase of every aspect of the program.

The relativist position is found in many colleges, but seldom in universities. Antioch College, Sarah Lawrence, Bennington, Berea, and other colleges developed on an experimental basis exemplify many elements of this stance. The General College of the University of Minnesota, as much as any unit in a large university, has operated on a relativist basis.

This presentation of three views does an injustice to the careful exposition of various philosophical points of view by qualified philosophers. Indeed, philosophers would not characterize these three brief statements of educational views as philosophies. A much more thorough exposition of various educational philosophies is found in *Modern Philosophies and Education* which includes discussions of Realism, Thomism, Idealism, Experimentalism, Marxism, Existentialism, and Logical Empiricism (3).

These distinctive philosophical views arise out of differing conceptions of reality, value, knowledge, and the nature and ultimate fate of man. Those who have wrestled with the nature and purpose of higher education may benefit from thorough study of them. However, few faculty members will do so, and, if they did, their differences might be magnified rather than resolved. With the exception of a few small colleges consciously committed to a particular position, institutions will not determine their educational programs by first agreeing on a philosophy. The threefold classification, in which a vague eclectic position is bounded by two extreme positions, is at least practical and realistic. Indeed, the structure presented at the beginning of the chapter (continuums, essential concepts, and facilitating agents) was introduced to avoid confrontation of philosophical differences and terminology meaningless to most faculty members. Curriculum choices ultimately imply a philosophy, but to determine its accepted name is rarely profitable. Likewise, a philosophy of education determines educational objectives, but it may be wiser to state objectives and let the philosophy remain implicit in them.

STEPS IN CURRICULAR DEVELOPMENT
(APPROACH NO. 3)

The identification of stages in the development of a curriculum or program falsely suggests that the steps are discrete and that a particular sequence is inviolable. Nevertheless, the identification of several stages helps to demonstrate the relation of program development and evaluation. Figure 2 on page 31 suggests the stages involved and the complex relations among them.

After the decision is made to develop, study, or revise a program or curriculum, the logical starting point is with objectives, which should be formally stated rather than assumed to be self-evident. Appropriate educational experiences are selected to realize these objectives and are organized into courses, curricula, or procedural patterns. Collection of data and evaluation of the program may then result in revision of the program through modification or replacement of any or all of the elements of the preceding stages (objectives, experiences, organization of the experiences, or evaluation).

Although the diagram clarifies the stages in development of an educational program, it fails to exhibit the essential role evaluation plays in the other three stages. This will become evident in the following discussion of each stage.

The diagram, and this discussion of it, may be too readily interpreted as applying only to the formal curriculum. Faculty and administrators must keep in mind that every practice and policy of a college affects students' learning. Priorities in expenditures of funds reveal values of boards and administrators and, thus, influence the values of students. Scholarship and loan policies, preferential treatment of athletes, social regulations, and student government, all constitute educational experience. As such, they are subject to the kind of analysis presented here.

SELECTION AND CLARIFICATION OF OBJECTIVES

The objectives of education arise out of a limited number of sources. As an instrument for the perpetuation and improvement of society, education is responsive to the needs of that society. Although conservative scholars may abhor this fact, historical and current events demonstrate its accuracy. Whether educators consciously sense social needs and initiate change or wait until inexorable pressures force it, education does conform to such needs. Narrow preoccupation with western culture

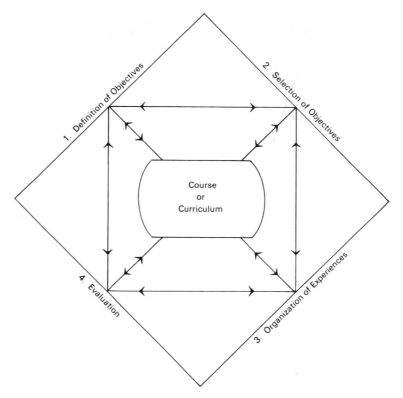

Figure 2. Stages in Curriculum Planning. (from Chapter II, Figure 1, "Basic Considerations in Curriculum Planning," in Paul L. Dressel, *The Undergraduate Curriculum in Higher Education*, The Center for Applied Research in Education, Inc., Washington, D. C., 1963, p. 25.

is giving way to an awareness of the significance of other cultures. Education for the contemplative life has long been replaced by the demand to earn a living. A flexibility which permits rational modification is preferable to a rigidity which prohibits even *necessary* change.

Objectives are also based on the needs of individuals and, in a democracy, these needs must be considered as important as the needs of society. Each college must determine the extent to which it will respond to the common needs of all students or to the individual needs of each student. Institutions of higher education must also determine the range of individual needs for which they will accept responsibility. They must decide whether intellect shall be their sole concern, or whether they will attempt to foster health and personality development as well.

Authoritative statements of individuals, conferences, and professional organizations provide a third source of objectives. Some educators feel that there has been no significant statement on education since Aristotle and Plato. Others are influenced by St. Thomas Aquinas, Milton, Newman, and more recent writers. Reports of the various presidential commissions on higher education are often influential. The objectives and content of mathematics and physics courses are currently being rewritten by scholars in these disciplines. Some teachers, unfamiliar with these sources, allow the writer of the textbook chosen to become, by default, the authority for both objectives and content.

A large and confusing array of objectives are found in these three sources. Some screening must be undertaken if the chosen objectives are to be (1) reasonable in number, (2) consistent with one another, (3) of approximately the same level of generality or specificity, (4) distinctive, but not completely independent, and (5) descriptive of attainable goals. Although psychological research has not yet provided full insight into human learning, certain known principles provide some guidance in selection of objectives. Thorndike's position on the possibility of transfer may have been extreme, but objectives based on a generalized mental discipline and unlimited transfer can no longer be defended. Objectives specifying neatness or desirable health habits are not adapted to the maturity of college students, although such habits may be indirectly required or reinforced by objectives appropriate to that age.

Objectives might be expected to grow out of a philosophy of education. However, few individuals have a fully developed educational philosophy, and more often a compromise, eclectic philosophy emerges from agreement on objectives. As this philosophy becomes explicit, objectives must be re-examined for their consistency with it. Even the philosophy itself, because of its eclecticism, may lack consistency. Only in a few denominational colleges are religious dogma and philosophical tenets sufficiently explicit to provide definite guides to objectives.

Departmentalization, course proliferation, and specialization have fragmented knowledge. Long lists of specific objectives may also be distorted by the specialized interests of the faculty in each of the several disciplines. Clearly stated, integrated objectives provide an antidote, but it is effective only if faculty members agree on a basic principle for unity of knowledge. Furthermore, the objectives must be limited in number and realistic enough to apply to all phases of college experience. Some objectives are more important than others; these few must be isolated and pursued with the confidence that, in attaining them, other, less important objectives will also be realized.

Evaluation is essential to the selection of objectives. The choice among many conflicting views should be made by evaluation of the rationale and logic underlying these views. One form of evaluation is the study of psychological research and its relevance to educational planning. Philosophical considerations necessarily involve consideration of values. Any significant factors omitted in selecting objectives may negate efforts to achieve the objectives. Objectives are like traveling in that one may go where he will only if he chooses to go where he can.

SELECTION AND PLANNING OF
EDUCATIONAL EXPERIENCES

The triteness of the saying that people learn by experience blinds us to the truth of it. However, people learn what is anticipated only if the experiences are carefully selected and planned with specific objectives in mind for each student. The following catalogue of a few instruments of learning reveals that possible learning experiences far outnumber those actually used.

1. Materials (textbook, supplemental required or optional readings, teaching machines, current periodicals, syllabus, slides, films, tapes, recordings, television).
2. Instructional methods (lectures, discussions, demonstrations, role playing, cases, problems, individual conferences, seminars, guest speakers, telephone interviews).
3. Assignments (readings, problems, papers, oral reports).
4. Activities (laboratory, field trips, independent study, observation, internships, work experience, travel, public lectures, concerts, plays).
5. Evaluation methods (objective tests, essays, papers, reports, participation, peer judgment, self-evaluation).

Certainly no limited credit course, extending over one quarter or semester, can employ all these materials, but the list does reveal the narrow range of experiences offered in many courses. Too often the instructor's choice of experiences is based on his own inclinations rather than the student's. The instructor implies that his interpretation of the significance of various experiences is more important than what the student understands and concludes. The student, in turn, infers that his reactions and ideas must be subjugated to the search for what the instructor wants. Often the student fails to reach the desired objectives because he has no experience relevant to them beyond that prescribed by the instructor.

If one objective of instruction is to enable students to relate ideas in solving problems, a model presented by the instructor may be beneficial. However, if the instructor continues to offer only his own solutions, the student may assimilate methods without developing insight or ability.

A limited conception of evaluation is that it reveals the value of an educational experience. Unless evaluation has first placed some significance *in* the education experience, evaluation *of* the experience is unlikely to be profitable. As one selects and plans, questions and alternatives arise, and evaluation can and should play a major role in reaching the required decisions.

Although evaluation of the worth of experiences usually is based on changes in students, it is possible to derive some criteria which apply directly to the experiences. Wynne has argued that evaluation by study of student change is difficult and, perhaps, impossible in a reasonable length of time (9). From careful analysis of educational objectives, he derives the following criteria for experiences: (1) contingency, (2) sociality, (3) interest, (4) originality, (5) intelligence, (6) purpose (9, pp. 31–47). If these are absent, he maintains that the experiences are inadequate. Such evaluation suggests rationalization, but it does assure that experiences will have some relevance to objectives.

ORGANIZATION OF EXPERIENCES

There are many ways of organizing courses and curricula. Some disciplines have an inherent logical order, although this may be historical accident rather than necessity. Others move from the simple to the complex, from the specific to the general, or from the immediate to the remote. Each of these may also occur in the reverse order; the general may be applied to the specific, or, as in history, the remote may precede the immediate.

These essential criteria already noted as elements in curriculum planning, may be used as principles of organization. There must be *continuity*, so that later learning experience will reinforce earlier ones. The full meaning and use of a significant concept, value, or skill is not grasped immediately. Monotonous repetition may impede mastery, but repetition with deeper insight and greater range of association promotes it. Thus, continuity in learning must be accompanied by *sequence*, so that continuing use of an idea leads to greater depth and complexity. Learning experiences must be cumulative rather than discrete. Finally, if the learning in a particular course or discipline is to be complete, it must be related to learning in other courses and disciplines, and to experiences outside the classroom. Some writers on curriculum theory call this quality *integration,* although integration, in the broadest sense, includes continuity and sequence.

These three criteria should be considered in planning both courses and the total curriculum. If a degree means nothing more than the fulfillment of certain course and credit requirements, integration is no problem. However, if education is to become a significant total experience, it must be based on more rigorous objectives. Even in small liberal arts colleges, the range of choice in courses, the turnover of staff, and the tendency toward overspecialization threaten to destroy the liberal education experience.

CONCEPTIONS OF INTEGRATION

The faculty of St. Olaf College identified four major concepts of integration in higher education (4, pp. 128–131). The *additive* view assumes that the integrated whole is not qualitatively describable, and that the parts are interchangeable. When course units add up to a specified number, subject to certain restrictions on distribution, grade average, and upper division credits, the degree is awarded. Except for minor restrictions, only budgetary considerations and student interest limit the range and choice of courses in the curriculum.

The *sampling* view maintains that each discipline or part of knowledge, adequately treated and pursued at length, ultimately involves all other parts. The personal qualities of the teacher and the work habits of the student are more important than the selection of courses. Both a highly restricted and an unlimited range of courses are consistent with the sampling view.

The *relational* view suggests that each discipline is unique in content, structure, and method. However, despite the relative independence of the disciplines, the curriculum should emphasize similarities and differences among disciplines and identify inclusive ideas and methodological concepts which underlie and relate the fields. The identification of unifying concepts in turn, leads to new course and curriculum organizations, particularly to interdisciplinary courses.

The *wholistic* view contends that the whole is more than the sum of its parts, that the choice of parts is largely fortuitous, and that each, although important, can be understood only in relation to other parts and the whole. In the extreme, such a view resulted in a completely prescribed curriculum integrated through a comprehensive world view or a highly explicit set of objectives.

The *additive* view, characterized by course credit requirements, and the *sampling* view, characterized by concentration in a particular discipline, both conclude that integration is no real concern in planning the college curriculum. The *relational* and *wholistic* concepts both make an explicit commitment to integration, but differ in their emphasis on the part or on the whole as the source of integration. The relational view emphasizes the content and method of each field and seeks for principles underlying and relating the fields. The wholistic view begins with a set of unifying principles and demands that these be made the central elements of all learning. Since pluralism rather than a monolithic religious or philosophical position characterizes most of our institutions of higher education, integration can be achieved only through acceptance of common educational objectives. These objectives must be limited in number and general enough to apply to all disciplines; at the same time, they must be sufficiently clear and specific to guide both the planning of instruction in all disciplines and the organizing of experiences outside the classroom. Unless the curriculum and associated experiences are carefully planned around these objectives to provide continuity sequence and integration, the student is not likely to achieve these ends.

EVALUATION

Although evaluation of objectives, experiences, and patterns of organization is an essential part of each phase of curriculum development, evaluation of the impact of the total program on students is also important. This impact can be measured only by comparing the students' statuses before the program with their status at its conclusion. The differences indicate the changes which have occurred and, to some degree the effectiveness of the experiences. If several patterns of experiences exist, crude comparisons of their effectiveness may be made by contrasting students who have had varying experiences.

If little or no change is found, several possibilities must be considered: (1) the objectives may be inappropriate, unclear, or unachievable; (2) the experiences may not be relevant to the objectives; (3) the organization of experiences may be inadequate; (4) the evaluation methods may be invalid. After one or more of these have been modified, the process should be repeated.

This concept of evaluation is oversimplified and unrealistic. A curriculum covering several years is too complicated, variable, and widespread to be appraised in this fashion. Thus, evaluation at each stage of the development of a curriculum is absolutely essential.

SUMMARY

In this chapter a number of considerations regarding curriculum planning have been introduced and organized under three different approaches. The first presented four major continuums upon which institutions differ. Various combinations of essential elements and facilitating agents were shown to be significant factors in determining the character of an institutional program. The second approach, the selection of an educational philosophy, clarified institutional programs but did not seem to be a promising approach to curriculum development. The third approach, which begins with clarification of objectives, expends too much energy in elaborating objectives and achieving agreement on them. The goal of a unified curriculum is as easily lost in a profusion of objectives as in a proliferation of disciplines and courses. All three approaches help clarify the process of curriculum development, although the first most closely approximates current patterns of thought.

REFERENCES

1. George A. Beauchamp, *Curriculum Theory*, The Kagg Press, Wilmette, Ill., 1961.
2. Edward A. Carlin and Edward B. Blackman, eds., *Curriculum Building in General Education*, Wm. C. Brown Co., Dubuque, Iowa, 1960.
3. Nelson B. Henry, ed., *Modern Philosophies and Education*, Fifty-Fourth Yearbook of the National Society for the Study of Education, Part I, University of Chicago Press, 1955.
4. Howard Hong, ed., *Integration in the Christian Liberal Arts College*, St. Olaf College Press, 1956.
5. Lewis B. Mayhew, *The Collegiate Curriculum*, Southern Regional Education Board, Atlanta, Ga., 1966.
6. A. Harry Passow, ed., *Curriculum Crossroads*, Bureau of Publications, Teachers College, Columbia University, 1962.
7. Paul C. Rosenbloom and Paul C. Hillestad, eds., *Modern Viewpoints in the Curriculum*, McGraw-Hill Book Company, Inc., 1964.
8. Harold Taylor, "The Philosophical Foundation of General Education," Chapter II in *General Education*, Fifty-First Yearbook of the National

Society for the Study of Education, Part I, Nelson B. Henry, ed., University of Chicago Press, 1952, pp. 20–45.

9. John P. Wynne, *General Education in Theory and Practice*, Bookman Associates, New York, 1952.

3

The Structure of Knowledge and Curriculum

The four continuums introduced in Chapter 2 raise significant issues regarding the role of the disciplines in curriculum planning.

1. Should the curriculum emphasize the disciplines or the interests, needs, and motivations of the individual?
2. Should the curriculum be theoretical and abstract, or should it confront the issues and the problems of the era?
3. Is a discipline an accumulation of knowledge or a mode of thought?
4. How is the attainment of breadth, depth, integration, coherence, and unity in learning related to the use of the disciplines as a basis for curriculum organization?

Too many attempts at curriculum reorganization fail to confront these questions. Clearly, the structure of knowledge and the role it plays in the curriculum must be considered. As the title of this chapter implies, the structure of knowledge (based on disciplines) and the structure of the curriculum (based on educational goals and learning experiences) are related but not identical.

Pace has noted that

In higher education today knowledge is organized around academic disciplines. This organization has a special relevance for scholars and researchers and it is certainly not irrelevant for the ordinary student. It is nevertheless a clerical organization of knowledge which serves most directly the interests of the academic priesthood. . . . (15, pp. 39, 40).

He adds that ". . . all students should encounter and come to understand and value . . . this organization but . . . it is not a sufficient organization

. . ." (15, pp. 41, 42). Knowledge, Pace feels, must be related to social and personal problems and the curriculum must include secular as well as clerical organizations of knowledge. Otherwise, education becomes totally irrelevant to life and often leads to anti-intellectualism.

The curriculum must consist of experiences ordered to, in the phrase of Phenix, "maximize meanings." Phenix suggests five areas which may be taught to maximize meaning:

1. Mastery—finding one thing which can be done very well.
2. Belonging to a community—finding meaning in a social whole.
3. Many sidelines—well-roundedness, a diversity of interests.
4. Integrity of the person—coherence, coordination of meanings.
5. Quality of understanding (17, pp. 268–269).

To achieve meaning, the curriculum must have structure—an ordering (both horizontal and vertical) and relating of content and educational experiences. The structure of knowledge and of disciplines relates to this problem, but does not solve it. As Bruner remarks, the curriculum must consider the learner and the learning process as well as the nature of knowledge itself (4, p. 72). Bruner omits a further consideration, the professor. Moreover, the structure of a discipline varies according to its content, and the several structures reveal little about how to organize knowledge as a whole (8, pp. 2,3). Too much emphasis on individual disciplines often leads to neglect of balance, relevance to life, interrelationships, sequence, and integration.

One might, of course, ignore the intrinsic worth and separate identities of the several disciplines and concentrate on individual interests, needs, and problems. However, this solution to the curriculum problem is not consistent with the nature of higher education since 1900, or with recent studies of the structure of knowledge and the disciplines by Phenix, Schwab, Bell, King, and Brownell, B. O. Smith, Bellack, and Bruner. As Phenix Says,

> The most impressive claim the disciplines have upon the education is that they are the outcome of learning that has actually been successful. A discipline is a field of inquiry in which learning has been achieved in an unusually productive way. Most human efforts at understanding fail. A very few succeed, and these fruitful ways of thought are conserved and developed in the disciplines. Every discipline is simply a pattern of investigation that has proved to be a fertile field for the growth of understanding (17, p. 36).

To this Bruner adds that understanding of the fundamental structures of the discipline is the best approach to transfer of training (5, p. 120).

Higher education, then, must impart to the student some understanding of the disciplines. One cannot deal effectively with problems which cross disciplinary lines without some comprehension of the essentials of the disciplines involved. Finally, one can scarcely keep abreast of new developments without some knowledge of the disciplines in which that revision is taking place.

STRUCTURE OF THE DISCIPLINES

It is difficult, but necessary to become familiar with the extensive writing on the structure of the disciplines. This study will present briefly the various questions, issues, and views which should be pursued in greater depth by those involved in curriculum development.

Is it possible to develop a theory of knowledge and content which gives specific guidance in curriculum planning? The various theories are so complex, disparate, and tenuous that identification and useful description of the disciplines seems almost impossible (23, p. 362). Nevertheless, the widespread dissatisfaction with departmental distribution requirements and interdisciplinary courses in science, social science, and humanities, demands that some description and definition be attempted.

What is a discipline? One view is that a discipline develops from the rules of procedure which define its scope and modes of inquiry. Disciplines differ according to the rules they accept. Each has its own body of facts, concepts, and principles, and its own specialized mode of acquiring that knowledge. Schwab poses three problems in definite disciplines:

1. How are the disciplines organized?

   This question implies three others: (a) What (for the purposes of instruction) are the distinctive disciplines? (b) What are the bases for distinguishing among them? (c) How do they relate to one another?

2. What are the substantive structures of each discipline?

   This question also implies several others: (a) What are the objects or subject matter of inquiry? (b) What concepts are used? (c) What kinds of questions are asked and what kinds of data are collected? (d) How does the conceptual structure encourage or inhibit understanding of the subject of investigation?

3. What are the syntactical structures of the disciplines?

   This question provokes the following: (a) What are the modes of discovery and verification of knowledge? (b) What criteria are used to evaluate the quality of evidence and how strictly can these be applied (19, pp. 6–10)?

The identification of disciplines is difficult and unanimity cannot be expected. Originally, philosophy included most of the social and natural sciences. Disciplines proliferate as increasing knowledge defines new or more specific subject matter, introduces new concepts, or develops new modes of investigation. Not all disciplines can be included in the undergraduate program, or even in the graduate program, of every university. Thus, the significance of the phrase, "**for the purposes of instruction,**" in Schwab's question about the identity of the distinctive disciplines becomes evident. Selection and classification of knowledge into disciplines is necessary in planning a curriculum, but further selection and classification of the disciplines themselves is essential to reduce the disciplines to a manageable number. The task of organizing knowledge into systematic categories requires principles, an architectonics of knowledge. Phenix notes that

> An architectonic is important for the educator because it provides a scheme for considering in orderly fashion the entire range of what can be known. By having a systematic view of the kinds of knowledge that can be acquired, he gains an essential resource for making intelligent decisions about the content of instruction. He can more easily evaluate existing or proposed curricula with respect to omissions and balance. In the architectonic categories he can also find suggestions concerning the organization of instruction and concerning possible productive relationships between studies in different categories (16, p. 44).

Such categories are useful only if (1) they make experiences more intelligible by pointing out meaningful distinctions and relationships; (2) they offer increased efficiency in learning; (3) they permit and encourage transfer of learning from one problem or situation to another. If learning is to be efficient and effective, the curriculum must be based on structural principles related to the different ways of knowing, but it must also recognize common problems which link disciplines and require utilization and synthesis of various modes of inquiry.

Before examining various approaches to classification, the problem of definition of the disciplines should be considered in more detail. Schwab notes four bases for identifying disciplines: (1) subject matter —objects or problems investigated; (2) practitioners—competencies and habits required; (3) methods (syntax) and modes of inquiry used in study of subject matter; (4) ends—kinds of knowledge sought (20,

p. 15). King and Brownell identify eight factors in defining a discipline: (1) establishing the most characteristic views held by the members of the discipline; (2) describing the mode of inquiry, skills, and criteria of the members; (3) identifying its domain and characteristic perspective; (4) determining its key concepts; (5) characterizing its substratum languages and particular terminology and notation; (6) noting its linguistic heritage and mode of communication; (7) setting forth the tradition and history of the idea of the discipline; and (8) explicating its instructive character (15, pp. 146–149). They add that the task of defining never ends, for disciplines are always changing. Moreover, because there are many "members of the community of discourse," there will rarely be just one correct or acceptable sequence for a discipline. The efforts of scholars and professional organizations in recent years to develop proposals for new programs in the elementary and secondary school in mathematics, physics, chemistry, biology, English, economics, geography, and anthropology reveal the difficulties of this approach. Each discipline is studied separately, and little attention is given to the relation of the disciplines or to the total curriculum. Yet relation among the disciplines are as important as relations among the ideas of each discipline. Bellack has outlined several interesting patterns of interconnection:

(1) Relations among disciplines that deal with similar problems or phenomena. For example, all social sciences have the common objective of explaining the social and cultural behavior of man.

(2) Relations among broad areas of knowledge, such as the sciences and the humanities.

(3) Relations of knowledge to human affairs so that the student can use his knowledge to achieve meaning and order in his life (2, pp. 28–29).

Phenix emphasizes that

the special office of education is to widen one's view of life, to deepen insight into relationships, and to counteract the provincialism of customary existence—in short, to engender an integrated outlook.

If this integral perspective is to be attained, a philosophy of the curriculum is necessary. By such a philosophy is meant a critically examined, coherent system of ideas by which all the constituent parts of the course of instruction are identified and ordered.

A unitary philosophy of the curriculum is important for many reasons, among which the following four may be cited: First, comprehensive outlook is necessary for all intelligent decisions about what shall be included and excluded from the course of study. If one subject is to be chosen instead of another, it is important to know how the one differs from the other and why the one is to be preferred to the other as a constituent in the complete pattern of the learner's experience and character.

Second, because a person is essentially an organized totality and not just a collection of separate parts, the curriculum ought to have a corresponding organic quality. Since it is one and the same person who undergoes each of the successive experiences in his course of study, the plan of study can best contribute to the person's growth if it is governed by the goal of wholeness for the human being.

Third, society, as well as individual persons, depends upon principles of community; corporate life, like the life of each individual, requires some overall plan. A curriculum planned as a comprehensive design for learning contributes a basis for the growth of community, while an atomized program of studies engenders disintegration in the life of society.

Fourth, a comprehensive concept of the structure of learning gives added significance to each of the component segments of the curriculum. The value of any subject is enhanced by an understanding of its relationships with other subjects, and its distinctive features are best comprehended in the light of its similarities and contrasts with other subjects (17, pp. 3–4).

Phenix also emphasizes the importance of relating the disciplines in curriculum building. He finds four major threats to meaning: destructive skepticism, resulting from the preeminent role of science; depersonalization and fragmentation of life, caused by extreme specialization; surfeit of cultural products, especially knowledge; and rapidity of change, which results in insecurity and transience (17, p. 5). The curriculum must be planned to alleviate these threats by giving meaning to life. A complete person, as defined by Phenix, should be:

> "skilled in the use of speech, symbol, and gesture, factually well informed, capable of creating and appreciating objects of esthetic significance, endowed with a rich and disciplined life in relation to self and others, able to make wise decisions and to judge between right and wrong, and possessed of an integral outlook. . . ." (17, p. 8).

These requirements are closely related to Phenix's six realms of meaning:

1. Symbolics, comprises ordinary language, mathematics, and various nondiscursive symbolic forms.

2. Empirics, includes the sciences of the physical world, of living things, and of man.
3. Synnoetics, signifies "relational insight" or "direct awareness."
4. Esthetics, contains the various arts, such as music, the visual arts of movement, and literature.
5. Ethics, includes moral meanings.
6. Synoptics, refers to meanings that are comprehensively integrative. It includes history, religion, and philosophy (17, pp. 5–7).

The classification proposed by Phenix contains both qualitative and quantitative considerations, seen in Figure 1. The meanings of the terms are sufficiently clear from the context. The figure demonstrates that there is no simple relationship between the generally accepted disciplines and Phenix's categories. Phenix readily admits that any classification is, to some extent, arbitrary. This classification organizes the disciplines according to similarity of their logical structure. Phenix believes that the student must receive instruction in all six realms to assure wholeness of meaning. He proposes four principles for selection and organization of content: (1) That content be drawn from fields or disciplines; (2) That it be representative of the field as a whole; (3) That it exemplify methods of inquiry and modes of understanding of the disciplines studied; (4) That it arouse the imagination (18, pp. 10–12). In this approach, disciplines maintain their identity, but each discipline provides experience in several realms of meaning. Although the Phenix analysis is very interesting, it is unlikely to have much impact on the

Quantity	Fact	Form	Norm
Singular, individual or specific	*Synnoetics* Philosophy, psychology, literature, and religion in their existential aspects	*Esthetics* Music, visual arts, dance, literature	*Ethics* Special areas of moral and ethical concern
General	*Empirics* Physical sciences, life sciences, psychology, social sciences	*Symbolics* Ordinary language, mathematics, non-discursive symbolic forms	*Ethics* Special areas of moral and ethical concern
Comprehensive	*Synoptics* History	*Synoptics* Philosophy	*Synoptics* Religion

Figure 1. Adapted from Philip H. Phenix, *Realms of Meaning*, McGraw-Hill Book Company, New York, 1964, "Logical Classification of Meanings," p. 28

planning of the higher education curriculum. Its terminology is too esoteric to be readily adopted by faculties, and its organization too foreign to traditional groupings.

Schwab suggests a threefold classification of disciplines: (1) theoretical disciplines which aim to know (natural science, mathematics, non-normative social science); (2) practical disciplines concerned with choice, decision, action (ethics, politics, education); (3) productive disciplines concerned with making (fine arts, applied arts, engineering) (19, pp. 20,21). This classification is presented not as a solution to the problem but as another basis for classification. Customary classifications of natural science, social science, and humanities are based on subject matter and practitioners. Phenix's is based primarily on ways of knowing or modes of inquiry, and on the level of generality of the knowledge sought, whereas Schwab's threefold classification (essentially the Aristotelian scheme of knowing, doing, and making) is based entirely on the nature of the product. Each suggests a type of experience which has some claim upon the curriculum, although the third applies primarily to vocational programs.

Bellack recommends that knowledge be viewed not only in terms of modes of inquiry but also in terms of modes of thought—analytic, empiric, aesthetic, and moral (23, p. 364). King and Brownell, like Phenix, argue for the primacy of the disciplines in planning the curriculum (14, pp. 62–90). They present ten different conceptions of a discipline, including the characterization of a discipline as a corps of human beings with a common intellectual commitment who make a contribution to human thought and to human affairs," as "a tradition," as "a heritage of literature and communications network," and as "a valuative and effective stance." They also present an informative review of the schemes of Plato, Aristotle, Vico, Descartes, Kant, and Comte (17, pp. 41–49). Aristotle's classification of disciplines into a hierarchy of knowing, doing, and making continues to influence our thinking about the nature and merits of liberal and vocational education. The Cartesian organization denies the existence of separate disciplines in favor of a universal science-mathematics. The current widespread application of mathematical models, statistical methods, systems analysis, and computer technology approaches the Cartesian scheme for unity of knowledge in mathematics. The emphasis on modes of inquiry owes much to Kant who saw judgment as the organized principle of knowledge. According to Kant, knowledge derives its structure from the human intellect rather than from the universe, and the ultimate unity is found in moral theology. Vico enlarged the concept of discipline to include emotional language and non-rational activity. In effect, he added the logic of imagination to the logic of reason. Comte arranged the "positive" disciplines, those based on sense experience and defined descriptively, in order of increasing dependence, particularly, and complexity. The traditional organization of school subjects and courses owes much to Comte's scheme. Study of biology assumes knowledge of chemistry, chemistry assumes prior contact with physics, and physics is based on mathematics. Such an organization today seems both arbitrary and artificial.

King and Brownell present a cogent argument for emphasis on the disciplines by negating various other organizing principles, such as values, problem solving, interdisciplinary study, usefulness, modernism, development of skills, and coverage (14, pp. 146–149). They point out fallacies in each of these proposals, and argue that the only way to knowledge, judgment or value commitments is by the concepts and modes of inquiry provided by the disciplines. On the other hand, having demonstrated the autonomy and diversity of the disciplines, they provide no solution to the problem of selecting the one or two disciplines which exemplify each mode of thought.

Others have attacked the problem of classification. Greene attempts to relate content directly to objectives by suggesting that language, mathematics, and art encourage clear communication; that the methodologies of the natural and social sciences, history, philosophy, and theology impart synoptic understanding; and that logic and mathematics teach valid reasoning (10). Greene proposes four basic skills: (a) logical linguistic (clear thinking and accurate use of language); (b) factual (knowledge about his physical, social, and cosmic environment); (c) normative (standards of values); (d) synoptic (integration, development of perspective) (9, pp. 121–123). He then classifies the disciplines which emerge from and communicate these skills:

(a) formal disciplines include mathematics, logic, languages, semantics, and linguistics (approximates the Symbolics of Phenix);

(b) factual disciplines include the natural sciences and the social sciences (approximates the Empirics of Phenix);

(c) normative disciplines include ethics, aesthetics, artistic and literary criticism, and religion (includes the Synnoetics, Esthetics, and Ethics of Phenix);

(d) synoptic disciplines include history (synoptic in respect to time), geography (synoptic in respect to space), philosophy (synoptic in respect to time, space, causes, and values), and religion (the ultimate attempt to relate life and eternity), (approximates the Synoptics of Phenix) (9, pp. 125–126).

Cunningham develops a wheel analogy in which language, theology, philosophy, and history are regarded as the hub and social science, natural science, mathematics, fine arts, and literature as the rim (6, p. 108):

Hong attempts a different solution:

1. *Receptive-focal* studies which draw upon other disciplines and relate them to a particular problem area—air science, music education, nursing, business education, speech.
2. *Receptive-contributive* studies which both draw upon and contribute to other disciplines—biology, physics, social sciences, literature, art, history, philosophy, theology.
3. *Basically contributive* studies which contribute to or are employed in other disciplines—logic (methods of reflective inquiry: mathematical, scientific, historical, artistic, literary, and philosophical methods); language, metaphysics (first principles, presuppositions of being and knowledge).
4. *Synoptic* studies which embrace the whole of knowledge and reality—history, philosophy, theology (11, pp. 163–170).

The schemes of Greene, Hong, and Cunningham deal with the relations of the disciplines rather than with the intrinsic nature of any one of them. Although the diversity of these approaches suggests that any institution could formulate its own definition of the disciplines and their relations, the problem of sequence remains. Education must be built on what has preceded and must relate to what follows. Thus, many unique solutions fail because students do not adjust to them or see how they relate to vocational preparation, or to graduate or professional school. It is unlikely that any one will be adopted at all levels of education. The diversity inherent in American education and the uniqueness of institutions of higher education prohibit such uniformity. However, a brief look at the thinking in two broad groups of disciplines— natural science and social science, may be instructive.

Science.   Science is both a major area of knowledge and a significant approach to expansion of knowledge. Its analytical methodology, its procedures for validation, and its self-corrective nature contain intellectual, cultural, and creative elements which make it as essential to liberal education as any other group of disciplines. However, science taught as a body of knowledge, rather than as a way of knowing is self-defeating. Students must grasp the sequential nature of knowledge in order to understand what they learn and to foresee and accept what is to come. Science must be presented not as a definite body of knowledge, but as a sequence of cumulative achievements which result from a discriminating and adaptive methodology.

This implies that the student must become familiar with many examples of scientific analysis. Concepts used in the several sub-disciplines vary greatly in their specificity and in their operational or experimental character. Some concepts are primarily for gross qualitative classification; some represent measurable characteristics; other are hypothetical constructs used in theory building. Hypotheses, principles, theories, and statistical or mathematical models present different scientific statements related in distinctive ways to observation and to experiment. A student with only a few of these concepts will develop an oversimplified view of science.

Science is not independent of social and political philosophies and institutions, and scientists do have human concerns for practical signifi-cance and personal satisfaction so that errors of commission and omis-sion do occur in scientific investigations. The history of science is full of poor logic, gross errors, faulty assumptions, and abandoned theories. Thus, exposure to a single science, particularly as a body of knowledge, will not impart clear understanding of science as a mode of inquiry.

The organization of science and mathematics in many schools is based on temporal rather than logical sequence in the growth of knowl-edge. This organization inhibits understanding of current scientific developments because the distinctions among the fields are based on outdated assumptions and the concepts and theories are frequently poorly chosen. Yet, any attempt to reorganize the sequence of courses will have to choose between conflicting views as to what concepts are fundamental and what relations are essential. As Chapter 5 demon-strates, the variety of possibilities is revealed in the number of different developments in recent curriculum work in these disciplines. Probably no science program will be widely adopted, but there may be an agree-ment to focus on structure and modes of inquiry rather than on partic-ular topics and sequences. If the student can grasp science as a mode of inquiry, he should be able to fill in gaps in his experience resulting from various structures used at different levels. Indeed, familiarity with two or more ways of structuring a discipline may help him to understand that any organization or structure is arbitrary and subject to change, and that an effective structure for current knowledge may be inadequate for fu-ture developments.

Social Science. Although the term "social science," suggests the application of scientific methods of inquiry to different subject matter, there are at least two significant differences. All natural sciences employ a scientific mode of inquiry. The social sciences, however, do not appear to share a common method or structure, and the term may be no more than a collective designation of a group of disciplines concerned with study of the personal and social behavior of man. Although some have tried to find a set of concepts common to the several social sciences, social science courses are rarely more than composites of ideas selected from sociology, psychology, economics, political science, and anthropology. The first difference, then, is that the existence of social science *per se* is less certain than the existence of natural science.

The second difference is that the social sciences rarely employ rigorous scientific methods. The disciplines use many poorly defined and highly subjective variables whose relationships may be unclear or impossible to determine. Research in these disciplines often results in ambiguous generalizations supported by insignificant statistics (51 percent generalizations). The results of many investigations are purely descriptive, and even the most sophisticated experimental designs have not yielded rigorous quantitative theories. Although Berelson urges that the ultimate goal of the behavioral sciences is not only to understand and explain, but also to predict human behavior, many experts doubt and resist this goal (3, pp. 1–11). Accurate prediction can lead to coercion and control. One can study, predict, and control the behavior of atoms without concern for the ultimate utility for good and evil, or for the fate of the individual atom changed from matter to energy by the process. In a democratic society, such manipulation of human beings is intolerable. If the social sciences ignore values, the use of achievable generalizations of quantitative theories to predict and control is inexcusable. Yet, to the extent that the social sciences consciously consider ethical and moral values, whether in patterns of investigation or in interpretation and recommendations, they fail to be fully scientific. The dilemma may be of no consequence, for Scriven asserts that the nature of social science makes realization of vast theories impossible (21, p. 88). In fact, Scriven asserts that no precise general definition of the social sciences or social studies is possible (21, p. 88).

The social sciences are characterized by relationships rather than by common syntax. Scriven suggests three different concepts of these relationships:

1. *Interdisciplinary* which views the several social sciences as specializations of a common subject matter.
2. *Multidisciplinary* which views the social sciences is indepen-

dent sciences concerned with human behavior and related only by the common source of that behavior.

3. *Reductionist* which views the social sciences as in the initial stages of developing a vast human macrophysics since human beings are, after all, but collections of atoms (21, p. 88).

Only the third view promises a complete unity of science. Scriven labels this view as "far out" and the interdisciplinary approach as unproductive in that no common subject matter has yet been isolated and defined. The multidisciplinary approach is the most promising, but it poses problems in the treatment of the social sciences in a curriculum. The study of a number of specific problems, such as poverty or urbanization, from the vantage point of the several social sciences, may be the only way to grasp the distinctions between social sciences, but this is not an approach based on the structure of the disciplines.

History is classified under both the social sciences and the humanities. For students, it too often becomes a catalogue of facts, dates, names, and events. History, as a discipline should teach the nature of evidence, the criteria for choice of sources and facts, and the conceptual structures employed by historians. Although history deals with the past, it is continually rewritten; its interpretations are always in doubt and often highly controversial. The student should see that there are recurrent problems in society (authority, relations of political, economic, and social systems, for example) which are resolved in different ways in different times and places. He should recognize that historical interpretations are always to some degree subjective, and that human motivations and purposes influence both the sequences of social change and those who later interpret them. Experiences in history as a discipline are available in most colleges and universities only to majors and to graduate students. But history, taught as a discipline to undergraduates, could engender continuing interest in historical problems and issues.

This brief discussion of the difficulties of developing disciplines in terms of their structure has but glanced at the problems in two broad groups of disciplines. One must conclude that, even in the sciences and social sciences, there is not general agreement on either concepts or syntactical structures, and the situation is even less promising in other disciplines.

PSYCHCLOGICAL ASPECTS OF THE
STRUCTURE OF KNOWLEDGE

The methods of initial discovery of knowledge and those of validation are rarely identical. A flash of insight cannot be described as a stage in a systematic method of inquiry, although the validated results may be so presented. Even in directed, organized inquiry, in which discovery and validation proceed systematically, the sequence of steps followed may differ from the order imposed to adjust the product to the larger body of previously existing knowledge. Although initial discovery is a learning experience, it is rarely repeated and is not a satisfactory way for others to learn. The learning process of a highly trained and motivated scientist is not suited to the undergraduate.

Two individuals confronted with a well-structured sequence of learning experiences will not acquire identical structures. Differences in intellect and in prior experiences result in different associations, interpretations, and degrees of understanding. Hence, we may distinguish two organizations of knowledge, the psychological order (idiosyncratic to an individual) and the logical order.

The structure of knowledge clearly has implications for curriculum organization and for instruction, but the nature of the learning process must also be considered. This task is closely related to the instructional process, and will be considered at greater length in Chapter 8. One of the underlying concerns of all education is transfer of knowledge. Knowledge and abilities which relate to nothing but their original context are worthless. The classical conception of training the mind by exposure to such subjects as Latin, Greek, mathematics, philosophy is supported by few psychologists and educators, but is still maintained by many faculty members. The view that there is no generalized transfer of knowledge and abilities developed from specific studies underestimates human capability and the power of education. The prevalent view maintains that transfer is possible, but that it depends on a similarity of the original learning situation to the new situation. Transfer results not from acquiring knowledge but from understanding the meanings and the sources of knowledge, from mastering of modes of inquiry, and from consciously seeking generalizations and applications. Thus, attention to the structure of dicsiplines is appropriate if transfer is desired, but effective only if transfer is a conscious goal reflected in the organization of the curriculum and learning experiences.

CONTINUITY, SEQUENCE, AND INTEGRATION

A college education includes a number of related elements: acquiring general knowledge and abilities; understanding the disciplines and one in particular; applying the disciplines to appropriate subjects or problems; relating the disciplines to each other; and integrating the disciplines to deal with common problems. These elements require ordering, which is a fundamental task of curriculum organization.

The task involves at least three problems. The first is the identification of continuity and sequence in each discipline. In the sciences and mathematics this seems simpler than in the humanities but, in fact, the organization is only *less* arbitrary because the cumulative nature of these disciplines is more evident. Furthermore, a completely logical order, in which each idea is introduced once and presumably mastered, is inconsistent with the way people learn. Seldom is any idea, concept, or principle mastered immediately; repeated contact at more sophisticated levels is required. Thus, sequence is only partially determined by the order and difficulty of ideas in a discipline. A second order is based on the degree of complexity of cognitive processes: rote knowledge, comprehension, application, analysis, synthesis, and evaluation (using the principal headings of the Bloom *Taxonomy*). There are, then, at least two possible sequences: the sequence of ideas and the sequence of cognitive processes. But the disciplines also relate to one another in a certain sequence. Ths student cannot study all disciplines at once, although some broad interdisciplinary programs attempt to achieve this goal. However, a structure cannot be built on an insecure base, so such courses have generally been isolated rather than sequential experiences. Clearly, a student must be proficient in English before pursuing any other college study, but the appropriate order of mathematics, biology, chemistry, and physics is not as evident. Of course, they can be taught independently, but the decision to do so insures that most students will forever regard them as independent. When students can take courses in several disciplines simultaneously, and particularly when the program is optional, few students or teachers attempt to explore common ideas and significant similarities, or to resolve or clarify inconsistencies and differences. Yet, even a sequential organization of disciplines may fail because teachers do not utilize the sequence or develop their courses within its framework. Perhaps continuity, sequence, and integration can be achieved in most colleges only through interdisciplinary or relatively unstructured learning.

SUMMARY

The number, organization, structure, and relationship of disciplines pose problems for which there is no final answer. Some solution must be found if many issues in curriculum development are to be resolved. If breadth is defined by distribution requirements, some meaningful grouping of the disciplines is necessary. If learning emphazises the structure and the mode of inquiry of a discipline rather than factual knowledge, then the structures and modes of inquiry must be more clearly defined. If double or triple majors are sought, then the relations of the disciplines must be clarified. If practical problems and experiences are included in a curriculum, then the modes of inquiry and the concepts of several disciplines may be required to deal with them. Finally, if integration, coherence, and unity are to be facilitated by curriculum organization, understanding of the disciplines and their interrelationships is essential.

REFERENCES

1. Daniel Bell, *The Reforming of General Education*, Columbia University Press, 1966.
2. Arno Bellack, "The Structure of Knowledge and the Structure of the Curriculum," Chapter 3 in *A Reassessment of the Curriculum*, Dwayne Huebner, ed., Bureau of Publications, Teachers College, Columbia University, 1964, pp. 25–40.
3. Bernard Berelson, ed., *The Behavioral Sciences Today*, Basic Books, Inc., New York, 1963.
4. Jerome S. Bruner, "Notes on a Theory of Instruction," in *Toward a Theory of Instruction*, Belknap Press of Harvard University Press, Cambridge, 1966, p. 72.
5. _____ , *On Knowing: Essays for the Left Hand*, Harvard University Press, 1962.
6. William F. Cunningham, *General Education and the Liberal College*, B. Herder Book Co., St. Louis, 1953.
7. Stanley Elam, ed., *Education and the Structure of Knowledge*, Rand McNally and Company, Chicago, 1964.
8. G. W. Ford and Lawrence Pugno, eds., *The Structure of Knowledge and the Curriculum*, Rand McNally and Company, Chicago, 1964.
9. Theodore Greene, "A Liberal Christian Idealist Philosophy of Education," Chapter IV in *Modern Philosophies and Education*, Part I, Fifty-Fourth Yearbook of the National Society for the Study of Education, Nelson B. Henry, ed., University of Chicago Press, 1955, pp. 91–136.
10. _____ , *Liberal Education Reconsidered*, Harvard University Press, 1953.
11. Howard Hong, ed., *Integration in the Christian Liberal Arts College*, St. Olaf College Press, 1956.
12. Dwayne Huebner, ed., *A Reassessment of the Curriculum*, Bureau of Publications, Teachers College, Columbia University, 1964.
13. Abraham Kaplan, *The Conduct of Inquiry*, Chandler Publishing Company, San Francisco, 1964.
14. Arthur King and John Brownell, *The Curriculum and the Disciplines of Knowledge*, John Wiley and Sons, Inc., New York, 1966.
15. C. Robert Pace, "New Concepts in Institutional Goals for Students," in *The Liberal Arts College's Responsibility for the Individual Student*, Earl J. McGrath, ed., Teachers College Press, Columbia University, 1966, pp. 38–47.

16. Philip H. Phenix, "The Architectonics of Knowledge," Chapter 2 in *Education and the Structure of Knowledge*, Stanley Elam, ed., Rand McNally and Company, Chicago, 1964, pp. 44–74.

17. _____, *Realms of Meaning*, McGraw-Hill Book Company, Inc., New York, 1964.

18. Oliver L. Reiser, *The Integration of Human Knowledge*, Porter Sargent, Publisher, Boston, 1958.

19. Joseph J. Schwab, "Problems, Topics, and Issues," Chapter 1 in *Education and the Structure of Knowledge*, Stanley Elam, ed., Rand McNally.

20. _____, "Structure of the Disciplines," in *The Structure of Knowledge and the Curriculum*, G. W. Ford and Lawrence Pugno, eds., Rand McNally and Company, Chicago, 1964, pp. 6–30.

21. Michael Scriven, "The Structure of the Social Studies," in *The Structure of Knowledge and the Curriculum*, G. W. Ford and Lawrence Pugno, eds., Rand McNally and Company, Chicago, 1964, pp. 87–105.

22. Hilda Taba, *Curriculum Development, Theory and Practice*, Harcourt, Brace and World, Inc., New York, 1962.

23. Daniel Tanner, "Curriculum Theory: Knowledge and Content," Chapter III in *Review of Educational Research*, Vol. XXXVI, No. 3, June, 1966, pp. 362–372.

4

Developments and Trends in Liberal Education

Although the distinction between liberal and vocational education has been over-emphasized, it is difficult to balance the practical, task-oriented aspects of education with the ideas, values, and vision which recognize the unique capabilities of man. For this reason, the discussion of developments and trends has been divided into three chapters. This chapter focuses on broad program developments in liberal education, the next, on developments in the disciplines, and the next, on professional and vocational education. This chapter discusses educational activity in both the small liberal arts colleges and the arts and science colleges of larger universities. The range of activity and program development is wide. Any discussion of curricular innovation must include independent study for, despite its antiquity as a mode of learning, this is one of the most revolutionary elements in the curriculum of higher education. Also, grades and examinations must be considered, for some programs rely heavily on the manipulation of grading patterns, Study abroad, work-study programs, and community service experiences are also new trends in liberal education. Any review must acknowledge the extensive curriculum studies and proposals in the various disciplines but, since these tend to be independent of each other, they will be discussed in the following chapter.

Many innovations are applicable to liberal, vocational, and professional education. Independent study and changes in grading or examination practices are as significant for vocational or professional education as for liberal education. Study and travel abroad can be as relevant for students in business, agriculture, or veterinary medicine as for students in the liberal arts. The rethinking of curricula in the various disciplines effects vocational and professional education as well as the departments in the liberal arts and sciences. Indeed, some developments in the basic disciplines result from the contributions of the applied fields. Finally, each of the experiences to be discussed could be specifically planned to provide a liberal education, a vocational education, or both.

BROAD PROGRAM DEVELOPMENTS

Independent Study

All learning is ultimately individual, but highly structured courses with common assignments are not concerned primarily with the specific needs of each student. Independent study is sometimes defined as individualized instruction outside of the formal class. Although independent study clearly refers to the student, individualized instruction focuses on the instructor. Some independent study programs, instead of teaching the student greater self-reliance, make him more dependent on his instructor. The student who is required to see his instructor several times a week may receive more detailed guidance than he ever would in the classroom.

Independent study may accomplish several things. First, through careful selection of the topic or problem of study and through recurrent contact and exchange with the instructor, the student may be more highly motivated. Second, the student may accept some responsibility for planning and conducting his own study and learn to criticize his own work. Third, the student, rather than simply assimilating the results of research or scholarly work, may initiate his own research or scholarly studies. Ideally, he learns a mode of inquiry by engaging in it rather than simply hearing or reading about it.

Two major problems have led to difficulty and discouragement with programs of independent study. It was once assumed that independent study would reduce both the burden on faculty members and the costs of education. Although some faculty members provide too much supervision, independent study projects are expensive and few institutions can introduce a significant number of them without greatly increasing the cost of education.

Another problem is that faculty members often discover that students do not readily assume responsibility for independent study. The freshman has very little experience or competence in guiding his own learning and must be taught, by a series of carefully planned steps, to engage in independent study in his senior year and thereafter. Otherwise, education has been a failure, for the student will not continue his learning on his own initiative. The faculty must determine a sequence of educational experiences which prepare the student to accept the responsibility of independent study.

Faculty members may be as ill prepared to direct independent study as students are to engage in it. Independent study may become little more than a scheduled course. The student signs up for three, four, or five credits of independent study. The faculty member, in turn, feels some compulsion to meet the student a reasonable number of times to justify the number of credits assigned. The student is usually enrolled also in formal courses with regular class meetings, deadlines, and tests, and independent study is easily postponed unless it, too, is structured. Independent study, thus, becomes a set of specific assignments and due dates which destroys its essential character. Some faculty members are reluctant to direct independent study because they already offer courses in every aspect of their own interests. They are not prepared to spend several hours with a single student when they could be doing the same thing with a larger audience. The faculty member may also wish to use an independent study student as a personal research assistant. This can be a very happy relationship, but a faculty member with highly specialized interests may sacrifice the student's desires and goals to his own.

An instructor cannot guide a student unless he is familiar with the materials the student is studying. But too many faculty members insist that they must read or reread everything they suggest to the student. They feel they must always know more than the student and must provide not just suggestions or guidance but firm leadership. Many students want such direction, but it does not result in independent study.

The most elementary approach to independent study is to allow the student to carry out on his own some portion of a course offered in conventional classes. Class meetings are reduced, oral or written reports increased, and oral or written examinations introduced. This approach may reduce the burden on the instructor, but he usually finds that he spends as much time with students outside of class as he would have spent in class meetings. An extreme form of this pattern is to give the student an outline or syllabus of a course and require him to complete the course requirements without class attendance. One college has found that asking the student to assume responsibility for a major portion of a a required course is a successful initial step toward independent study. Since other students are taking the course, the student has opportunities for exchange with other persons, but he himself must determine how much he does and how quickly he moves in preparing for the examination.

Independent study courses are often programs of systematic and supervised reading based on a bibliography prepared by the instructor or a specialist in the field. Occasional group conferences or seminars of students doing related reading provide incentive and tutorial direction. These conferences can be dominated by the instructor and based on a schedule of reporting by individual participants. They also can be self-directed groups, in which each individual contributes to the analysis and possible solution of a problem either by thorough investigation of a particular aspect of the problem or by general reading on the topic. In this case, responsibility to the group provides motivation and incentive. Indeed, members of a seminar may be more brutal in detecting and denouncing lack of effort than a faculty member would be.

There is always a question of what constitutes an adequate amount of work in independent study. Those students who are challenged by it will probably spend much more time than the credit hours justify; others may do little or nothing. Thus the issue of standards and grading arises. If independent study is put on a pass or fail basis, few will fail because the grade involves an appraisal of the student's worth as well as of the quality of his work. One good solution is to agree initially on the nature of the independent study project and then let the student continue working until it is completed.

Many studies suggest that the freshman year is crucial, especially for the most able students. The transition from senior year high school courses, which often include honors or independent study programs, to freshman introductory courses may result in disenchantment and apathy. To alleviate this situation, a number of institutions have introduced freshman seminars, required or optional, and occasionally ungraded. Prominent, outstanding, and provocative scholars are selected to instruct the seminars. Topics may be derived from frontier research in a field, from broad interdisciplinary problems, or from concerns or issues of specific interest to freshmen. If seminars are offered in a wide variety of fields, a student who has already selected a specialization may confront advanced problems in his field, while completing the relatively routine requirements in other courses. Other students will find a challenging introduction to a significant area of study, or become familiar with the institution's resources and research opportunities. Experience in one or more such seminars may also help the student make a wiser decision as to his major or concentration.

Despite the success of the optional non-graded freshman seminar, it poses a number of problems. Outstanding faculty members may be challenged by the novelty of the experience, but they soon find it an additional burden and rarely continue with it for more than a year or two. Thus, it may become very difficult to staff such seminars with challenging and prominent scholars once the initial enthusiasm has worn off.

Also, because freshmen receive no credit for the seminar, many will not or cannot spend much time outside preparing for one course. Moreover, such seminars only alleviate rather than resolve the basic difficulty. If freshman students are unchallenged or bored by the regular freshman program, it seems wiser to alter the total program than to provide a diversion from it.

The goal of independent study is not complete independence which, in the extreme, only isolates the student from other scholars. Independent study should lead to increasing self-reliance in learning and increasing insight and understanding through sharing learning with others. Such sharing provides much of the excitement of learning and also forces one student to analyze his understanding in a deeper and more exacting way. The resulting interaction provides the sense of accomplishment and achievement which motivates and sustains learning.

Honors

"Honors" is one of the more ambiguous words in American higher education. One university has an Honors College which frees the student from all university requirements and imposes no requirements of its own. Thus, the student may graduate as a member of the Honors College without having done any honors work. A student may also graduate with honor or with high honor solely on the basis of his point average. This same institution also offers honors courses and honors sections of courses which students not enrolled in the Honors College may attend. In other institutions, there are departmental honors as well as general honors. Although, in England, only the honors degree is respected and the ordinary, general, or pass degree has relatively little status, there is little evidence that honors status or honors college graduation has achieved such respect in this country. Graduate schools and employers often select solely on the basis of point average. The reaction of one young woman graduating from a state university with a 4-point average typifies the situation. When asked why she was not in the honors program in her major field, she replied that there was too much work for what one would get out of it and that it might have lowered her average. Finally, she remarked that her sorority offices and student activities were probably more valuable to her than an honors program, and she could not have done both.

Honors work is basically independent study, although the term, "honors," is sometimes applied to special courses or sections of courses which cover more or different material, probe more deeply, or use different techniques. For example, seminars or conferences are preferred to lectures and recitations in honors courses. One possible difference between independent study and honors lies in the initial selection of students. Some insist that honors work is for the elite and that the students admitted to honors work must already have demonstrated unusual capacity. Others maintain that the honors experience is valuable for all students, although a different label may be chosen for those who are less outstanding.

Honors work, traditionally and perhaps by British influence, has emphasized probing deeply into a given body of knowledge and doing research in source materials. Thus, honors work has been related to depth rather than to breadth. However, honors work focusing on problems which cut across disciplines is often permitted. In any case, honors work involves reading, research, and the preparation of reports, essays, and papers. It may include laboratory research, creative projects, or field studies. Traditionally, honors work differs from independent study in referring to a cumulative experience over a period of time. The honors student is usually committed to a two-year program, and his work culminates in a thesis or special project and comprehensive examination. The examination rarely has the same significance in institutions in this country as in British institutions. In this country a limited number of students take honors work and, although the formality of a final comprehensive examination may be maintained, it is less decisive than in England where the examination alone determines the honors degree level. However, some new English universities do include course work achievement in determining honors. An institution revising its curriculum might well emphasize independent study for all, and award honors on the basis of unusual performance rather than on completion of an unusual program.

Integrative Seminars

Perhaps because the seminar was imported as a mode of graduate instruction, seminars at the undergraduate level are associated with probing in depth into a particular discipline. Seminars do perform this function, and are still the preferred mode of formal instruction at the graduate level. However, the graduate seminar may have an integrative impact because, in a group of advanced students and professors, individuals may achieve new insights, perceive previously unnoted interrelationships, and arrive at different and more coherent organizations of their knowledge. A seminar can be highly specialized in focus and yet be integrative in impact.

Seminars can also be integrative by emphasizing, through the inter-action of students from different fields, pervasive concepts, principles, or modes of inquiry or by seeking the particular contributions of several disciplines to understanding and solving a specific problem. Such seminars seem best adapted to students with some depth of specialized study. Obviously, there must be some correlation between the composition of the group and the content of the seminar. Art, mathematics, and science students might, with imaginative leadership, profitably investigate the concept of symmetry. Mapping poses problems of common concern to geographers, demographers, historians, and mathematicians. Social science and science students might gain from investigating common modes of scientific inquiry. Problems of classification concern all disci-plines, and representatives of several disciplines might consider the various bases for and assumptions underlying different systems.

A second focus for an interdisciplinary seminar is a problem of sufficient complexity to require for its understanding concepts, prin-ciples, and skills from several fields. Poverty, juvenile delinquency, un-derdeveloped nations, the scientific-humanistic schism, and conserva-tion of natural resources are a few such problems. A seminar of foreign students and students who have spent some months in a foreign culture might profit from a re-examination of the values of American society.

At one college, a seminar required for all juniors studied the City of Florence in the year 1500. Students followed their various interests in probing into the social, scientific, medical, economic, architectural, artistic, philosophical, political, and literary accomplishments of that era. This period was chosen because so much research had been done on it, the library holdings were excellent, and a very able teacher had long been interested in it. The students discovered the relations between various facets of a culture and developed new insights into each of the disciplines used to study the culture. Each student, to some degree, be-came a practitioner of a discipline and educated other students in its concepts, structure, methodology, and subject matter.

The integrative seminar can promote breadth, depth, and integra-tion. It encourages both *independence* and *interdependence* in study. However, it cannot be successful unless inspired leadership is provided by one or more faculty members. Such persons must have a breadth of scholarship, and must be willing to sacrifice their own specialized in-terests. The dearth of such individuals is perhaps the major reason why so many enthusiastic attempts at integrative seminars have failed.

One popular development of the integrative seminar was the "Great Issues" senior seminar. Courses in this pattern were surveyed by Stickler in "Senior Courses in General Education" (28). Great issues are both timely and timeless: freedom and responsibility, conflicts of labor and management, communism and democracy, religion and science. Such seminars allow seniors to assess the significance of their education and its implications for facing the problems of adult life. Guest lecturers may be used; readings, including current newspapers or journals, may be required; and discussions among students and faculty may demonstrate the relevance of various disciplines and of college education to pervasive problems in all areas of human experience. Students may be required to pursue a particular problem in some depth, as well as participate in discussions and lectures. Although students need not be graded, at Dartmouth there was a consensus that examinations and grades were necessary to insure the active participation of students.

Climate for Learning

The term, "climate for learning," refers to attempts to restructure the physical environment and academic program in such a way as to alleviate or eliminate conflicts which interfere with learning. A climate for learning attempts to introduce some measure of coherence and unity into the student's total experience. Its development involves one or more of the following:

1. A merger of two competing and sometimes conflicting cultures, that of the classroom and that of the residence.
2. An emphasis on teaching and on individual learning rather than on content coverage.
3. Close and continuing contact between a group of students and a group of faculty, so that classroom and informal contacts can ripen into close and friendly association.
4. Increased homogeneity in background and ability, and increased commonality of experience to promote independent and interdependent learning.
5. Integration of experiences in and out of class and on and off campus.
6. Encouragement of greater individualization and interdisciplinary learning.
7. An effort to join students, faculty, administrators, and student personnel workers into a unified scholarly community.
8. Elimination of pointless moving from place to place.
9. Economies in organization of instruction by reduction in number of courses and possibly of class meetings per course.

10. Opportunity to develop new patterns of instruction, such as seminars, tutorials, independent study.
11. Replacement of tests and grades with intrinsic motivation derived from the excitement of learning and the continued interaction with other learners.

Few ventures in the development of a climate for learning offer all these possibilities. Some public university administrators question the desirability of homogeneity in background, although the requirements and emphases of university courses inevitably result in some uniformity. For example, if foreign language is to be a major part of the experience of a group of students, then some admission requirement in foreign language must be established. Furthermore, students who dislike foreign language will avoid the program. If the program emphasizes the humanities, few science students will enroll. Some ventures have not explicitly accepted economy as a determining principle but, when several hundred students are involved in a common set of educational experiences, economy in instruction and courses will result. Publicly supported institutions usually limit the cost of new ventures to that of previously existing programs.

The reasons for developing a climate of learning suggest some of the elements in planning it. One of the more obvious elements is size, the number of faculty and the number of students. Universities with enrollments in the tens of thousands may think 1,200 an appropriate size to develop close relationships between faculty and students. Smaller institutions may think of 100 students and 5 faculty members. The new English universities prefer groups of 300 students.

A second element is the degree of involvement of both students and faculty in one program. Those strongly in favor of such units within a larger institution argue that both the faculty member's teaching duties and the student's courses should be within the unit. However, in large institutions, the departmental emphasis is so strong and the demand for research time so prevalent that faculty members prefer to spend less than half their time in such a unit, and often resign from the program after two or three years. Also, resources are expensive to duplicate so that the student usually spends only fifty or sixty percent of his time in unit programs, and the rest in developing a departmental concentration.

A third consideration is the relation of any given unit to other units. This involves shared use of certain facilities, development of common programs, joint membership of students or faculty in two or more units, and financial considerations. Several issues can be pointed out by a few questions. What is the relation of the dean of students' office in a university to the small, autonomous residence college? Are students free to take courses in any unit? Can a student enrolled in such a unit fulfill concentration or major requirements of another unit or department in the university? Is such a unit free to employ its own faculty, or must the appointment first originate in a department?.

A fourth issue is programing and scheduling. A small living-learning unit can be much more flexible in scheduling classes and providing free time for trips, special lectures, and seminars. If the unit is heavily dependent upon offerings of other units or departments, this flexibility may be lost. If the unit is dependent on a part-time faculty, informal contact of students and faculty is limited.

A fifth issue is the degree of autonomy. Obviously, the nature of the program largely determines the necessary degree of autonomy. In a Master of the House program, in which house activities such as seminars and discussions, occur outside of normal class hours, autonomy may not be an issue, although conflicts between the Master of the House and the residence hall personnel may arise over food service, use of facilities, rules, and discipline. If the institution is a small cluster of independent colleges which have pooled their resources to provide certain expensive and important facilities and programs, then almost complete autonomy may exist in the individual units, as is found at Oxford or Cambridge. When small units are set up within a large university, complete autonomy is difficult to achieve. The deans and department chairmen resist such autonomy because it infringes upon their own and because they fear it may lower university standards. On the other hand, a part-time faculty will endanger the success of the program, because the faculty will not be available to engage in continuing interaction with students and in mutual education and extensive curricular planning.

A sixth element in planning is the basis for admitting students and selecting faculty. There are several conflicting views on admissions criteria. One is that a cross-section of students should be sought. This is especially important if the program might ultimately be used extensively in the institution. Another method is to publicize the intended program and let students select it. A third method is to develop a program which requires certain competencies and select students on the basis of their attainment of them. Another is to allow interested faculty members to set up a program which will attract its own students. Yet another approach selects a group of students and an experimentally-minded group of faculty, and allows them to work out the program together. This method is rarely found in institutions of higher education, but it has been used in some programs for the underprivileged.

The emphasis on living together characteristic of these programs raises the issue of whether students not residing in the unit should be permitted to participate in it. In the formative period of the program, it may be advantageous to restrict it to resident students. In the long run, such restriction is unreasonable unless the program requires an eighteen to twenty-four hour day. However, nonresident students should be provided study space and expected to join in many non-class programs, even to the extent of eating one or more meals with the group. The living-learning conception cannot be successful unless there is continuing and pervasive interaction of students and faculty.

The nature of the program, of course, is a major element in planning. Many programs have developed a particular theme, such as intercultural studies, area studies (Europe, Asia, etc.), or scientific studies which involve an interdisciplinary approach and use elements of history and philosophy of science. Other programs emphasize independent study and research and stress a method rather than a theme.

The development of climates for learning follows closely the pattern developed in Chapter 2, which presented the various continua, essentials, and facilitating elements basic to curriculum development. Patterns for a climate of learning are quite varied. The house plan involves a small group of students and faculty, in a ratio of fifteen or twenty to one, who participate in common structured learning experiences. It emphasizes independent study, and concentrates on the total activity of the group in educating each other. Thus, this plan can lead to a self-contained college. If a number of these were operating in a given institution, the degree of independence might approximate that of the Claremont cluster pattern, even though the separate units would be part of one college on one campus. However, one residence hall or part of one residence hall could operate in this way, while the rest of the institution continued in the more traditional pattern of departmental course organization and separation of academic and residence living.

A second pattern might be described as a residence hall instructional program. This pattern is most successful in institutions with a common core of required courses. If all freshmen and sophomores must take certain general courses, then offering these in a residence hall insures that a large proportion of the students will be enrolled in classes there. The inclusion of offices, class rooms, laboratory, and library facilities in a dormitory achieves a climate which embraces both learning and living. Such a program, to be effective, should provide halls which house both men and women, with common dining and recreational areas. If there are no requirements which apply to a large proportion of students, it is difficult to develop a residence hall living-learning situa-

tion. Assigning faculty to a dormitory for classes or for office space does
not have any marked impact on one character of the hall unless programs for interaction of faculty and students are provided. If classes
offered in a residence area include large numbers of students from
other areas, the living-learning climate is confused and diluted. However, with capable and inspired leadership, the character of a residence
hall can be considerably modified by an extensive informal and cultural
program.

Another pattern is the development of semi-autonomous or
autonomous liberal arts colleges based in a residence hall. This plan is
similar to the house plan, but the college is likely to be somewhat larger
and more self-contained because college status implies a head or a dean
with an established position in the hierarchy of the institution. Yet, the
college will be different from other colleges because the faculty and students will live and work together, and they will tend to develop their
cultural, social, and recreational programs around the college unit. The
usual college in a university exists as an academic unit only and, except
possibly in vocational or technical colleges, attracts no allegiance from
its students.

Another pattern developed at Rutgers establishes several equivalent liberal arts units at some distance from one another, each with its
own faculty, who also participate in university-wide departments. This
development is largely determined by problems of size and space rather
than by thorough exploration and development of the living-learning
concept.

Finally, there is the cluster college pattern of Claremont in which
essentially independent institutions band together to provide certain
common programs, facilities, and graduate instruction. In a sense,
this is the antithesis of the small, autonomous units in a university.
Whereas universities develop smaller units which combine the character of a small college with the advantages of a large university, the
cluster college pattern begins with small units then combines the resources of the colleges to develop programs characteristic of a university.
Educationally, the results may not differ greatly but certainly the units
in a cluster college are more independent and unique than those im-
bedded in an overshadowing university.

Grades and Examinations

The elimination of grades and examinations is a recurrent theme in
curricular review and innovation. Grades and frequent examinations
reinforce the course-credit pattern in which the student learns because

he must rather than because he wants to. Any discussion of grades and examinations gives rise to diametrically opposed points of view. In one state university, two proposals were being entertained simultaneously. One maintained that the existing A, B, C, D, F pattern provided insufficient differentiation, and proposed that pluses and minuses be added to each letter. The other proposed that the letter grade system be replaced by a pass/fail pattern. Similarly, those in favor of examinations argue that more frequent tests place greater pressure on the students and insure higher standards. Those who de-emphasize grades usually feel that examinations should be replaced either by essays and papers or by comprehensive examinations scheduled at intervals of a year or more. Some argue that, without grades, students will not work; others argue that, with grades, students will not do worthwhile work. There is no evidence to support either position.

The examination and grades controversy involves basic issues about the nature of education. Those who view educational objectives as primarily cognitive or factual can accept a single grade. Those who wish to emphasize attitudes and values, or to attain a number of reasonably distinct objectives view the grade as a totally inadequate reflection of the student's accomplishment.

Human fallibility is a significant factor in the reaction against grades. Many doubt that the average instructor can grade fairly or accurately, or that he takes the time to do so. Grades often do incorporate factors of attitude, attendance, and prejudice which are not relevant to achievement. Part of the difficulty is that grades serve many functions, and the meaning and relative importance of these functions vary among instructors, students, and college administrators. Grades are used to (1) distinguish between students who will receive credit for a course and those who will not; (2) distinguish levels of performance among those who receive credit; (3) summarize for the official record the student's enrollment and achievement in the course and provide for transferability of the credit; (4) inform the student of his achievement in the course; (5) inform parents of the achievement of thier children; (6) maintain scholastic standards by eliminating the lazy or inept; (7) motivate students to worry about low marks and appreciate high ones; (8) discipline students who fail to attend class or otherwise fulfill the contract implied by enrollment; (9) provide a basis for determining the award of honors and scholarships and for selection in advanced programs of education; (10) carry out research studies on prediction, placement, and comparisons of social groups, departments, and colleges; (11) evaluate instruction.

The first and third of these functions, credit determination and records, encourage the use of a single letter or number so that official records can be economical and simple. In addition, the importance of granting credit forces some judgment, on at least a pass or fail basis, of all aspects of student performance. In large institutions, especially those on a quarter system, the instructor's contact with his students is so limited that any more than a single letter grade is difficult, if not impossible. Other tasks, such as honors awards, scholarship awards, probation, and elimination, are also simplified by use of the letter grade and point average. Despite the imprecision and ambiguity of the grade and average, they provide a sense of precision and permit decisions based on the second or third decimal place.

There are not a great many alternatives to the five-point grading scale. The most extreme is the complete elimination of grades. Institutions accepting this pattern stress small classes, close contact between students and instructors, and independent study. The student presents reports, orally or in writing, and the instructor informs the student directly of the quality of his work. The instructor may also prepare a written appraisal of the student, and possibly review it with the student before consigning it to the permanent record file. Students are often asked to write a personal evaluation of their experience. In at least one college, student papers are filed as part of the record. One problem with this system is the difficulty of obtaining a written report which clearly analyzes the student's strengths and weaknesses. One can usually determine the really outstanding students, but it is difficult to eliminate inadequate students. The combination of subjectivity, ambiguity, and charity renders the permanent record system a bulky, expensive, and not very serviceable instrument for evaluating student performance. One institution found that the sheer bulk of a student's file meant that, when a student transferred or applied to graduate school, a clerk in the registrar's office had to prepare a brief summary of it.

A second alternative of the A-F pattern is the pass/fail or pass/no report system, which can be applied to all or to some segment of the student's program. One pattern uses grades only in courses in the student's major field to encourage the student to explore other fields without fear of lowering his grade point average. Experiences with this pattern are mixed. One university reported a large number of students electing courses outside their major under the pass/fail pattern in the first year, but a marked decrease in the second year. Also, students enrolled simultaneously in two patterns of courses, one using the standard five-division letter grade system and the other using a pass/fail system are very likely to concentrate on the courses providing the widest range of grades. One state university recently announced that students could choose between the ordinary grade system and the pass/fail system. Only experience will reveal the results of such an option. One might hypothesize that outstanding students will use the option less than average or weak students, and that the latter will use it primarily in difficult courses. Although the system has not been used enough to draw conclusions on its impact, some hypotheses emerge from informal reports of the experience. The distinction between pass and fail usually is not the interval between D and F, because D is generally accepted as unsatisfactory, though passing, whereas pass is regarded as C or better. The distribution on the two-point scale depends largely on the instructors but, since F's may have to be justified, probably fewer will be given than under a five-point system. Some minimum standards for passing might be set, but for many students this minimum would become the maximum. The use of the pass/no report eliminates failure, and implies that the student may be able to pass the course with additional work. The pass/no report system takes the radical step of saying to the student, "continue until you do an adequate job or discontinue, if you wish, without penalty." This pattern is highly disruptive to the usual organization of the academic year, and raises serious questions as to how long a student may be permitted to continue working on courses without achieving a satisfactory level of work. Failure to pass an adequate number of courses in a specified period would have to be made the basis for dropping the unmotivated and incompetent.

A third alternative is a three-point scale providing distinction or honors, pass, and fail. This eliminates one major dissatisfaction of both faculty and students with the two-point scale, that it eliminates recognition of the outstanding student. A few institutions have switched to the two-point scale, added the category of distinction or honors, and then interpolated two intervals, one between pass and fail, and one between honors and pass, thus arriving back at the five-point scale. No doubt each addition was an innovation.

One pattern of grading occasionally used by individual teachers is the contract system. Under this system, the instructor indicates in advance that a C will be awarded for completing a certain specified amount of work at an acceptable level. For additional work, again clearly specified, the student will receive a B or an A. Under this system, the student is asked to contract at the beginning of the term for the grade he wishes to earn, and he then must fulfill the indicated obligations for that grade. In the two instances in which this was observed, students seemed to react favorably to the pattern, but one wonders whether quantity had not usurped the role of quality in appraising the student's work.

There is some support for grading scales which require greater discrimination. The addition of pluses and minuses to a five-point scale yields a fifteen-point scale. The percentage scale permits one hundred distinctions but, in practice, usually shrinks to forty or fifty. All objections to the five-point scale can be leveled with even greater force against these extended scales.

Considering the widespread use of the five-point scale, it is doubtful that any alternative will be satisfactory for long. The novelty of a new pattern may produce some enthusiasm and transient satisfaction. However, the elimination of grades usually requires more effort for faculty to provide an effective substitute than does the grading system itself. The necessity of transferability, readily satisfied by a common five-point system, and the demand that outstanding students be distinguished from the mass of satisfactory students will ultimately lead to a great deal of dissatisfaction with any alternative. The five-point system generates as much dissatisfaction as any other, but its prevalence makes it tolerable.

Although examinations are often used for grading, they are by no means synonymous with grading. They tend to come under similar scrutiny because many instructors base their grades on a final examination or on a midterm and final. The fact that "midterm" and "final" are universally understood terms in American higher education suggests the extent of their usage. An examination, in the best sense, informs students and teachers of their mutual progress. The assignment of a grade to an examination, however, tends to defeat the purpose of informing and motivating the student, and ignores the responsibility of the instructor. A system could easily eliminate grades and continue to use examinations as a means of assisting students to evaluate their own progress. In a sense, this is what programed learning does.

Examinations prepared especially for the purpose of grading at the end of a course and read by persons other than the instructor may eliminate some problems of grading. Well-constructed examinations often provide uniformity of appraisal and a better evaluation than grading by individual instructors. Institutions of higher education in England, even the new ones which have introduced continuous appraisal, still lean heavily on examinations for the final appraisal of a student's progress. However, these are usually essay in form and comprehensive in nature, rather than attached to individual courses. Both students and instructors in the United States usually dislike the use of examinations as a substitute for instructor grading. The examination dictates what the instructor must teach and what the students must learn, and the student's grade depends entirely upon one performance. Moreover, the size of institutions in this country usually necessitates the use of objective examinations which too often degenerate into rote recall.

Comprehensive examinations of work done over a year or more, with or without course grades, offer one solution to the problem of grades. Course grades may be maintained, but they become purely informational. The ultimate decision as to the student's competency depends on his ability to pass a comprehensive examination. Faculty members at one college that instituted a comprehensive year-end examination and dropped course grades reported difficulty in maintaining student motivation and activity during the year. By focusing on broad educational goals, both students and faculty can be freed from specific course requirements taught to a specific syllabus. However, many institutions find there is a demand for preparatory courses for the examination. Students and faculty appear to want security more than freedom.

Comprehensive examinations can be used to assess student achievement over a shorter, as well as a longer period of time. Increasingly, institutions accept the idea of acceleration or credit by examination, but they rarely accept the idea of taking a longer period of time to satisfy certain educational goals. Students resist extra time, partly because of the added expense and partly because it suggests inadequacy. A time-bound concept of education exists, which assumes that everybody should be able to complete a given program of study in a given length of time. Finally, many state supported institutions argue that students who spend extra time are costing the state extra money, and that they ought to be replaced by students who can complete the program in the normal period of time.

Another difficulty with the comprehensive examination as a replacement for course grading is the specificity of the material. Comprehensive examinations are accepted more often in the humanities than in any other area. Scientists and mathematicians argue that mastery of specific materials is most easily appraised at the completion of a course. The broader objectives which might be appraised in a comprehensive examination are of little interest to such faculty members.

One of the difficulties with grades and examinations is that both tend to be oriented toward the present or the past. Grades and examinations reflect the student's mastery of what he has learned. An examination which determines to what extent the student has mastered competencies which he will use in his later life might alleviate the situation. In a sequential area, such as mathematics or science, one might determine whether the student, having had a year or two of work in this field, is able to read and interpret materials in advanced courses. In the humanities and social sciences, one might determine whether the student has sufficient grasp of an area of knowledge to apply it to a problem or to the interpretation of materials he has not seen before. A real innovation in grades and examinations would be to replace the pattern which emphasizes the present or the past with a program which focuses on the student's progress toward his degree.

To summarize, since people learn at different rates and achieve different levels of mastery, there should be no time requirement other than a demand for reasonable progress. Grading and evaluation should motivate the student to improve, and help him too appraise his progress toward a future goal. The methods of appraisal should be continually reevaluated and improved. Grades, as presently used, have no rational basis, and become ends in themselves rather than appraisal of progress toward ends. However, grades will probably remain, at least in large institutions. Thus, the student must recognize that the grade does not measure what he is getting out of college, it only indicates whether his educational development merits continued investment of funds. There is a relation between the student's grade and the faculty member's salary check. Any faculty member who carefully adjusts the amount of work he does to the size of his salary check is not to be tolerated in an institution of higher education. Students must develop a similar point of view. Yet, as we discuss the problems and evils of grades for students, there is much talk about initiating a program to determine and maintain the quality of faculty instruction.

Study and Travel Abroad

The 1966 edition of *Undergraduate Study Abroad*, a publication of the Institute of International Education, documents the astounding growth of undergraduate study abroad since 1956 (30). The essay by Stephen A. Freeman describes this development, and points out many problems arising from it. Freeman reports that the half a dozen junior year abroad programs in 1950 increased to 208 by 1966 (30, p. 7). Summer programs of resident study and of travel and study have also increased. In addition, Freeman points out that the number of American students going to foreign countries on their own for travel or study is unknown. He also notes a marked increase in the quality of many of the study programs.

It is never easy to assess why a particular development in higher education becomes popular. Certainly American educators realize the importance of developing in young people a sensitivity to and an understanding of differences in world cultures and values, but the American people may be equally concerned with "keeping up with the Jones." Admissions counselors who lose a few prospective students to institutions with a program abroad soon demand that this be added to the educational program. Presidents and deans, equally concerned with enrollment and innovations, are sometimes easily persuaded that a sound undergraduate education must involve travel and study abroad. That such programs may require travel abroad by administrators and faculty members is not openly considered but is certainly influential.

The educational value of programs which offer a rapid tour of several different countries is doubtful. There may be no serious objection to awarding some college credit for such an experience, provided the student engages in serious reading and discussion and presents some evidence of a thoughtful approach to his experiences. Worthwhile study abroad, however, must involve intellectual effort; it must be a well-organized experience and, to be justified as part of a college program, it must relate to what precedes and follows it. In short, study abroad must be planned, administered, and evaluated so that it is a significant and integral part of the total program.

Unless experiences abroad will develop the student to a greater extent than the same period on the home campus, the wisdom of adding such a program is questionable. Such programs seldom pay for themselves, and students usually spend more money than originally indicated. The programs present many problems to the administration and faculty, and result in discontinuities and dislocations which interfere with the educational program on the home campus.

The first step in planning a program abroad is to clarify its objectives. Some institutions view such a program as a vital part of a liberal or general education for all students. They feel that the liberalizing and humanizing effect of extended contact with a different culture cannot be achieved in any other way. This objective will be a part of the experience of any student living abroad, but it is likely to be more fully realized if the program includes one or more other objectives. If the student studies the language, literature, civilization, and culture of the country he is to visit prior to his trip, he will be able to rely on his personal observations and interpretations rather than being dependent on those provided in his own language. A third objective might be specialized study relative to the country the student will visit in a field in which he is particularly interested. This requires that the student's competency in language be such that he can pursue a particular field or problem in depth.

As Freeman points out, the vast majority of American students abroad do not enroll in a foreign university (30, p. 14). Either they have not mastered the language or they find the educational programs of foreign universities confusing and unrelated to their American educational experiences. Students take special courses taught by selected foreign teachers or courses taught by faculty members of their own university. Too frequently the students live together, travel together, and talk together in their own language. For many students, the experience resembles an extended guided tour. Such programs can relate meaningfully to the home campus program, but they do seem to promise more than they deliver.

The traditional junior year abroad program is based on different assumptions. The student studies the language of the country he intends to visit for two or three years. He is expected to be intelligent, knowledgeable, well adjusted, and dependable. He enrolls as a regular student or an auditor in a foreign university, participates in cultural events, and spends most of his time with students of the county. He observes the country directly and achieves a much better understanding of its people and problems than large groups of students sent primarily for the cultural benefits. However, if every junior year abroad program required these prerequisites, the number of students and programs would decrease markedly.

A third program involves students whose competency in language and whose prior work in a particular field enable them to study abroad independently or as regular students in a foreign university. Students of this caliber, even at the graduate level, are rare, and attempts to extend such a program, while highly desirable, should be undertaken with caution.

Students should be carefully selected and prepared for any foreign program. Students unfamiliar with the language and culture of a foreign country rarely find their visit to it a rich and coherent educational experience. Directors, too, should be carefully selected on the basis of their competence in the foreign language, their knowledge of the locality, and their professional stature. The selection of a director poses a number of problems. Relatively few American faculty members are proficient in a foreign tongue. This often results in the employment of a language professor or an expatriate of the country as director of the program. If the program's primary concern is with language facility, this may be appropriate. However, foreign language teachers and expatriate professors rarely understand fully the principles and procedures of American education. Such directors often fail to consider the educational experience of the student, and often are not familiar with all aspects of the foreign culture. Thus, they do not fully orient the student to the foreign culture, and often they emphasize and enhance the discontinuities involved in moving from the campus to a foreign country and back again.

Other serious problems affect study abroad. Many foreign cities and universities resist these programs because the universities are crowded and housing facilities are limited. Too often the financial success of the program depends on low tuition fees and low costs of living. Although foreign study programs could be established in institutions in different parts of a number of foreign countries, the tendency is to select capital cities and tourist meccas. If such programs are to be maintained and extended, groups of institutions in this country will have to collaborate on programs, establish new foreign contacts, and work out more equitable financial arrangements. Also, highly qualified people in all disciplines will have to be trained to direct foreign study. If institutions initiating such programs are willing to learn from the experiences of cooperative groups, such as the Great Lakes College Association, the Indiana Colleges, the Associated Colleges of the Midwest, California State Colleges, Minnesota Colleges, the New York State Colleges, and the Pennsylvania State Colleges, many difficulties and weaknesses may be avoided. Clearly, more American college students will be going abroad in an increasing variety of programs. Thus, each institution which sponsors or gives credit for such a program must carefully analyze its objectives, initiate a program of preparation of students, organize a program of reintroducing the student into the campus life, and insist that the quality and results of the educational experience abroad be equal to those which could be achieved on the campus.

Study abroad must be a meaningful and integrated part of a total experience. If all students cannot go abroad, those who remain on campus should benefit from the experiences of those who go abroad. It is especially important that the campus not be divided into two classes of students, those who have been able to study abroad and those who have not. Moreover, certain programs are not conducive to study abroad. In mathematics and the sciences, for example, the continuity of a four-year experience can be seriously disrupted by a year's absence, particularly since equivalent experiences in these disciplines probably will not be provided abroad. Programs abroad should not be undertaken without more careful study and exploration than most institutions can afford. Study abroad glamorizes a curriculum but, unless this innovation is preceded by a thorough examination and adjustment of the curriculum, the actual impact may be much more harmful than beneficial.

WORK AND SERVICE EXPERIENCES

Work-Study Programs

Wilson and Lyons, in their volume on work-study college programs published in 1961, reported over sixty baccalaureate institutions with such programs, and, in addition, many technical institutes, junior colleges, and a few graduate schools (33). It is difficult to determine when the combination of work and study first appeared in American higher education, but Herman Schneider introduced a cooperative program at the University of Cincinnati in 1906. The pattern developed at that time has had continuing influence. Believing that education would be enriched by applying to a job the concepts and principles learned in college, he grouped engineering students into two sections which alternately attended class and worked. Schneider's first program alternated work and study on a weekly basis, but later experience tends to favor alternation on a quarter or semester basis. This adjusts the work program to typical patterns of course organization in higher education and permits the work program to be optional or restricted to special groups of students. Another current variation establishes an interim period between regular terms during which many or all students work in business, industrial, or service organizations.

Wilson and Lyons suggest that cooperative education achieves several significant educational values. They include among these:

1. Students find greater meaning in their studies by relating theory to practice.
2. Students are motivated by seeing the practical significance of what they are learning on campus.
3. Work experience develops responsibility, self-direction, and maturity.
4. The interaction of students with adults provides a significant experience in human relations.
5. Students develop some orientation to a field of work and have an opportunity to explore their own interests and aptitudes.
6. The combination of work and study provides financial assist-

ance and makes education more meaningful for students coming from low income families.

7. Faculty members profit from interacting with business, industry, and the professions in curriculum planning.

8. The rotation of students so that only half of them are on the campus at one time permits more efficient use of facilities.

9. The work experience eases the transition from college into employment. For girls who marry and do not continue working, the work experience provides a background of satisfaction and confidence if they wish to return to work at some later date.

10. Cooperative education provides an area of common concern in which higher education and business and industry can work together on a problem and gain insight and understanding of each other (33, pp. 6-8).

Work-study programs do pose problems for the institution. While most students, according to Wilson and Lyons, easily shift back and forth between campus and work experiences, some find it disconcerting. Some faculty members are disinterested in or even antagonistic to the work aspect of the program. Work and study are not completely separated, however, for students do continue to study and participate in social and cultural activities during the work period.

While cooperative programs generally take more time because the work experience is not awarded as much credit as on-campus course work, the additional time is not as disadvantageous as it might initially seem. The income from the job helps cover the costs and the work experience frequently permits the student to obtain a better position after graduation. Financial considerations, however, may make students refuse lower paying jobs despite obvious educational advantages.

One of the major problems with work-study programs is the extensive planning and coordination involved. To be fully effective, the institution must provide staff members to work with the students on the job and with their employers. Generally, the institution helps the student find a job, and maintains contact with him while he is working, although one institution regards the student's finding his own job as a major part of the experience. While this institution reports some satisfaction with the program, greater coordination and supervision usually are essential. Some students cannot find a job; some acquire, through the intercession of friends or relatives, a nonpaying assignment created to satisfy the work requirement. Students usually cannot find significant work experiences for short periods of time, whereas institutions can establish long-term relationships with organizations so that a succession of students can be employed. Furthermore, institutions which require all students to work at the same time cannot replace students who are returning to campus.

Cooperative programs are not without disadvantages to employers. Although the programs allow employers to observe and attract prospective employees, they are expensive. Since the term of employment may be quite short, the tasks are severely limited. Student workers may be assigned to relatively unimportant activities which can be dropped or continued by other workers when the student leaves. As a result, cooperative jobs are often eliminated in periods of recession.

Some businesses which endorse cooperative education may object to a particular program. Some programs rotate students from one organization to another over a period of years, whereas many companies prefer to have an able student work only for them and join their regular staff on the completion of his program. In a program in which an organization provides work for the same students on a rotating or part-time basis, the responsibility for the program is shared equally by the organization and the college. The student may acquire seniority and other benefits which rotating from firm to firm prohibits. On the other hand, familiarity with only one organization may restrict the educational opportunities inherent in the program.

Wilson and Lyons conclude that the advantages of the cooperative work-study program far outweigh its disadvantages. Yet many work-study programs are not fulfilling their potential, and the number of institutions involved in cooperative education remains relatively small. The reasons for this are obvious. The institution must establish a close working relationship with business and industry to assure a stable level of cooperative employment and a satisfactory work experience for students. For faculty and students in highly cumulative sequential fields, such as mathematics and the sciences, recurrent absences from the campus raise serious problems, particularly since the student's work experience rarely corresponds to his advancement in the discipline. Accordingly, the campus experience and the work experience may be unrelated or even conflicting. Brunel University in England attempts to resolve this difficulty by having both a campus tutor and an industrial tutor to help the student relate his experiences.

In relation to continuity, sequence, and integration, the work-study program contains both obvious advantages and obvious disadvantages. The relating of theory to practice certainly helps to achieve integration, but only if the student's work experience is related in a meaningful way to what he is doing on the campus. This does not require that a chemistry major work in a chemistry laboratory every work term, but it does require that the chemistry major not be assigned to typing and filing.

There are other conceptions of a work-study program. The original concept was to have students work in small industries or in small communities to help transform their immediate environment and, perhaps, ultimately their whole society. Most current programs, however, emphasize work experiences in large cities, large corporations, and national and international organizations. The student learns to adapt to rather than change his environment. In a few colleges the old ideal continues to exist in two slightly different versions. One version has students assist in the maintenance and operation of the institution. This often reduces costs and also involves students and faculty in a community or family type of living in which each learns to accept some responsibility. In other cases, students help construct buildings, usually with some expert supervision. Another pattern which exists in a very few small colleges, requires students to manufacture and merchandise small handmade goods. However, such learning experiences have little relevance to the formal curriculum, and can be justified only as helping to develop responsibility, maturity, and citizenship. Probably all institutions employ a considerable number of students in various jobs. However, these jobs rarely relate to the student's course work, although occasionally a student will find work in his own department which involves and develops competencies related to his course of study.

Work-study programs, when contained within the campus, have some value, but they fail to attain the objectives of travel, increased responsibility, and introduction to the world of work. Work-study programs are more difficult to establish for students in liberal arts than for those in engineering, business, and other applied fields. Nevertheless, Antioch College's statistics, which are instructive and impressive, demonstrate that such a program can be effectively worked out for all students.

In 1963–64, the 1,700 Antioch students, alternating between work and study every three or six months, worked for 580 organizations in 35 states and 25 foreign countries. Thirteen staff members handled the extramural phases of the program. The director of the extramural program reported that it involved negotiation with parents, deans, faculty advisers, alumni, police, psychiatrists, prospective employers, girl friends, and boy friends. Obviously, such a program is expensive, although the student earns at least his maintenance, and the institution uses one plant and a slightly enlarged staff to instruct two student bodies.

The Antioch experience reveals that size is a complicating factor. A large university with 20,000 or more undergraduates would find an extensive work-study program an impossible task. The task of placement and coordination would be monumental, and probably many full-time employees would begin to view students as competitors for their jobs. The general movement of students to large publicly supported institutions suggests that extensive expansion of coordinated work-study programs is somewhat unlikely. On the other hand, the increasing number of community colleges and large urban institutions, in which most students hold outside jobs, suggests that some coordination of work and study might well be explored.

Social and Community Service Experiences

Some recent curriculum developments provide for social or community service experiences. Students may engage in service activities while on the campus, or on a full-time basis during the summer, interim term, or a full term. In some respects, these programs are analogous to work-study programs but they are directed toward adult citizenship rather than toward vocational experience. However, a student planning to engage in youth service activity will find work with underprivileged youth a vocational, as well as a community service experience. Participation in a community survey or pre-election assistance to a political party also may have vocational implications for the sociology or political science major. Ideally, the student's ultimate vocational goal should be related to his area of service but, in any case, the student will become aware of the many social problems and tasks which every citizen should confront and help solve. The service experience may also be combined with a period of residence abroad, perhaps in an underdeveloped country.

One problem with service projects is that the student is rarely paid for his work and is likely to incur additional expenses unless he works in his home community. Another problem is that most undergraduates are untrained, so that their duties may be routine and insignificant. Inexperienced assistance places an additional burden on the responsible personnel, and they may actually find such short-term aid more of a nuisance than a help. Unless the institution sufficiently values such experience to provide staff to assist in placing the student, coordinating his activity, and helping him relate it to his educational experiences, the student will derive little benefit. Colleges with many students and limited budgets usually find that they can offer such experiences only to students with appropriate interests and contacts, or to students enrolled in specific programs.

One college currently requires twelve credits of independent, field, or foreign study. This broad characterization was deliberately chosen to avoid difficult and ambiguous distinctions among the three educational experiences. The goal of the requirement is to remove the student from the closely supervised classroom or laboratory and force him to accept responsibility for planning and carrying out his own education. This requirement can be satisfied by such diverse activities as:

1. A project or program of independent study carried out by the student on or off campus.
2. A field experience, such as helping VISTA volunteers plan educational programs for migrant workers.
3. Working with Navajo Indians.
4. Assisting in an Upward Bound project in a southern Negro college.
5. Working in a program for emotionally disturbed children.
6. Reference and research service in the Library of Congress.
7. Assisting in translation of research literature.
8. Counseling in small schools which do not have such services.
9. Special projects in business, industry, social work, education, or government.
10. Residence and study or service in a foreign culture.
11. Assisting in a community survey or a political campaign.
12. Travel with a specific educational goal in mind.

This particular institution recommends such experience for the junior year or the following summer, but it may be scheduled any time after the freshman year. Students are *not* permitted to receive pay, and they must file a detailed proposal describing the project and their specific objectives. Upon completing the project, students must submit a report of activities and accomplishments in order to receive credit. The flexibility of the requirement allows students to relate it to their preceding experiences and long-term educational goals.

If social and community service experiences must be offered off the campus, then the campus community itself cannot or is not providing such experiences. Since service and work experiences do disrupt the students' participation in the campus community, the willingness of colleges and students to do this implies that there is something lacking in the campus community experience. Perhaps more effort should be expended to make the campus itself a worthwhile experience in living and working together. It is interesting that faculties who have criticized student absences and weekend egressions are now advocating programs which disrupt both the formal curriculum and the campus community.

The Community Service Role of Colleges and Universities

Much innovative thinking in recent years about college and university programs views the institution as a community and attempts to develop a more integrated or radically different community. The phrases "learning environment" or "living and learning centers" indicate this pattern of thought. However, there is also concern with the college *and* the community, a concern which may compete with the former or may enlarge and enhance it. Despite the pride most communities take in having a college in their midst, there continue to be town and gown distinctions and controversies. Professors are no more likely than other groups to feel superior, to refrain from participation in community activities, or to make Olympian pronouncements on matters in which they have no special competency, but this behavior on the part of a few individual professors does not endear the group to a community. The professor, accustomed to respect from his students and to esteem as an expert in his field, can unintentionally appear pompous and dictatorial. Even his insistence on academic freedom irritates these who mistakenly view it as a demand for personal privilege rather than as an essential condition for pursuit of truth.

Another difficulty often complicates the interaction of faculties with the community in certain regions of the country. The professor is regarded as a representative of his institution, and a remark to which conservative business, political, or religious groups take strong exception can involve both the professor and his institution in a quarrel which is seldom completely reconciled. If the behavior of one faculty is sometimes irritating to the community, the behavior of students can be even more so. The liberalism and occasional irresponsible radicalism of college students antagonizes certain segments of adult society. Student activists often reject the policies and rules developed to control and direct student behavior and to smooth the relations between institution and community. They often are convinced that they are exploited by both the institution and the surrounding community. Such attitudes generate widespread distrust of the value of higher education. As institutions expand their enrollment, acquire more land, build more buildings, and seek more money, the community begins to fear that it has generated a monster which it can no longer control.

A college's attempt to relate itself more firmly to the community is a mixture of self-preservation, a sense of obligation, a desire for increased support, and a concern for more realistic education of both students and faculty. The first three of these motivations are obvious, but the fourth calls for some discussion.

Baker Brownell, in his book, *The College and the Community*, emphasized that an institution of higher education is an enemy of the small community and a proponent of the metropolis (7, p. 24). The values, standards, and culture of the small community are discounted and even ridiculed by comparison with outstanding cultures of the past and with the cultural opportunities of large communities. Some students regard the college as an escape from a home community and as a sanctuary from the responsibilities of living. The institution fosters this attitude by rules, regulations, and special supervisory personnel, all designed to eliminate some kinds of behavior and enforce others. Thus, the college student may be doomed to an inveterate juvenilism. The student who most readily accepts this is regarded as the most adult, and the one who rejects it and tries to attain maturity and responsibility is the most juvenile. Also, students are transients; they usually remain for no more than four years, and many transfer from one institution to another. Considering dropouts and transfers, the average student stay in many institutions is well under two years. Thus, faculty and administrators find it difficult to accept students as having a significant role in the conduct of the affairs of the institution. It is even more difficult for people in the community to regard students as anything more than a source of profit or a source of irritation. Many faculty members are also transients, and have limited loyalty to the university and even less to the community.

Although institutions of higher education generally accept an obligation to prepare students for citizenship, institutional policies and the models provided by many of the faculty are rarely consistent with this goal. Some institutions feel this situation must be rectified through a program which actively involves faculty and students in the concerns of the surrounding community. They feel that the college and the community must confront their common problems together, that the student must participate in the community, and that the faculty member must be a model of the citizenship role of the educated individual. Some of this was discussed in connection with work and service experiences, but these experiences were planned specifically for students, whereas we are now discussing acceptance by the total institution of a community involvement which includes both faculty and students.

One approach to a joint college-community enterprise is through adult education. Such a program can include conferences with church, business,government, and fraternal groups. The institution should avoid becoming simply a meeting place, and insist that all conferences have definite educational significance and that they include some faculty and students. The college can also offer noncredit recreational and cultural programs in which students, faculty, and representatives of the community participate. For example, an expert in bridge may conduct a class in which students, faculty, and townspeople pursue this common interest. Credit or noncredit vocational skills courses in typing, bookkeeping, and other fields can also involve faculty, students, and townspeople to their mutual advantage.

Some institutions have set up special adult degree programs as alternatives to the usual degree requirements. Such programs, taken on a part-time basis, are rarely completed in less than seven or eight years. A program of credit by examination may shorten the period but, if examinations rely heavily on courses, few credits will be amassed in this fashion. Many required courses for the usual baccalaureate degree are offered only during the day and require laboratory hours. This complicates the procedure for an adult who holds a full-time job. Special degrees with their own evening courses, requirements, and sequences eliminate some of these difficulties. Increased flexibility in evaluating general education gained through travel, reading, and work, flexible residence requirements, coordination of on-campus course work with correspondence and educational television courses, work-study programs, and independent study will also help the adult attain a degree. Several institutions (University of Oklahoma Bachelor of Liberal Studies, the Goddard College A. B. for Adults, and the Syracuse University Bachelor of Liberal Education) have developed programs especially geared to adults which emphasize general interdisciplinary area seminars, independent study, one or more residential experiences of two or three weeks, and extensive off-campus projects. Papers or examinations can be used to evaluate progress. Goddard College combines the desire to be of service to adults with the feeling that the participation of a large number of faculty and students in this program will have a significant impact on their concept of education and its relation to adult life.

Adult education programs raise problems of time and cost. If faculty or students are expected to work on such programs in addition to their regular course loads, they may become so involved that they have no time to engage in inquiry in any depth. By doing too much, nothing may be done well.

Evening adult education programs are rarely self-supporting. The overhead cost of the use of buildings, attendant services, and utilities and the unrealistically small stipends paid to faculty or students assisting in the program are usually discounted or ignored. A recreational and cultural noncredit adult program staffed by students and faculty on a voluntary basis may be developed at minimal cost. There are, however, obvious risks in depending on volunteers or in imposing any general requirement for student or faculty service. There is no justification for forcing faculty members to teach full-credit day courses on an overload or cut-rate basis at night.

Another approach to relating the college and the community is the establishment of a cultural center. Such a center can do much to overcome the separation between the institution and the community, but an auditorium and a program of cultural events is not sufficient. In order to be fully effective, members of the college and the community should plan the center together and work out programs of mutual interest to both groups. The center should provide not only a meaningful interaction among community and college groups, but also a level of cultural experience which neither group could attain by itself. The figures on utilization of auditoriums are far lower than those on classrooms and laboratories. Thus, there could be gains in economy as well as in quality by the town and gown joining forces.

Colleges may also serve the community through consultation, assistance to committees, and supervision of surveys. These were discussed earlier in relation to work-study and service programs. Advanced classes in sociology, for example, may take surveys for certain community committees seeking an objective appraisal of what people think about a problem. In such circumstances, students take their work far more seriously because it has practical applications and may lead to meaningful results. To schedule such activities on a large scale would require an office where people could register their needs and where professors and students could register their willingness and availability. The success of any program of interaction between the community and the college usually depends on the enthusiasm of a limited number of people. The schedules of professors and students do not always permit them to meet the needs of the community. The professor who is in demand as a consultant to government or business may not appreciate being asked to volunteer his services to a local group or to sit on a committee which does not recognize his established competency in the area of concern.

Although colleges often list public service as a function of their faculty, they rarely assign time for this activity or delineate precisely what they mean by it. Industries ordinarily expect most of their executives to give a considerable amount of time to community activities. Lower-level employees need do so only if they wish. However, the peculiar nature of the educational institution is that, although presidents are in great demand for a wide range of community activities, real competency exists at the faculty level. While the college or university recognizes that the chief executive officers will be heavily involved in off-campus activities and provides additional assistance for this, it rarely provides similar assistance for faculty members. When a few faculty members are given time to engage in service activities with the community, such activities are curtailed for other faculty members and students. It appears that meaningful involvement of a college or university in a community depends either on personal contacts in small institutions and towns, or, in larger institutions, on a special agency, office, or group established to develop community interaction. Continuing education centers in large universities represent such an answer to the problem. However, these centers seem to have been much more successful in obtaining faculty involvement than student participation.

SUMMARY

The broad program developments discussed in this chapter demonstrate how specific facilitating agents are used to modify the overall character of the college experience. Independent study and honors work focus on the student as an individual rather than as an assimilator of knowledge. They attempt to provide increased flexibility in learning and a measure of coherence and integration through self-education. The development of a climate for learning demonstrates a concern for the total individual, for unity and coherence in the student's experience, and for integration of the classroom with the practical considerations of daily living.

Programs of study and travel abroad and work and service plans attempt to balance the ivory tower campus experience with practical, realistic experiences, which may have vocational significance or may simply broaden the student's understanding of cultural differences and social problems. The limitations of grades and examinations in assessing the objectives of such experiences have forced the reconsideration of grading patterns, although some discussions seem to overrate the impact of grades. Variations in the calendar, such as the January or interim term, have been mentioned at several points. Such variations are commendable if they allow a different pattern of experience or structuring of a program than would otherwise be possible. Interdisciplinary and interclass seminars, work and service projects, problem-oriented readings, lectures, and discussions may be offered during an interim period. Yet, some colleges have been known to include such a period in the calendar and then confront the problem of deciding what to do with it.

Many of these programs, however, fail to confront the more basic and problematic issues of course offerings and instruction in the basic disciplines. A circus with ten distracting but rather commonplace rings might add an array of continuously performing aerial artists to liven up the show. Conceivably, this might unify the whole performance, but it is more likely to result in total confusion. First, the circus should see to the quality of activity in the ten rings, and so we turn to developments in the disciplines.

REFERENCES

1. Irwin Abrams and Winslow R. Hatch, "Study Abroad," *New Dimensions in Higher Education* No. 6, Office of Education, U. S. Department of Health, Education, and Welfare, 1960.

2. Samuel Baskin, ed., *Higher Education: Some Newer Developments*, McGraw-Hill Book Company, Inc., New York, 1965.

3. Samuel Baskin and Winslow R. Hatch, eds., "Quest for Quality, *New Dimensions in Higher Education* No. 7, Office of Education, U. S. Department of Health, Education, and Welfare, 1960.

4. George M. Beckmann, "Curricular Methods of Introducing Foreign Area Studies," *The Educational Record*, Vol. 47, No. 2, Spring, 1966.

5. Percy W. Bidwell, *Undergraduate Education in Foreign Affairs*, King's Crown Press, New York, 1962.

6. Robert H. Bonthius, et al, *The Independent Study Program in the United States*, Columbia University Press, 1957.

7. Baker Brownell, *The College and the Community*, Harper and Brothers, New York, 1952.

8. Malcolm B. Campbell, "Nonspecialist Study in the Undergraduate Curricula of the New Universities and Colleges of Advanced Technology in England," *University of Michigan Cooperative Education Dissertation Series* No. 10, University of Michigan, 1966.

9. Marjorie Carpenter, ed., *The Larger Learning*, Wm. C. Brown Co., Dubuque, 1960.

10. Joseph W. Cohen, *The Superior Student in American Higher Education*, McGraw-Hill Book Company, Inc., New York, 1966.

11. Barbara M. Cross, ed., *The Educated Woman in America*, Teachers College Press, Columbia University, 1965.

12. "The Experimental College," *New Dimensions in Higher Education* No. 3,

Office of Education, U. S. Department of Health, Education, and Welfare, OE-50010, 1960.

13. Winslow R. Hatch and Alice L. Richards, "Approach to Independent Study," *New Dimensions in Higher Education* No. 13, Office of Education, OE-50041, U. S. Department of Health, Education, and Welfare, 1965.

14. Ralph C. Leyden, ed., *The Stephens College House Plan*, Stephens College, 1966.

15. Helen M. Lynd, *Field Work in College Education*, Columbia University Press, 1945.

16. Lewis B. Mayhew, *The Smaller Liberal Arts College*, The Center for Applied Research in Education, Inc., Washington, D. C., 1962.

17. Earl J. McGrath, *The Liberal Arts College and the Emergent Caste System*, Teachers College Press, Columbia University, 1966.

18. Margaret Mead and Frances Kaplan, eds., *American Women*, Charles Scribner's Sons, New York, 1965.

19. Franklin Patterson and Charles R. Longsworth, *The Making of a College: Plans for a New Departure in Higher Education*, The M.I.T. Press, Cambridge, Mass. and London, England, 1966.

20. Renee and William Petersen and Warren Rovetch, *University Adult Education*, Harper and Brothers, New York, 1960.

21. *Planning College Union Facilities for Multiple-Use*, Association of College Unions—International, Cornell University, 1966.

22. Willis Rudy, *The Evolving Liberal Arts Curriculum*, Teachers College Press, Columbia University, 1960.

23. George P. Schmidt, *The Liberal Arts College*, Rutgers University Press, 1957.

24. Clarence A. Schoenfeld and Neil Schmitz, *Year-Round Education, Its Problems and Prospects from Kindergarten to College*, Dembar Educational Research Services, Inc., Madison, Wis., 1964.

25. Albert E. Sloman, *A University in the Making*, Oxford University Press, Inc., New York, 1963.

26. Stanley Spector, "The Coordination of High School and Undergraduate Studies in Non-Western Languages and Cultures," *The Educational Record*, Vol. 47, No. 2, Spring, 1966.

27. W. Hugh Stickler, *Experimental Colleges*, Florida State University Press, 1964.

28. W. Hugh Stickler, "Senior Courses in General Education," *Journal of Higher Education*, Vol. XXV, No. 3, March, 1954, pp. 139–146, 171.

29. Richard N. Swift, *World Affairs and the College Curriculum*, American Council on Education, Washington, D. C., 1959.

30. *Undergraduate Study Abroad: U. S. College-Sponsored Programs*, Institute of International Education, New York, 1966. (The introductory essay by Stephen A. Freeman is especially significant.)

31. Myron F. Wicke, *The Church-Related College*, The Center for Applied Research in Education, Washington, D. C., 1964.

32. Howard E. Wilson, *American College Life as Education in World Outlook*, The American Council on Education, Washington, D. C., 1956.
33. James W. Wilson and Edward H. Lyons, *Work Study College Programs*, Appraisal and Report of the Study of Cooperative Education, Harper and Brothers, New York, 1961.

5

Developments and Trends in the Disciplines

After the successful launching of the first Russian satellite in the fall of 1957, American education faced serious charges of inadequacy. With support from a number of sources, particularly the National Science Foundation and the U. S. Office of Education, numerous curriculum reform groups were established. Discussions of the *new* mathematics, the *new* physics, and the *new* biology became commonplace. The University of Illinois Committee on School Mathematics initiated the School Mathematics Study Group, which influenced other programs in mathematics, such as the Greater Cleveland Mathematics Program, the Syracuse University-Webster College Madison Project, the University of Illinois Arthmetic Project, the University of Maryland Mathematics Project, and the Suppes Experimental Project in the Teaching of Elementary Mathematics. The 1967 *Report of the International Clearing House on Science and Mathematics Curriculum Developments* lists twenty-six projects in mathematics (39, p. XXVIII). The Physical Science Study Committee and the Biological Sciences Curriculum Study have developed new curriculum materials in physics and biology. The biology group developed three distinct sets of materials, the "green," "yellow," and "blue" series, which treat the same material but differ in approach. Extensive work in chemistry has been done by the Chemical Bond Approach Project at Earlham College in Richmond, Indiana, and the Chemical Education Materials Study at the University of California, Berkeley. The same 1967 *Report* lists eleven projects in Biology, eleven in Chemistry, and fourteen in Physics.

In addition to these, twelve projects in Earth Science, twenty-four in Elementary Science, twelve in General Science, and seven in Physical Science are reported. There is some duplication because many projects involve curricular work in several fields, but it is clear that the science curriculum is under intensive scrutiny. The 1967 *Report* also lists twenty-three natural science and mathematics projects at the tenth to twelfth grade levels.

The social sciences curricula are similarly inadequate, although less energy has been expended on them. The report of the American Council of Learned Societies and the National Council for Social Studies, entitled *The Social Studies and the Social Sciences*, attempts to determine what concepts and techniques students should know by the end of high school (42). The Joint Council on Economic Education, in its publication, *Economic Education in the Schools* prepared by the Committee for Economic Development, attempts to define what a high school graduate should know about economics. The High School Geography Project and the Anthropology Curriculum Study Project have had to contend with the problem that neither geography nor anthropology has a defined place in the secondary school curriculum. In English, several groups have been at work. The National Education Association sponsored a project to improve writing. "Project English," supported by the Cooperative Research Program of the U. S. Office of Education, encouraged several attempts to improve curriculum materials. In foreign languages, the Modern Language Association has sponsored various conferences, workshops, and curriculum materials to improve the teaching of foreign language. John Goodlad has evaluated many of these developments (21). Although they have had a marked impact on many teachers, it is not clear how extensively and in what direction they will influence the secondary school curriculum. The impact has been sufficient to force some review of college programs which, for a long time, were untouched by the radical developments at the lower levels.

One criticism of the new curricula has been that the materials, particularly in science, are too difficult for many students. A second is that the programs have not been adequately tested in the classroom. Most programs have been tested only in school systems enrolling primarily middle and upper middle-class children. This fact, coupled with the dominance of college faculty in curriculum development, may account for the inappropriateness of the materials for students of lower ability or deficient cultural background. Another difficulty is that the projects have been isolated from teacher education and from graduate students interested in curriculum reform and teaching. The programs do not provide methods for extending, revising, and developing the ideas generated in these studies. Finally, each of these ventures in a particular discipline has ignored problems of the total curriculum. Yet, at the elementary and secondary levels, the disciplines are not clearly defined and isolated from one another, and a total view is essential. For example, the Commission on Engineering Education has developed a course in engineering which is essentially a history of the impact of developing technology on civilization. Such a course must inevitably include mathematics, physics, and social science, but simultaneous and unrelated curriculum projects are developing separate courses in each of these areas. Thus problems of duplication and sequence must arise. However, the new curriculum ventures are to be commended for their search for better sequential organization, more interesting materials, and an approach which requires thought and understanding rather than rote memorization of facts.

New curriculum ventures at the college level often have more impact on elementary and secondary education than projects directly concerned with those levels. Perhaps only the urgency of a Sputnik could generate curriculum studies at the lower levels of education. Such studies, to be effective, require a vast national program for re-education of teachers and perhaps even national directives and specifications for curriculum development. Traditional organizations of knowledge and approaches to education are entrenched in the organization of schools, in the books and materials used, and in the minds of teachers and parents, who resist changes they do not understand. Furthermore, no curriculum change which involves a restructuring of the disciplines will be effective unless there is a correlated restructuring of the college curriculum. Currently, many professors are educating teachers to use a curriculum which other professors are trying to replace.

A number of commissions are now working on problems in the college curriculum. These include the Commission on Undergraduate Education in the Biological Sciences, the Commission on the Undergraduate Program in Mathematics, the Advisory Council on College Chemistry, the Council on Education in the Geological Sciences, the Commission on College Physics, the Commission on College Geography, the Commission on Education in Agriculture and Natural Resources, and the Commission on Engineering Education (10).

To indicate some possible results of these and other ventures, studies in each of the major groups of disciplines will be briefly considered in the following paragraphs. The discussion will indicate major issues rather than provide a complete picture of developments. In fact, the picture cannot be complete, for discussion and deliberation rather than conclusions characterize current studies.

Science

One common concern in the sciences is to reduce the gap between course organization and research activities. There is also concern for sequential organization and proposals have been made to develop a core of courses required for study in any of a group of closely related disciplines.

In biology, the problem of balancing the classical concept of anatomical and morphological differences in major plant and animal phyla with the more recent quantitative experimental approach is a major concern. Sequential considerations involve mathematics, physics, and chemistry, for much current biological research cannot be understood without some knowledge of these disciplines. Numerous methods of structuring biology courses have been proposed. Some biologists feel initial courses should be experiences in inquiry or in the scientific method. Some view complete living organisms as the proper focus, and others select the relation of the organism to its environment and the problem of adaptation. Some wish to avoid themes and use a series of problems; others propose the introduction of history and philosophy of science. Few biologists accept any reduction in the laboratory requirement, but many accept the idea that the laboratory should be open-ended, an experience in learning rather than a verification of something already learned.

Biology for liberal arts students is often discussed but, for the scientist, this usually means biology for non-majors. One proposal suggests a special course for non-majors which examines the scope, history, philosophy, and probable future of science. Some biologists have suggested that this might also be an excellent introductory course for majors.

A very interesting proposal recommends a core sequence of biological science courses integrating the study of plants, animals, and microorganisms and replacing the introductory departmental offerings. This interdisciplinary development is not related to earlier general education biology courses because it grows out of a research emphasis and it involves a sequence of as many as seven courses (as at Purdue and Yale) for biology majors. Nevertheless, it does confirm the interdisciplinary principle of the earlier general education courses. Some biologists have even suggested postponing biology until the sophomore year, and requiring chemistry and mathematics, and perhaps physics and biochemistry as prerequisites.

In the physical sciences, the pressure for curriculum change is focused on the independent disciplines. A few institutions (usually small liberal arts colleges) have developed a physical science sequence which includes chemistry, physics, and mathematics, but this pattern is not likely to be widely accepted. Most studies attempt to reorganize course content utilizing basic concepts and to integrate content, course structure, and current research. Some chemists feel that several core courses should be required of all majors, and that electives in the major should be available only in the third and fourth years. A few chemists have attempted to define the number of courses or hours essential for a sound major, but nothing definitive has emerged. The requirements for the Bachelor of Science in Chemistry continue to set a standard which complicates curriculum reorganization in liberal arts colleges.

Biochemistry presents two problems: the possibility of a special chemistry sequence for prospective biochemists, and the need for some biochemistry in the chemistry major sequence. Chemistry has become a somewhat vague, intermediate field between biology and physics, although the development of biochemistry, chemical physics, and biophysics suggests that new relationships are emerging.

Some chemists feel that lecture demonstrations and experiments can partially replace the laboratory. There is some concern for a chemistry course for non-science majors, and there is clearly a need for special chemistry sequences for students in engineering, agriculture, home economics, and other science-based vocational fields.

Some physicists feel that forty semester hours including introductory physics, but not related mathematics can achieve satisfactory undergraduate preparation in the field. They regard additional courses for those preparing for graduate study in physics as desirable and sometimes necessary. Competency in a foreign language and in one other science are also deemed desirable for the physics major. However, many physicists feel that overemphasis destroys not only the liberal arts tradition, but also the student's enthusiasm for his field. The Commission on College Physics has also considered the problem of physics for non-science students, and has issued course outlines, techniques, materials, and a bibliography of appropriate science books.

The Council on Education in the Geological Sciences has given some attention to new approaches to the introductory course, to the course sequence and content for the major, and to cooperation with other disciplines. It recognizes the importance of requiring some mathematics and statistics for majors, and the necessity of further education of most geology professors so that the requirement will be functional.

The Commission on the Undergraduate Program in Mathematics

has developed detailed programs of courses and course sequences for students in various fields requiring mathematical and statistical competency. These include programs for five levels of teaching, from elementary school mathematics to college mathematics. Except for the recommendation of four courses in mathematics for elementary school teachers, which poses serious difficulties when related to the many other requirements for teachers at this level, the recommendations appear reasonable and feasible. Courses in curriculum and methods of instruction, including objectives, content of proposals for change, teaching techniques, and literature of mathematics, are suggested but are not included in the recommended program.

The Commission also proposed special programs for students interested in computing, graduate study, and research and applications. A minimal six-course sequence was developed for "Biological Management and Social Science" majors. Although there is some duplication in the courses proposed for these programs, the total range of courses could be offered only by an institution with a large undergraduate enrollment. The small college must limit itself to a more general curriculum. Recognizing this, the Commission proposed a fourteen-course general curriculum in mathematics, which could be taught by four teachers. However, the Commission reveals no concern for what the student takes outside his major or for the place and problems of a liberal education distribution requirement in mathematics.

These activities and recommendations are both encouraging and disillusioning. Most reveal an awareness of the need for better sequential organization and for interdisciplinary thinking. Although many emphasize study in related fields, they usually stress only those competencies demanded by the major. Most reports acknowledge that the undergraduate major may require only one-third of the student's time, and occasionally they recognize that the major may not even be the most significant part of his undergraduate education. It is too early to judge the work of these national groups, but their failure to evidence any concern for the relation of science to the arts and humanities reinforces the tendency of scientists to propagate their own kind rather than to provide a coherent, interdisciplinary undergraduate education.

Social Science

Various disciplines in the social sciences have recognized the need for curriculum restudy, but support for such projects has not been readily available. The Commission on College Geography encourages new programs, and has developed new materials and four new approaches to introductory courses. The Commission is also concerned with interdisciplinary cooperation and with the improvement of instruction, which has too often emphasized memorization of details. There are so many approaches to the content of geography that the significant relations between various factors of a geographic region or several regions, and between geographic features and man may be lost to the student.

The dissatisfaction of economists, particularly with introductory courses in economics, is reflected in the volume, *The Teaching of Elementary Economics* (28) and in the current efforts of the Joint Council on Economic Education and the Test Committee of the American Economic Association to develop tests which emphasize applications. The introductory course in economics, like those in mathematics and chemistry, is taken by many non-majors. Few departments have attempted to separate majors and non-majors, but many have found problems in relative emphasis on various topics, since the course is often required and is also a popular elective. Quantitative economics which often utilizes a computer, necessitates additional changes in the curriculum and requires the interrelating of economics, mathematics, statistics, and computer science. Many economists would prefer greater emphasis on economic policies in the introductory course, so that the student would not only learn facts and principles but also analyze problems and make policy decisions.

The volume, *Teaching Political Science*, criticizes and evaluates courses and instruction in political science (12). Rogers believes that present offerings condemn the student "without trial to serve sentences of confinement within the walls of specialized vocational minutiae" (12, p 29). Connery remarks that ". . . a very good case might be made for studying Far Eastern governments or underdeveloped countries in the first college course, since these would be completely new and different from anything that a student has had in high school" (12, p 246). Connery also suggests that course content and sequence may be insignificant, although individual departments might find some rationale for a hierarchy of courses (12, pp. 248, 249). At the moment, however, no definite trends are evident.

History has a universal appeal to mankind, perhaps because it provides a sense of continuity. The uncertainties of the future and the tribulations of the present seem to be borne with better grace by those familiar with the past. Popular interest in history is based on biography, and few people care whether these historic figures determined the course of events or were created by them. Few effectively differentiate history from fiction, perhaps because history, however well investigated and written, is a recreation of the past based upon incomplete and possibly inaccurate evidence. History belongs both to the humanities and the social sciences, and the materials, research, principles, and modes of inquiry of all the humanities and social sciences are available and useful to the historian. In addition, all disciplines have a history; their history tells the story of man's continuing search for explanation and understanding.

The writing of history requires defining a subject, collecting materials and verifying sources, extracting and organizing data, and preparing a report. In each of these endeavors, subjectivity is inevitable. Unrecognized bias, tentative commitment to a new hypothesis, incomplete evidence, and sheer stupidity have all effected the writing of history. The student must recognize the subjective aspects of history if he is to learn what history is. Ideally, every student should play the role of an historian by questioning an interpretation of history or by working out his own. As he does so, he will compare his own values and patterns of thought with those of others. He will apply methods of inquiry, and he will acquire a sense of what history is and is not. Consider, by way of contrast, the following quotation:

> The variety of history courses in the colleges is encouraging. It makes teaching in the colleges attractive to trained historians, and offers a range of education to undergraduates that is to be applauded. But care should be taken to offer history courses to undergraduates that suit their broad needs and their limited time for the study of history.

> An awareness of the discipline as a whole can be conveyed to undergraduate history majors by requiring a patterned distribution of courses in three or four broad fields of history, by providing a comprehensive reading course for senior majors to fill gaps in coverage, or by the introduction of a comprehensive examination for history majors. In addition, majors ought to be acquainted—the earlier the better—with historical method, changing philosophies of history, and the classics of historical literature. Early competence in foreign languages should be strongly encouraged. Neglect of the non-Western areas should be ended. . . . (36, p 84).

The quotation is not totally inconsistent with the view suggested above, but its emphasis on the value of a variety of courses "attractive to the trained historian" appears to sanction proliferation of courses. However, courses in relatively obscure periods of history tend to emphasize facts rather than insight into the essential nature of history.

Despite the extensive search for new structures and concepts for social studies curricula at the secondary level, no widely accepted answer has emerged. It seems highly unlikely that any structure of history or any set of historical concepts will be acceptable to all historians. Some social scientists are concerned about the wide range of courses and the failure of many of them to challenge the student. Interest in non-western areas has led to course proliferation in political science, history, and other social sciences. However, no concerted effort has been made to develop a tighter curriculum. One difficulty is that no criteria for sequence exist in the social sciences. As noted in Chapter 3, the structure and methodology of the social sciences are unclear and provide little guidance.

English

Although a Commission on English, set up by the College Entrance Examination Board, has worked for several years on the improvement of English at the college and secondary levels, English has not received the intensive scrutiny given to the sciences. "Project English," of the U. S. Office of Education, has supported many projects in the field, but most of these have concentrated on precollege English or on the freshman course. One of the problems of the discipline of English is defining what it includes. English literature, American literature, linguistics, creative writing, and the history, principles, and practice of rhetoric and literary criticism are offered in most English departments. In some institutions, speech, journalism, and drama are also affiliated with the department of English.

There are many different approaches to literature. Some professors feel that appreciation of literature is the major objective. This approach is intuitional and impressionistic, rather than analytical or critical. The philological approach treats literature genetically and attempts to demonstrate its sources, connections, and relationships. The sociological approach considers the social and political concerns which give rise to and are involved in literature. Some professors regard literature as history or a record of ideas and do not attempt to judge its value, while others are concerned only with its moral and ethical qualities. The New Criticism analyzes the individual work in great detail, looking for unity, coherence, ambiguity, paradox, and the relation of the work to social conditions and political developments. It emphasizes internal evidence rather than external influences.

These different conceptions of English give rise to a proliferation of courses organized by author, by literary form (drama, novel, poetry, expository writing, creative writing), by period, and by philosophy (romanticism, realism, naturalism). History, criticism, linguistics, and aesthetics suggest still other methods of organization. This confusion poses almost insolvable problems of coverage and sequence.

Few English departments can provide adequate majors in all these areas, but too many of them try. One clearly discernible trend in the major, as indicated by the U. S. Office of Education publication, *Curriculum Patterns in English*, is an increase in requirements in the study of the English language, and in the historical, analytical, and advanced grammar approaches (47). Another trend is the replacement of the survey course with a course dealing with major forces and figures. Another development is the addition of requirements in world literature. Unfortunately, these new courses and requirements are not always accompanied by the elimination of others.

The problem of what English includes leads to the problem of what the major in English includes. Faced with a formidable array of courses, most students, and many professors, are confused about what specialization in English means. The student may be advised to select a program in literature, composition, creative writing, or linguistics. Some departments refuse to prescribe courses, but indicate that the student should plan his own program with his adviser, an approach which is fine in theory but unsatisfactory in practice because it usually fails to produce a sequential program. One problem in English, as in many other disciplines, is that course offerings represent the specialized interests of the faculty rather than a meaningful program for students. This deficiency will be resolved only by the formulation of a clear conception of desired competencies, and by the development of one or more sequences of courses and requirements (perhaps reinforced by a senior seminar or comprehensive examination) which will achieve those competencies. Wayne C. Booth, in his chapter on the undergraduate program in *The College Teaching of English*, effectively points out that most programs for undergraduate English majors lack coherence and sequence, and that only a complete rethinking of the major will remedy its present weaknesses.

A continuing problem of the English department is the freshman composition course. Concern and responsibility for writing should be shared by the entire faculty rather than arbitrarily imposed on the English department. Introduction to English through a composition course does an injustice to the discipline, and to the professors who are forced to teach a course in which they have little interest. The only advantages the English department derives from this course are that it provides teaching assistantships for many graduate students, and it requires a large staff which can be selected to cover all the essential subspecialties of the field. The only solution to the problem of freshman English is the drastic one of eliminating the requirement. Responsibility for spelling, punctuation, and elementary grammar should be returned to the elementary and secondary schools. The importance of writing itself should be emphasized in all the disciplines the student studies. He must write on some topic, and he will probably prefer to write about what he is studying than about the artificial issues posed in freshman composition courses. Writing, as a method of organizing and expressing one's ideas, is a mode of learning as much as a skill. The importance of writing, both as a means of communication and as a means of learning, must be impressed upon the student by the concerted effort of the entire faculty.

Foreign Languages

The recent emphasis on international affairs has enhanced the value of foreign languages. Government support of area and language centers has encouraged the introduction of African, Asian, and additional European languages into many colleges and universities. Much of this work, particularly in the more esoteric languages, has been at the graduate level and limited largely to individuals having strong research or service interests in that particular culture.

In the more common foreign languages, several notable shifts in emphasis have occurred. Many institutions now require a specified level of competency rather than a certain number of credits in a foreign language. This results from the great variation in the language backgrounds of students, many of whom have studied foreign languages extensively in high school, or even in elementary school. Furthermore, the many foreign students and American students who have lived abroad have made it clear that, if the objective is the ability to use a language, then competency rather than credits must be recognized. In a few cases, the emphasis on competency grows out of another concern. With the pressure for more hours in the major and with the increasing importance of supporting work in mathematics or other cognates for many fields, the specification of a level of competency encourages the student to reach that level by starting his language in high school, studying it during the summer, or taking additional, non-credit work. Finally, the competency specification encourages the student to attain fluency in one language rather than passing familiarity with two or more languages.

A second development emphasizes the oral-aural approach and the use of the language laboratory. Evidence on the effectiveness of this approach is incomplete. Some enthusiasts claim that, after a year or two of a language emphasizing the oral-aural approach, a student is able to carry on a reasonable conversation, and has made excellent progress in reading, grammar, and understanding of the culture. Others feel that, if reading competency is the major concern, there are more direct routes to it. There is also some question whether the level of facility attained by the oral-aural approach will be retained unless the student almost immediately resides in a country where that language is spoken.

A third development is the study of foreign languages as preparation for a period of study abroad. However, many of these programs are so planned that students do not need much foreign language facility and have little opportunity to use what they have. Thus, the demand for fluency is not sufficiently stressed to reinforce the program and motivate the student. If foreign study were restricted to students who could demonstrate a reasonable level of aural-oral competency, both foreign language study and study abroad would undoubtedly benefit.

One problem in foreign language study is the small proportion of students required to study a foreign language who actually make use of it. An optimistic view suggests that, if a student studies language *long enough* (and this may require three, four, or five years), he will find some opportunity to use it. The pessimistic view asserts that the usual level of competency achieved by language study does not provide the student with a usable skill, and that the competency deteriorates very rapidly. One difficulty results from the compartmentalization of the curriculum. The student rarely uses his facility in foreign language in any other aspect of his undergraduate study. The problem is similar to that of the freshman composition requirement. Everybody wants the student to be able to write, but few faculty members are willing to take responsibility for it by reinforcing or maintaining whatever writing competency might be developed by the requirement. Likewise, faculty in other disciplines rarely care how much foreign language their students know, and make no attempt to insist that the student continue to use his language competency. Thus, the language requirement becomes artificial to the student, for he rarely sees his professors use or need a foreign language. Furthermore, the one opportunity the student might have to use his foreign language would be in connection with a major interest or field of work. When this does not occur, foreign language is isolated and becomes one more of the traditional minimal requirements in American higher education which are both expensive and unprofitable. If we are concerned with verbal fluency, we will have to extend and intensify foreign language programs. If we are concerned with continuing use of the language, we will have to find ways to demand and utilize language competency in other aspects of the student's work.

Physical Education

According to Brubacher and Rudy, students in the early American colleges had little opportunity for physical exercise (8, pp. 49, 50). College authorities became concerned about the effect of lack of exercise on student health, and also thought that an active physical training program might eliminate rebellions and other undesirable forms of student activity. These two objectives were somewhat inconsistent. The stories of early student rebellions indicate considerable student activity and, furthermore, one doubts that the young men of that day were any more inclined to sit around with folded hands than the young men of today. In any case, an historical precedent was set in 1826, when the Harvard faculty authorized a new German instructor to establish a college gymnasium with an elaborate program of exercise based on contemporary German principles. Although Harvard students found the program quite disagreeable, the movement spread rapidly and, after 1840, a number of gymnasiums were built. Since then, physical education has become an almost universal requirement in the undergraduate programs of American colleges and universities. Those who object to the traditional requirement are often regarded as irresponsible, anti-American, and atheistic. Coaches and directors of athletics, who are not always models of the physical proficiency they demand, are the most ardent proponents of physical education requirements, perhaps because the staffing of such courses provides a large coaching staff for various intercollegiate athletic activities. Few members of the health and recreation staff defend the physical education requirement on the grounds that it contributes to student health. They recognize that two or three hours of physical training a week can, at most, make a limited and temporary contribution to the student's physical development. Instead, they view the program of physical education as an important contribution to social and emotional development, and as an experience in health education, recreation, and safety and prevention. They feel that the program develops not only physical skills, but also more efficient physiological function, more effective movement, and improved human relations. The several physical education associations, such as the American Association for Health, Physical Education, and Recreation, the College Physical Education Association, and the National Association for Physical Education of College Women, claim much greater benefits than a minimum requirement in physical education can possibly achieve. The 1959 revision of *Physical Education for College Men and Women* is full of such phrases as "realization of maximum potentialities," "development and improvement of democratic behavior," "acceptable ethical code," and "appreciation, understanding, and accepting of individual and cultural differences" (37). These are impressive goals to which some small contribution may be made by physical education requirements. However, one doubts that the average physical education instructor can keep all these objectives in mind, and certainly few students will recognize these benefits as ensuing from the requirement.

The suggestions for exercise prepared by the Joint Committee of the American Medical Association and the American Association for Health, Physical Education, and Recreation are: (1) A program of exercise should be started at an early age and continued throughout life, with certain adjustments as life advances and needs, interests, and capabilities change; (2) the amount of vigorous exercise that is desirable each day is largely an individual matter, although a minimum of thirty minutes to an hour daily is recommended; (3) something of interest can be found for every individual to make exercise satisfying and enjoyable (16). In addition to numerous sports, suggested activities include walking, bicycling, and gardening. It is not clear that the standard physical education requirement fulfills these suggestions. Clearly, a requirement limited to one or two years is not necessarily continued through life, even though it may emphasize the development of skills and interests which the individual can use as an adult. Moreover, despite efforts of physical education teachers to adjust programs to the interests and needs of students, the reality of the registration system often forces students to select a physical education course they dislike. Not only may the activity be irrelevant or even distasteful, but also the hour at which it is scheduled may be unreasonable. A physical education class at 8:00 in the morning or squeezed in between two demanding courses is not conducive to a satisfying experience. Also, the general unwillingness of physical education instructors to accept different patterns of exercise which are equally vigorous and healthful is often disconcerting and irritating. For example, the exercise suggestions noted earlier include walking, bicycling, and gardening. Yet most physical education instructors will not accept these as a basis for waiving a requirement. They often refuse to excuse even students who are engaged in intercollegiate athletics.

There is a tendency at the college level to emphasize theoretical knowledge and understanding of physical education. Textbooks are used, readings are assigned, and examinations cover various aspects of the history of a sport, its role in our culture, and an analysis of techniques, skills, rules, and organization. Such activities seem to be contrived to add some academic respectability to the requirement. Yet, instead of encouraging students to exercise, they often force students to spend additional hours memorizing facts and rules. Moreover, one wonders whether the best way to learn, let us say, the terminology and rules of tennis is by reading and lectures or by additional experience on the court where the rules and terminology are essential.

There are numerous inconsistencies in the physical education requirement. For example, page 6 of *Physical Education for College Men and Women* gives an excellent analysis of student needs, such as development and maintenance of personal and social efficiency, opportunity for leadership, activity on a coeducational basis, development of recreational skills, greater muscular strength and endurance, quick judgment in physical and emotional adjustments, and individual adjustment to a group. Many of these, such as leadership experience, coeducational activities, the development of satisfying recreational skills, and individual adjustment to a group, seem to have no particular relation to the physical education requirement. Individuals can and do have all of these experiences in other contexts. Many people, for example, learn golf, bowling, tennis, and various team sports without a structured physical education course. Similarly, the long list of program elements on pages 6 and 7, which emphasize healthful functions of the organs, adjustment to tension and emotional strain of daily living, and cooperative experiences in group problem solving, is impressive, but it does seem a great deal to claim for a requirement limited to a year or two and to one to three hours per week. Another inconsistency is found in the requirement of specific courses. For example, some schools require every student to take swimming and demonstrate some competency in it. Presumably, swimming is regarded as an essential safety skill. However, the imposition of specific requirements seems inconsistent with the objective of finding activities of interest to students. Even in an elective program, however, the student rarely has complete freedom of choice. As already noted, the individual who prefers walking, bicycling, or gardening will find that these skills and activities, will not satisfy the physical education instructor. Finally, certain inconsistencies in the physical education requirement are imposed by external pressures. For example, evening college students and students over some arbitrarily determined age are often excused from physical education. It is hardly consistent to impose a requirement upon freshmen and sophomores and then discard it for juniors, seniors, and graduate students. Perhaps it is expected that the student, once introduced to such activities, will continue his involvement in them. There has been no study to determine the validity of this expectation, and it is unlikely that such study would effect the program. The requirement is emotional rather than rational, and is based on the assumption that college is otherwise a completely sedentary mental experience. Thus, a requirement which is expensive, ineffective, and basically unrelated to the goals of higher education is perpetuated.

Various professional associations in the field do recognize many of the inconsistencies noted. Their recommendations include the following:

> Physical education, properly conceived and implemented, has potentials for continuing beneficial results; therefore, instruction in physical education, properly adopted, should be required of all students throughout their entire undergraduate college career (37, p. 11).

Clearly, this recommendation is based on the realization that a requirement limited to a year or two is not likely to achieve the stated goals. They also recommend that all students participate in the physical education program. They feel that substitution of such activities as band, dramatics, military drill, ROTC courses, veterans' experiences, and varsity sports for instructional class work should seldom be permitted. Although a student might use freshman or varsity sports to meet his physical education requirement, he should be permitted to use the same intercollegiate sport only once during a year, and he should be required to return to his physical education class at the close of the season. A careful reading of the materials and recommendations of physical education and recreation instructors indicates that their unwillingness to recognize other physical activity as a substitute for a physical education class is based on an awareness that physical skills must be developed continuously over a long period of time. Perhaps they also believe that the theoretical elements of the courses are an essential part of the physical education program. Certainly the barring of substitutes is consistent with this point of view.

One final issue in physical education should be considered. Many colleges and universities have maintained the requirement, but have discarded grades and credits. In some cases grades are recorded but are not counted as part of the student's point average. Physical education instructors, however, argue that physical education should be a recognized and accepted instructional area, and that students should receive grades and credits for demonstrated knowledge and proficiency.

The attention given to the physical education requirement is perhaps excessive. However, the requirement is not only an expensive anachronism, but also an excellent example of how tradition, politics, patriotism, and administrative fears of public reaction combine to defeat an objective examination of an outdated program. Requirements, like rules and regulations, are too often a facade to avoid criticism and responsibility.

Interdisciplinary Courses

Developments in interdisciplinary courses may be classified into three groups. The first is the interdisciplinary or interdepartmental course developed by two or more departments for majors in those fields. A good example is the biological science sequence for all students majoring in any one of the biological sciences. This approach has not been used extensively in the physical sciences, the humanities, or the social sciences. Some of the new residence colleges which base their program on a particular theme, such as policy applications of the social sciences, develop a number of interdepartmental courses appropriate to the theme. Courses of this first type may be regarded as interdepartmental efforts for majors. Some English universities have developed two or three discipline honors programs which concentrate on a particular problem or vocational possibility. Interdepartmental efforts in this context are also directed toward the major.

A second interdisciplinary development is directed toward non-majors and concentrates on general education courses. Although these courses appear to be losing popularity, many institutions continue to experiment with them. For example, a state university recently announced an interdisciplinary three-hour freshman humanities course using materials from history, philosophy, English literature, music, art, and theater arts. Such a course may too easily become an ill-assorted collection of facts and ideas unless a coherent theme or set of principles unifies the various disciplines and materials. The interdisciplinary approach in biology, in contrast, arises out of a conviction that there are certain fundamental ideas, facts, principles, and techniques common to all biological sciences. It is unfortunate that interdisciplinary attempts to develop courses for majors are not extended to provide an appropriate experience for non-majors.

A third interdisciplinary development is the non-western civilization program. Non-western courses are not necessarily interdisciplinary, and many of the disciplines, such as geography, history, literature, sociology, and political science, do introduce their own courses in non-western cultures or countries. By taking several departmental non-western courses, the student might obtain a comprehensive view of the culture of a particular area, but he might also learn about the geography of West Africa, the history of China, and the anthropology of the South Sea islands.

If large numbers of students are to be exposed to non-western experiences, it might be preferable to infuse non-western materials into established courses rather than add new ones. Many English departments have introduced courses in world literature and comparative literature. Such courses are equally appropriate in philosophy, religion, and art.

The argument for an interdisciplinary course which covers all aspects of a particular culture is that a culture exists as a whole rather than a series of arbitrary segments corresponding to the established academic disciplines. The student may more easily perceive certain relationships between American culture and foreign cultures in a course which compares and contrasts specific elements of several cultures, but he is not likely to perceive the essential character of a foreign culture unless he studies its history, government, literature, art, religion, and society in a single course. No undergraduate can study every culture, but an interdisciplinary course in one or two cultures can give the student insight into his own culture and make him more receptive, tolerant, and considerate to those of different cultures. The interdisciplinary course will be even more beneficial if some departmental courses use a comparative or cross-cultural approach.

American colleges and universities are still exploring ways to incorporate non-western languages and cultures into the curriculum, and there are few accepted patterns, standards, or norms. Often, the most significant impact of a non-western course or specialist is that it forces curriculum evaluation. Traditional compartmentalizations are inadequate to deal with such material and, by contrast, the usual departments and disciplines appear to be poorly organized collections of materials which give little meaningful insight into either a culture or a discipline.

UNRESOLVED PROBLEMS

This chapter has raised so many issues and provided so few solutions that the heading of this section is somewhat anticlimatical. However, many of the problems posed are based on certain fundamental difficulties which make it impossible to arrive at a satisfactory solution.

The departmental organization poses very serious problems in attempting to develop a comprehensive undergraduate program. Each department is concerned with its own enhancement, and each department member is concerned with his own specialty. Thus, the department is a source of the course proliferation which makes it so difficult for the undergraduate to obtain a coherent view of the discipline. Since the institution is made up of several such departments, the unity and coherence of the undergraduate experience are lost in a maze of unrelated and unrelatable experiences.

Emphasis on vocation and specialization in the departments also threatens the quality of the undergraduate experience. A vocational motivation, if broadly conceived, can enhance a liberal education, but too many vocations are narrowly conceived and fail to prepare the student for future changes by developing his ability to relate and use materials and ideas from a number of fields. Likewise, specialization can be beneficial, but emphasis on preparation for graduate school can lead to a very narrow program. The student interested in both history and economics can restrict himself to a very narrow specialization, history of economics, or he can study the broader implications of the role of economics in history. The first is a specialization appropriate to graduate study but unreasonably narrow for the undergraduate, whereas the second takes advantage of an interest in two specialties to develop a more thoughtful and integrated approach involving both.

A third unresolved problem concerns education for women. Much has been said about the multiple roles of women, and many programs have been developed to accommodate the various roles of wife, mother, professional, and civic and social volunteer. However, educational institutions offering such programs usually find that most young women are not interested in programs different from those taken by men. The conflicts about the role and education of women arise from the mores of society, and it is not likely that any undergraduate curriculum can solve them. For the intellectually capable woman, continuing education may offer the best solution. However, there is no unanimity among women as to what role they seek in society, and, for many, marriage, home, and family remain the major goal.

A fourth unresolved problem is that of faculty selection and training. Major curricular reforms in higher education rarely achieve complete success because it is so difficult to generate enthusiasm among faculty members for any program which differs from their own undergraduate training. Curriculum reform which begins with an existing faculty usually ends in complexity and compromise. Curricula developed by planners and administrators prior to the employment of the faculty undergo extensive modification as soon as the faculty arrives. Every faculty member considers himself well and liberally educated, and he readily assumes that his pattern of education brought about this desirable result. Unfortunately, his most recent training was highly specialized and he tends, therefore, to emphasize specialization for undergraduates. Thus, faculty selection, training, and orientation constitute one of the major problems in curriculum reform.

REFERENCES

1. Joseph Axelrod and Donald Bigelow, *Resources for Language and Area Studies*, American Council on Education, Washington, D. C., 1962.
2. Jeffrey J. W. Baker, ed., *Biology in a Liberal Education*, Reports of the Colloquium on Biology in a Liberal Education, Stanford University, August 2–13, 1965, CUEBS Publication 15, Commission on Undergraduate Education in the Biological Sciences, Washington, D. C., February, 1967.
3. A. Cornelius Benjamin, *Science, Technology and Human Values*, University of Missouri Press, 1965.
4. Bernard Berelson, et al, *The Social Studies and the Social Sciences*, Harcourt, Brace and World, Inc., New York, 1962.
5. Louise Berman, ed., *The Humanities and the Curriculum*, Association for Supervision and Curriculum Development, National Education Association, Washington, D. C., April, 1967.
6. Elizabeth Berry, *The Careers of English Majors*, National Council of Teachers of English, Champaign, Ill., 1966.
7. J. Bronowski, *Science and Human Values*, Harper and Row, Publishers, New York, 1965.
8. John S. Brubacher and Willis Rudy, *Higher Education in Transition, An American History, 1936–1956*, Harper and Brothers, New York, 1958.
9. P. Carpenter, *History Teaching: The Era Approach*, Cambridge University Press, 1964.
10. "The College Commissions," (Agriculture, Biology, Chemistry, Engineering, Geography, Geology, Mathematics, Physics), Commission on Undergraduate Education in the Biological Sciences, Washington, D. C., July, 1967. (Each Commission has its own newsletter and publications.)
11. Henry S. Commager, *The Nature and Study of History*, Charles E. Merrill Books, Inc., Columbus, Ohio, 1965.
12. Robert H. Connery, ed., *Teaching Political Science*, Duke University Press, 1965.
13. "Core Studies for Undergraduate Majors," A Conference Report, *BioScience*, Vol. 14, No. 8, 1964, pp. 25–29.
14. *Curricular Change in the Foreign Languages*, 1963 Colloquium on Curricular Change, College Entrance Examination Board, New York, 1963.
15. *Economic Education in the Schools*, Committee for Economic Development, The Joint Council on Economic Education, New York, 1961.
16. *Exercise and Fitness*, A Statement on the Role of Exercise in Fitness by a Joint Committee of the American Medical Association and the American Association for Health, Physical Education, and Recreation, National Education Association, Washington, D. C., 1964.
17. James A. Fisher, ed., *The Humanities in General Education*, Wm. C. Brown Co., Dubuque, 1960.

18. Dorothy M. Fraser, *Current Curriculum Studies in Academic Subjects*, Project on Instruction, National Education Association, Washington, D. C., 1962.
19. John C. Gerber, gen. ed., *The College Teaching of English*, Appleton-Century-Crofts, New York, 1965.
20. Bentley Glass, *Science and Ethical Values*, University of North Carolina Press, 1965.
21. John I. Goodlad, *School Curriculum Reform in the United States*, Fund for the Advancement of Education, New York, 1964.
22. G. B. Harrison, *Profession of English*, Harcourt, Brace and World, Inc., New York, 1962.
23. Robert R. Haun, ed., *Science in General Education*, Wm. C. Brown Co., Dubuque, 1960.
24. Robert W. Heath, ed., *New Curricula*, Harper and Row, Publishers, New York, 1964.
25. G. Holton, ed., *Science and Culture*, Beacon Press, Boston, 1967.
26. Gail M. Inlow, *The Emergent in Curriculum*, John Wiley and Sons, Inc., New York, 1966.
27. W. T. Jones, *The Sciences and the Humanities*, University of California Press, Berkeley, 1965.
28. Kenyon A. Knopf and James H. Strauss, eds., *The Teaching of Elementary Economics*, Holt, Rinehart and Winston, New York, 1960.
29. Mark M. Krug, *History and the Social Sciences: New Approaches to the Teaching of Social Studies*, Blaisdell Publishing Company, Waltham, Mass., 1967.
30. Clarence B. Lindquist, *Mathematics in Colleges and Universities*, Final Report of a Comprehensive Survey of Graduate and Undergraduate Programs, Office of Education, OE-56018, Cir. 765, U. S. Department of Health, Education, and Welfare, Washington, D. C., 1965.
31. Lewis B. Mayhew, ed., *Social Science in General Education*, Wm. C. Brown Co., Dubuque, 1960.
32. J. Michel, *Foreign Language Teaching: An Anthology*, Macmillan Company, New York, 1967.
33. Leo Nedelsky, *Science Teaching and Testing*, Harcourt, Brace and World, Inc., New York, 1965.
34. Howard L. Nostrand, et al, *Research on Language Teaching*, University of Washington Press, 1965.
35. William R. Parker, *The National Interest and Foreign Languages*, Third Edition, U. S. Government Printing Office, Washington, D. C., 1962.
36. Dexter Perkins and John L. Snell, *Education of Historians in the United States*, McGraw-Hill Book Company, Inc., New York, 1962.
37. *Physical Education for College Men and Women*, American Association for Health, Physical Education and Recreation, National Education Association, Washington, D. C., 1955.
38. *Report of the Commission on the Humanities*, American Council of Learned Societies, New York, 1964.

39. *Report of the International Clearinghouse on Science and Mathematics Curricular Developments*, A Joint Project of the Commission on Science Education, American Association for the Advancement of Science, and the Science Teacher Center, University of Maryland, J. David Lockard, Director, 1966.

40. J. Carter Rowland, chm., et al, *An Annotated Bibliography on the College Teaching of English, 1957–1963*, National Council of Teachers of English, Champaign, Ill., 1966.

41. Francis Shoemaker and Louis Forsdale, eds., *Communication in General Education*, Wm. C. Brown Co., Dubuque, 1960.

42. *The Social Studies and the Social Sciences*, American Council of Learned Societies and the National Council for the Social Studies, Harcourt, Brace and World, Inc., New York, 1962.

43. Edward M. Stack, *The Language Laboratory and Modern Language Teaching*, Revised Edition, Oxford University Press, 1966.

44. Robert Stover, *The Nature of Historical Thinking*, The University of North Carolina Press, Chapel Hill, N. C., 1967.

45. J. A. Stratton, *Science and the Educated Man*, M.I.T. Press, Cambridge, Mass., 1966.

46. *This is Physical Education*, A Statement Prepared by the Physical Education Division of the American Association for Health, Physical Education and Recreation, National Education Association, Washington, D. C., 1965.

47. Donald R. Tuttle and Helen O'Leary, *Curriculum Patterns in English—Undergraduate Requirements for the English Major*, Office of Education, OE-33027, Bulletin 1965, No. 21, U. S. Department of Health, Education, and Welfare, Washington, D. C., 1965.

48. Glenys G. Unruh, ed., *New Curriculum Developments*, Report of the Commission on Current Curriculum Developments, Association for Supervision and Curriculum Developments, National Education Association, Washington, D. C., 1965.

49. Erich A. Walter, ed., *Religion and the State University*, University of Michigan Press, 1964.

50. Arthur Weston, *The Making of American Physical Education*, Appleton-Century-Crofts, New York, 1962.

6

Developments and Trends in Professional Education

The title of this chapter raises the question of what is meant by the word "professional." Few people agree on what vocational fields are included in the term. The ministry, medicine, and law are traditionally accepted as professions. Dentistry is usually regarded as a profession, but home economics, nursing, journalism, social work, engineering, and even teaching are not always accepted as professions. One solution is to distinguish between professional and technical fields, yet the word "technical" can apply to vocational fields which do not even require a college degree. Thus, to define home economics, nursing, or engineering as technical fields may seem somewhat derogatory. The confusion as to what constitutes a profession results from the vagueness of the definition of a profession. Lieberman, in his book, *Education as a Profession,* has defined several characteristics of a profession (44). If such characteristics as control over entry into the profession, a statement of ethics formulated and enforced by the professional group, and self-employment are essential aspects of a profession, then the field is quite limited. These standards exclude even the university professor, both as a teacher and as a practitioner of his particular discipline. However, this chapter is concerned not with definition but with discussion of some representative undergraduate and graduate professional fields. The fields of engineering, business, social work, journalism, agriculture, teaching, home economics, nursing, law and medicine will be considered. This chapter will not examine in detail the developments in each of these fields but, rather, will point out some major issues in current thinking about curriculum and instruction in professional fields.

Engineering

Eric A. Walker asserts that "There seems to be a basic dilemma in engineering education—the fact that for at least fifty years, engineering educators have been trying to achieve two separate, fundamental goals—two goals which to a large extent are irreconcilable: singleness of purpose and professional unity on the one hand, and broadening diversity and fragmentation on the other (66). This dilemma, as Walker points out, has led to three different educational patterns. The first provides a broadly based liberal science curriculum, increasingly diverse and general in its nature and gradually replacing the traditional four-year curricula. This development recognizes the need for a basic understanding of science and mathematics before moving into complex engineering problems which demand a high level of professional competence. Thus, graduate study in engineering becomes more significant and represents a second major attempt to answer the dilemma. The third solution emphasizes the relations of many branches of knowledge, and attempts to develop an integrated and sequential program of study.

One pattern emerging from these developments is the five-year integrated study program, which awards a bachelor of science degree after four years and a master of engineering degree after five. Cornell, Rennselaer, and the University of California have all developed programs along these lines. The *Interim Report* suggests that ". . .before long only the full five years will constitute a fully recognized engineering curriculum suitable for commencing a professional career" (34, p. 42).

Engineering is changing rapidly as a result of technological developments, and requires a broad approach which will enable the student to continue learning throughout life. Even so, formal programs of continuing education will probably be necessary to enable the engineer to keep up with his field. Independent and productive research play such a vital role in engineering that engineering education must also develop research competency and attitudes.

The problem of specialization is a serious one. While a broad base in mathematics and sciences appears to be essential in all fields, new fields of specialization are continually emerging which often involve new patterns of relationship with the basic fields of science. Engineering science, engineering physics, nuclear physics, and computer sciences are examples. The systems approach is another field which is both highly specialized and rather broad in its implications. Moreover, many persons trained in engineering move quickly into management and administrative posts. Thus, engineering education should include some social science.

Holstein and McGrath report that engineering schools will probably become more scientifically oriented but that most will continue to include some liberal arts requirements to broaden the student's over-all intellectual growth (32). The *Interim Report* recommends greater emphasis on liberal education and interdisciplinary experiences (34, p. 24). Holstein and McGrath also report an increase in honors and advanced placement programs for talented students in engineering (32). The quality of instruction in engineering has been a source of considerable concern. A study conducted by a committee of the American Society for Engineering Education in 1960 indicated that few institutions encourage or assist the young engineer to become a teacher (22). The project carried out by Otis E. Lancaster at Pennsylvania State University is perhaps the most realistic response to this need (1). Response to this program was enthusiastic, and it had a strong impact on those who participated.

In summary, engineering education is wrestling with the problems of preparing students for a professional world in a state of flux. Engineering faculties have to use traditionally structured departments to develop integrated, interdisciplinary, inter-departmental programs. Finally, engineering educators are trying to develop an educational program which enables and motivates the student to continue learning throughout life.

Business

College programs in business have been the subject of several studies. Gordon and Howell, in their study in 1959, emphasized that academic standards in business schools tend to be low because admissions standards are low, and faculties cannot introduce programs too rigorous for their students (27). The result is that there are more mediocre students in the field of business administration than in any other professional field. Pierson's study emphasized the same problem and added that, because of the diversity of careers in business and the lack of extensive work on the curriculum, the subject matter is disorganized and unrelated to academic work in the traditional fields (54).

One problem that has received considerable attention is what proportion of the undergraduate program in business administration should be in the arts and sciences. Recent studies generally recommend that at least fifty percent of the program be in general education, whereas the American Association of Collegiate Schools of Business for a long time suggested forty percent. The four-year program has been under increasing pressure to provide both general education and the special skills and training needed in modern business administration. To correct this, the Gordon and Howell report recommends a five-year undergraduate program and a two-year graduate program. The undergraduate program would emphasize basic preparation and avoid specialization.

The situation is complicated by the existence of two different kinds of professional preparation, one which emphasizes knowledge and skills to deal with finance, production, sales, and personnel, and the other which develops broad administrative skills. Many students do not continue to work in their undergraduate specialty, which justifies the trend toward basic skills and fundamental knowledge, including problem-solving, organization, interpersonal relationships, and communication. There is also an increasing interest in the behavioral sciences, management science, business games, and the problems of ethics and governmental relationships. This naturally leads to greater interest in the social sciences and the humanities. While many schools provide education in business only at the graduate level and require a liberal arts degree prior to entrance, many other institutions are responding to the demand to continue the undergraduate program and to provide a wide variety of specialties.

One continuing irritation in the field is the disparity between the views of executives and personnel offices. Although top-echelon businessmen insist that they are looking for a broad liberal education and qualities of integrity, resourcefulness, and judgment, their employment offices continue to require highly specific preparation for some aspect of business.

There is increasing dissatisfaction with the quality of instruction in business. Business practices change rapidly, and often instructors fail to keep up with current methods. The uses of programed learning materials and educational technology have not been fully explored, although business faculties tend to adjust more readily to such methods because of their extensive use in business and industry. The use of the computer in management games relates a method of teaching and a technological development which have widespread use in business and industry.

Most discussions of business education are not primarily concerned with sequence and integration. Yet, the search for new and more meaningful relations between liberal education and business education, and for a fundamental or core program basic to all specialties clearly reveals a concern for the over-all unity of the program.

Social Work

Social work education has been extensively studied. The 1942 report of the Study Committee of the American Association of Schools of Social Work recommended a broad liberal arts education as preparation for professional study in social work (21). The 1949 report of the American Association of Social Work emphasized again that the best foundation for social work is a broad undergraduate course of study in the liberal arts, with a major in the social sciences (62). This report allowed a few courses in the social work field itself, but maintained that they should be general and nontechnical. The 1951 report by Hollis and Taylor also emphasized the need for a broad liberal education with avoidance of overconcentration in any one area (31). This report argued that the undergraduate and graduate programs should be a continuous educational experience leading toward professional responsibility. This recommendation contrasts with the attitude of many schools of social work that undergraduate education is irrelevant to graduate work. In one state university, an undergraduate major in social work operates quite independently of the graduate school of social work; although the two are housed in adjacent buildings, there is little communication and no exchange of staff.

In 1955, the Council on Social Work Education initiated a study of the social work curriculum under the direction of Warner W. Boehm which produced a fourteen-volume report (6). This report, too, examined the significant question of the relation between the undergraduate and the graduate curricula. Although there is a need for an undergraduate major in social work which would qualify the student to fill some of the many positions in the field, the profession rejected this idea until quite recently. Yet, the number of graduate social workers is inadequate to meet the demands in the field and, as a result, persons with all types of college degrees and even some without degrees are employed to do social work. Some schools do offer an undergraduate program in social work, and Gordon Aldridge and Earl McGrath present some evidence that students with a background in social work are more successful in professional school (2). However, their evidence is based on a very few cases, and more extensive studies which attempt to correlate undergraduate work and graduate school success in social work are less definitive. Most evidence indicates that a sound liberal education is adequate preparation for study in social work, although various studies in the field have recommended a solid background in the social sciences. This recommendation seems reasonable but it poses several questions. How much background is desirable, and should the student concentrate in one or two fields, or sample all the social sciences? Could the undergraduate program include a limited amount of work in social welfare so that the student might become more familiar with the field and have a basis for choice? If the undergraduate major is irrelevant to graduate social work, is it possible that a college degree is not essential for professional study in the field? Would students with two or three years of college do just as well as those with four? Finally, with the tremendous demand for social workers, can schools of social work continue to ignore the necessity of an undergraduate program which qualifies the graduate to work in certain areas of the field? Although graduate training in social work once emphasized specific techniques, more recent curricula are oriented toward general preparation for work in the profession. This has been paralleled by a unification of the seven professional associations into a single national association of social workers. The school of social work is now accredited for its basic curriculum only, and not for its several specialized programs.

Journalism

The term "journalism" no longer means what it meant in the last half of the nineteenth century when the first formal attempts at journalism education were initiated. Originally, journalism referred to the collection and dissemination of news, including managing, editing, and writing. A definition proposed by Kearl in 1943 included all of human communication (38, p. 42): "Journalism is the conveyance of timely information, ideas, counsel, guidance, emotions, attitudes and advertising to a varying audience by means of organized media and written, oral, or pictorial symbols." The appropriate content and degree of difficulty of journalism education are sources of disagreement. Journalism schools continue to offer courses in copy reading, typography, photography, picture editing, radio news writing, sports coverage, sports writing, advertising, and salesmanship, which emphasize rule of thumb procedures and tricks of the trade rather than comprehensive knowledge. Some journalism schools discourage practical experience, while others encourage, or even require, work with the student paper or with radio and television broadcasting units. Many journalism educators feel these technical courses should be replaced by a broad liberal program which emphasizes the social and behavioral sciences and the field in which the student plans to write. Thus, the journalist interested in scientific writing should have extensive education in science.

The relationship between liberal education and professional education is particularly problematic in the field of journalism. The journalist cannot write on a subject in any depth unless he is familiar with the relevant facts, principles, and ideas, and is able to select and interpret pertinent materials. Journalism professors often criticize liberal arts courses because they emphasize facts, are unrelated to significant problems, and are so numerous that the prospective journalist cannot obtain an overview of the major ideas of a particular discipline. This difficulty results in criticism of journalism education itself, for journalism majors often take a few courses in a large number of disciplines and fail to grasp the essential nature of any one of them.

A good journalism program can be a significant experience in liberal education. Journalism classes are generally small. Students are expected to write, and their writing is read and extensively criticized. When this criticism is skillfully done, it includes not only style and quality of writing but also adequacy of documentation and accuracy of statements. The journalist is asked to draw on his background in liberal arts to write about practically every aspect of human activity and experience. To do this well, the student must organize his past experience, engage in additional reading, and adequately fulfill his requirements. The liberal education experience provided by the continual demand for writing can be enriched by courses in the history of journalism and the law of the press which deal with significant problems and concerns of a democratic society.

The American Council on Education for Journalism, which is the accrediting agency for programs in this field, has long recommended that journalism majors devote only a quarter of their time to journalism courses and the rest to courses in liberal arts. As Dressel indicates in *Liberal Education and Journalism,* journalism schools frequently violate this recommendation (18). Even when they adhere to it, electives may be so used by the student and the adviser to violate the principle. However, the ratio becomes a somewhat meaningless criterion if the professional work itself provides significant liberal education experiences. In some of the best journalism programs, the total undergraduate experience may be as effective or more effective than that of the best undergraduate liberal arts colleges. On the other hand, the requirement that three-fourths of the student's work be in liberal arts courses and the possibility that many of his courses in journalism will have a liberal arts content does not necessarily result in a liberal education. The quality of the liberal education attained by journalism students depends on the quality of the journalism faculty. The existence of numerous technical courses in a journalism curriculum is less devastating than what it reveals about the mentality and point of view of the faculty.

The problem of sequence also exists in this field. In some respects, it is desirable for the student to complete his liberal education requirements before beginning professional study in journalism. Thus, some schools, such as the Medill School of Journalism at Northwestern University, insist that professional preparation in journalism be at the graduate level, although undergraduates can enroll as journalism majors and take courses approximating one-fourth of the total degree requirement. Sequence, is also a problem within the undergraduate program, both in the relation of liberal education and journalism courses, and in journalism courses themselves. A sequential, integrative approach to advanced journalism courses is needed, and some consideration should be given to the balance of journalism core courses and specialties in television, advertising, radio, and newspaper work. The problems in journalism education are not unique; most fields are facing the same or similar difficulties.

Agriculture

Although agricultural education is traditionally associated with the land-grant colleges and universities, agriculture is also offered in many other institutions. The latter, however, emphasize undergraduate education, whereas the land-grant institutions increasingly stress graduate education. Agricultural research in the land-grant institutions is also shifting from applied to basic research. At the same time, the mechanization of agriculture and the increased productivity of land have markedly decreased the percentage of the population involved in agriculture. The implications of these developments for the undergraduate curriculum are not fully known, but it is clear that more students in agriculture are interested in graduate study as preparation either for positions in business, industry, and government, or for careers in research and teaching.

It is difficult to distinguish between terminal programs and preparatory programs for graduate study. Students often change their majors and programs while undergraduates, and their career plans both during and after their undergraduate education. Any distinction is complicated by the scope of the undergraduate program in agriculture, which includes soil, plant, and animal sciences, food science and technology, agricultural engineering, agricultural economics, and forestry, fisheries, and wildlife. The Commission on Education in Agriculture and Natural Resources (CEANAR) and six action committees in animal sciences, bio-engineering, food sciences, natural resources, plant and soil sciences, and social sciences have studied many problems in agricultural education (56). They agree that the basic goal of agricultural education is to prepare the student to continue to expand his knowledge and to live a life useful to himself and society. They also agree that agriculture must emphasize interdisciplinary and problem-solving approaches. The natural tendency is to increase requirements in basic sciences and mathematics, to decrease agricultural science and technology, and to seek interdisciplinary cooperation in the consolidation and development of new sequences of agricultural courses. Those concerned with the improvement of undergraduate agricultural education are primarily interested in the development of integrated sequences in chemistry and biology which stress fundamental concepts, and in the reduction of duplication. Many are investigating the possibility of a core program in agriculture which provides both a common, basic educational experience and an increased economy through concentration of students in a small number of courses.

The diversity of the undergraduate program in agriculture makes it possible for some students to begin study in agriculture at the graduate level. Undergraduates in other fields may also be interested in such basic world problems as food supply, conservation of natural resources, and population problems. Thus, the program in agriculture can make some contribution to the liberal and general education of students majoring in other fields. One of the most encouraging aspects of the study of the agricultural curriculum is that no effort has been made to develop special programs or courses in the various scientific areas. Educators in agriculture face problems of content, emphasis, and prior preparation, but they appear to be committed to working out a solution with the cooperation of the basic science departments. With this cooperation, the agricultural program will very likely become preprofessional training in the agricultural sciences, rather than education in agricultural technology.

Teacher Education

Diversity characterizes the current education of teachers. While most educators recognize that there is no essential conflict between the science or art of teaching and the disciplines or subject matter to be taught, certification continues to be a state function strongly influenced by the prestige and power of individuals and groups. The influence of the National Council for the Accreditation of Teacher Education as a unifying and mediating force is not yet clear.

Teacher training programs at the elementary and secondary levels include fewer professional courses than most other curricula. Three major problems must be faced by those who wish to develop a new synthesis of content, educational theory, and supervised experience.

One continuing problem is that faculty members teaching courses in the basic arts and sciences are primarily concerned with their disciplines, and are rarely interested in questions of philosophy, curriculum, and educational methodology. Thus, the prospective teacher learns his discipline from professors who are only interested in teaching at the college level, and often discovers that his professors have no interest in students who plan to teach at the elementary or secondary level.

A second problem results from the independence of college and university curricular reorganization from curriculum reform at the elementary and secondary levels. Although prominent mathematicians and scientists have given unsparingly of their time to develop new courses and curricula in the sciences for the elementary and secondary levels, their efforts and programs have had minimal impact on the courses provided in their own colleges and universities. The prospective teacher continues to be educated according to traditional disciplinary patterns, and receives little or no instruction in current methods of teaching. It is encouraging that college and university professors in the basic disciplines are concerned with elementary and secondary curricula, but too few attempt to relate their discipline to the total curriculum at these levels, and even fewer succeed in relating the college curriculum to developments at lower levels.

A third problem results from the changing character of colleges and departments of education. Increasingly, these units are concerned with graduate education which prepares students for a wide variety of positions other than classroom teaching. Thus, within colleges of education, those primarily concerned with the preparation of elementary and secondary school teachers have little prestige. The requirement of a fifth year or a master's degree for permanent certification tends to make undergraduate preparation preliminary rather than professional in nature, and also poses questions about the relation of undergraduate to graduate work. Teachers, especially in the sciences, must continually update their knowledge of their discipline, which suggests that graduate study should emphasize the discipline. However, a single year is hardly adequate for this purpose. The teacher must engage in a continuing process of self-education which requires a good undergraduate foundation in the discipline. But other areas of knowledge and skills compete for attention. Teachers should be informed of developments in educational technology and in testing and evaluation. They need to know something about counseling and guidance. Every teacher should be familiar with general curriculum developments and current curriculum studies. Since the undergraduate program cannot cover all these areas, the graduate program must consider some of them.

Practice teaching, which constitutes the internship or preceptorship of this professional field, continues to be scrutinized. Although some colleges and universities continue to have students teach in campus schools, many educators feel this experience is unrealistic. Even practice teaching for a few hours or few days a week in an off-campus school is frequently regarded as inadequate work experience. Full-time teaching and residence in a community provide a more realistic internship but raise problems of sequence in academic work on the campus. However, as more institutions provide or require off-campus study or service experience, practice teaching may become only one example of a generally-accepted pattern, which will ease current difficulties in combining work and study.

Home Economics

Home economics, once a single field covering the tasks of the housewife on the farm or in the small town middle-class home, now includes a multiplicity of activities and vocations. Although a major in home economics might be helpful to the housewife and home manager, a very small percentage of the future homemakers take home economics, and a very small percentage of those who do select home economics choose it for this reason. Home economics, as a single field, once led to a career as an extension worker, who served the needs of housewives in all aspects of home economics. Increasingly, however, a group of extension workers in home economics forms a team, in which each member has a particular specialty. One field in which the single-field concept continues to have significance is that of teaching home economics in the secondary school. Few secondary schools are able to employ three or four home economists to cover the various specialties. Sources of financial support tend to specify that certain courses be taught by home economists, even though individuals teaching in other areas might be as well or better qualified. For example, some biologists or physical scientists might teach nutrition and foods as well as the home economist.

One can argue that home economics is a unified field involving a central core and a limited number of undergraduate specialties. The nature of this unifying core, however, poses some difficulties. It can hardly be defined as a set of skills or minimal competencies in the several specialties of home economics. The core might consist of fundamental concepts and principles but, since these have not been defined and organized, the case for a unified field seems to rest either on ethical and value concepts or on general orientation and history of home economics. There are essentially four specialties in home economics: nutrition and foods, textiles and clothing, related or applied arts and housing, and child development and family relations. Nutrition, foods, and dietetics are closely related to the biological and physical sciences. Textiles requires a sound background in organic chemistry, whereas clothing construction emphasizes design and skill. Applied arts and housing also emphasize design, but include business and economics. Child development, family relations, and home management are concerned primarily with psychology and the social sciences, but also demand some knowledge of budgeting, consumer economics, insurance, and simple bookkeeping. These several specializations are related in such diverse ways to the basic disciplines that it is very difficult to isolate a common focus or unifying theme. Even engineering and architecture are related to certain aspects of home planning and equipment, and sociology, psychology, medicine, social work, and education are all related to marriage, family, child development, and mental and physical health. Home economics includes specializations in several fields also covered by specific disciplines, and the recurrent contention of home economists that their unique contribution is the interpretation of the impact of these specialties on the home and family falsely implies that other fields have no such concern.

Home economics suffers in the present day from its traditional orientation to the middle class. Many of the most serious problems in the general field of home economics exist in large urban centers and slums. However, home economists have resisted involvement with these problems. Home economics also suffers from traditional exclusion of men. Men are interested in and make significant contributions to many areas of home economics. However, the name "home economics," the predominance of women in the field, and the feminine orientation of much of the curriculum are unlikely to attract men to the program, either as staff members or as students. The recent emphasis of home economics on the sciences has even discouraged many women of average or lower ability from entering the field.

Home economics thus faces several major problems in curriculum planning. One is the clarification of the several specialties in the field and of the relation of these specialties to the basic arts and sciences. A second problem involves the sequence of courses in the various specialties and the relation of these sequences to required work in the basic arts and sciences. Home economists also must decide whether the field is to be a single, unified professional field or a disparate array of specialites. Must each student sample all the basic areas in the program? Are there basic concepts, principles, and methods of analyzing problems common to all specialties or is the continuing association of the several aspects of home economics based on sentiment and tradition? Another problem involves the question of whether home economics is a vocational or a liberal arts field. Home economics may provide a general education for women and some courses in the field may supplement or contribute to a liberal education. However, home economists recently have become professionally oriented and the curricula emphasize preparation for careers in education, business, and public service. Few home economists have even attempted to structure courses which would have widespread appeal to majors in other fields by offering them the opportunity to examine certain general materials and problems from a home economics point of view.

Home economics presents many difficult curriculum problems. No satisfactory solutions will be found until the goals of home economics, and the relevance of the concept itself, are objectively reassessed.

Nursing

The multiplicity of programs in the field of nursing complicates any discussion of educational problems in this field. Although the number of nurses per hundred thousand persons has increased from approximately 60 in 1910 to 280 in 1960, and many technicians and aides, now perform traditional nursing duties, there still are not enough graduate nurses to meet the demand. Many graduate nurses now become involved in supervisory and administrative duties rather than in bedside care and personal relationships with patients. Other health related vocations, such as physical therapy, occupational therapy, dietetics, and medical technology, infringe upon the traditional sphere of the nurse. Thus, the role of the nurse and her relationship to the doctor, to the dietitian, and to other paramedical personnel must be reassessed.

No single definition of the role of the nurse is possible. Many hospital schools of nursing still provide an education which is highly specific and task-oriented. There are junior college programs, baccalaureate degree programs, and programs of specialized graduate study. Those who hold the R.N. differ in educational background and in degree of competency; yet distinctions based on such factors are not consistently made because the R.N. constitutes the recognition of professional status.

In baccalaureate degree programs, a major issue (as in all university technical and professional programs) is the relation of liberal education to professional content. Should general education courses in the program contribute to or support professional courses? Is the objective of the program to produce a liberally-educated person who also has nursing competencies? The central issue is whether the baccalaureate degree program should emphasize a high degree of technical competency or such qualities as compassion, understanding, and capacity for growth. The ideal seems to be the latter, but most programs fail to attain this ideal for several reasons. First, the nursing task is poorly defined, especially for those in baccalaureate degree programs. Second, nursing faculties tend to be clinically-oriented, and often do not have the educational background to make them at ease with other university faculty members. Also, many of them have not mastered the current scientific and social science knowledge deemed essential for nursing students. Third, nursing has not had an extensive research program to help analyze the problems of nursing and develop appropriate solutions. Thus, the nursing profession tends, though reluctantly, to remain supportive and dependent on the medical profession.

The nursing curriculum inevitably reflects these problems. Since a number of disciplines are relevant to the field of nursing, and since the graduate nurse may be a supervisor and administrator as well as a bedside nurse, the curriculum must emphasize the total development of the individual rather than mastery of content. Because knowledge in the area of medical care and practice is changing so rapidly, it is essential that the nurse be able to understand, contribute to, and adjust to changing patterns. Reasonable balance between theory and practice will continue to be a matter of concern, but hopefully the current pattern of fixed periods of time in specified types of clinical experiences will be replaced by clinical experience which emphasizes fundamental concepts and principles and which can be adopted to the preparation and interests of the individual student.

Educators in nursing must also confront several questions relating to the problem of sequence. How much basic work in the sciences and social sciences should be required prior to professional courses which apply knowledge and insights developed in these courses to nursing problems? How much basic science should be included in nursing courses? When should the student be introduced to clinical experience, and how is this experience to be related to continuing on-campus study? Should clinical experience be postponed until the end of the program and become a period of internship prior to assumption of full-time nursing duties? What can be done to develop habits of continuing professional study and inquiry? Should research be included in the nursing program, as it is in many medical school curricula?

The problems of nursing education clearly relate to the four continuums discussed earlier, and they cannot be solved in isolation from the central concerns of the university's total undergraduate program.

Law

Professional training in law usually requires three years of education beyond the baccalaureate degree, and culminates in an LL.B. or J.D. degree. Although innovations in legal education are less apparent than in some other fields, criticisms and suggestions for change are no less common (25, 63). Even the appropriate degree is a matter of some concern, and there is a trend toward greater use of the J.D. (perhaps by analogy with the M.D.). Comparison with medical education raises the issue of clinical or practical experience. Legal education traditionally has concentrated on minutiae and abstraction rather than on practice. The case method, which emphasizes precedent and procedure rather than theory, has little relation to law office practice and tends to concentrate on professorial analysis and commentary rather than on the cases themselves. Moreover, the expansion of materials and specializations has favored the lecture system rather than the discussion or seminar. The isolation of the law schools in most universities prevents interaction with other disciplines. This is particularly detrimental in view of the recent juridical trends and the involvement of lawyers in policy decisions which require familiarity with sociology, psychology, and natural science. Law, as a central element in culture, also should receive more attention in other disciplines. The law school is rarely the center of innovation, critical comment, and research which its role as a professional school requires.

The appropriate length of the law program has often been debated. A six-year program resulting in both an A.B. and an LL.B., which requires the cooperation of liberal arts colleges and law schools, was once fairly common and continues to be of some interest. There is also interest in an additional optional or required year leading to an LL.M. One factor in the concern about length is dissatisfaction with the third year which too often concentrates on the impending bar examinations to the exclusion of all other educational concerns. Thus, the three-year program lacks a strong sequential, unified organization.

The 1966 report of the American Association of Law Schools suggested four models for a law school:

1. A policy-directed law school devoted to producing lawyers capable of making policy decisions.

2. A legal-doctrine-directed law school aimed at preparing lawyers to understand and apply legal doctrine to client problems.
3. A skills-oriented law school which concentrates on development of basic skills with very limited coverage of legal doctrine.
4. A combined-purposes law school which attempts to provide training in policy, doctrine, and skills (63, pp. 544–570).

The first three models are viewed as inadequate, but useful in helping to grasp the objectives which legal education must attain.

The dilemmas of legal education are similar to those of liberal education and other professional programs. Its relation and its contribution to liberal education are unclear. Proliferation of content has encouraged specialization and the use of the lecture and has thereby detracted from the relevance of the student's experience to practice. Examinations and grades are disruptive and encourage the substitution of rote recall for demonstration of proficiency and judgment. Legal educators must consider the role of practical experience, independent study, research and interdisciplinary courses in the legal curriculum, and must look for new methods to achieve unity and coherence.

Medicine

The traditional medical school program emphasizes general practice, but many medical students are now primarily concerned with specialization and research. Faculty members of the better medical schools also are involved both in research and in the direction of graduate study. Specialization is encouraged by conferences and courses sponsored by agencies and professional societies, by the importance now attached to advanced degrees, and by the specialty certification program. Of the more than eighty schools of medicine, fifty-one were reported in a recent unpublished summary to have sponsored some form of curricular innovation. Moreover, these fifty-one institutions reported fifty innovations in the area of research and graduate study, including provision for research activity during the regular year, degree combinations (M.A.-M.D. or Ph.D.-M.D.), summer research, and research during a nonresident year.

Research and graduate study usually imply specialization, which may be narrowly based on a discipline rather than generally applicable to medical practice. Diagnosis and treatment and the research problems directly related to them demand an interdepartmental organization and an integration of knowledge from the natural sciences, the behavioral sciences, and the humanities. Forty-one of the fifty-one schools had initiated interdepartmental courses in the basic sciences, clinical sciences, and behavioral sciences.

These approaches may be attempts to find a more meaningful organization of knowledge than the traditional disciplines. They may also be attempts to break away from a theoretical orientation to a practical orientation. Finally, they may be attempts to free medical education from its preoccupation with the organization of knowledge in order to emphasize that, in educating a physician, one must educate a total individual to work with other individuals. Thus, another major area of curricular innovation has been that of patient contact. Some medical schools have students work with patients throughout their training. Many provide clerkships and preceptorships for students, which involve both general and specialized practice, and family contacts as well as clinical or hospital experiences. More medical schools realize that the physician is one member of a paramedical team which includes social workers, nurses, clinical psychologists, counselors, laboratory technologists, occupational therapists, and physical therapists. Thus, they encourage the prospective physician to learn something of the role of each of these specialists, and to work closely with them.

After completing the M.D. degree, many graduates spend several years in specialty internships. However, any physician who is to keep abreast of the field must continue his education. To facilitate this, many medical schools are initiating programs which require the student to accept greater responsibility for self-education. Students are offered electives and are given free time for research or independent study. Advisers have greater autonomy in helping students plan individual programs, which often include honors work and independent study. Overseas study and exchange programs are permitted in a few medical schools. The possibility of eliminating grades has also been considered by many schools.

This rather lengthy list of curricular innovations provides a good argument for lengthening the medical program. Stanford University requires five years for the medical degree, in addition to a four-year premedical program. However, several institutions are investigating ways to abbreviate the total length of the program by combining portions of the baccalaureate and professional programs.

Medical educators are also concerned about examination problems, improvement of teaching, and the adaptation of educational technology to the problems of learning. In fact, medical schools have been leaders in the introduction and application of color television to instructional and research problems. That several medical schools wish to incorporate the social sciences and the humanities into the medical program is particularly interesting in view of the current emphasis on scientific research and specialization.

SUMMARY

The preceding review of several fields of professional education indicates that vocational education faces the same problems that concern educators in the liberal arts and sciences. Vocational programs not only depend on the liberal arts disciplines for significant segments of their educational programs, but also face the same problems in seeking a balance between the individual and abstract knowledge, practice and theory, flexibility and rigid structure, and unity and compartmentalization. Specialization, research orientation, and course proliferation not only pose problems for the arts and science student in planning a unified program, but also force vocational and professional faculties to specify those courses in the arts and sciences which are relevant to the student's later study. Thus, the efforts of faculties in the various basic disciplines to reorganize courses, develop new and more meaningful sequences, and to provide opportunity for greater student responsibility are of great interest to vocational faculties who are demanding broader and more basic undergraduate preparation.

The sharp distinction between liberal and professional programs is gradually being erased. Faculty members in the basic arts and sciences are often professional in their orientation toward graduate study and research, whether or not they acknowledge it. Professional programs, on the other hand, are emphasizing research and graduate study and thus are more readily accepted by other segments of the faculty. Finally, the rapid expansion of knowledge requires that a student in any area of professional activity have a firm basis in the relevant disciplines.

Most professional fields recognize some responsibility for educating citizen leaders, for relating the professional area to other professions, and for teaching the student to educate himself. These objectives make value considerations and social and psychological concepts and principles relevant in most university-affiliated vocational fields. The problems posed by the expansion of specialties and knowledge also cause educators in all areas to combine forces. Storage and retrieval of knowledge, use of educational technology in the improvement of instruction and learning, and widespread commitment to the development of certain broad competencies combine to convince educators that

liberal and professional education are interrelated and mutually reinforcing.

Liberal education can no longer be defined as knowledge of a set
of subjects called the liberal arts; indeed, liberal education is defined
not by knowledge, but rather by behavior and by the quality of actions
and thought. The objectives of liberal education, then, should describe
what constitutes a liberally-educated person. First, such a person
knows and understands the essential ideas and concepts necessary
to live effectively in *his own* culture. Second, he is familiar with
the modes of thought of several disciplines, and is able to utilize these
appropriately in making his own judgments. Third, he communicates
effectively with others by assimilating their ideas through reading and
listening and by clearly expressing his own ideas in writing and speaking.
Fourth, he understands the values upon which his society is based; he is
aware of some of the differences between these and the values of other
societies and cultures; and he consciously accepts a personal set of
values which guide his own judgment and actions.

Not everyone will agree with this definition of the liberally-educated man. However, too often we think of these objectives in a purely
quantitative way: a student should know more, think more, communicate
more and understand more about value differences. The essential concern is with qualitative rather than quantitative outcomes. Not only
should the student know more, but also he should acquire *more significant* ideas and should make *sounder judgments.* He not only should
communicate more, but also should communicate in *clearer, more precise,* and *more effective* ways. He not only should understand values,
but also should *use* them as a conscious basis for his own judgments
and actions. Thus, it is not what a person knows, but rather the character of his thoughts and actions that determines the quality of his education.

Earl McGrath defines the objectives of professional education as:
(1) orientation to the profession; (2) vocational flexibility; (3) understanding of basic principles; (4) cultivation of professional attitudes
and motivation (48). At first glance, these seem to differ from the
objectives of a liberal education. However, orientation to a profession
surely requires an understanding of the essential facts and ideas upon
which the profession is based and of their application to a general area
of service. This, coupled with the third objective of providing basic
principles, indicates that a major goal of professional education is knowledge and understanding of concepts and principles, most of which
originate in the basic arts, sciences, and social sciences, but which are

synthesized in new ways for new purposes. The second objective, to provide vocational flexibility, emphasizes that a professional education cannot produce a fully-competent professional, for the profession is constantly changing. The individual may specialize, but he must always adapt his knowledge to particular and changing circumstances. Vocational flexibility means the ability to think and to make sound judgments about each individual case or set of circumstances. Finally, the fourth objective of professional education, to cultivate professional attitudes or ethics and motivation, clearly involves a set of values and the relating of these values to one's judgments and actions.

Thus, both the liberally-educated and the professionally-educated person must be rational and compassionate; he must be committed and tolerant; and he must be purposeful and flexible. He must be well based in his basic disciplines, but also interested in his impact on people; he must be aware of and understand significant ideas and theories, but also committed to solving or alleviating the difficulties of individuals and society; he must understand and accept the necessity for rules and requirements in organizations and society, but also accept the need for flexibility in the application of these rules; he must sense and accept the existence of distinctions and differences, yet seek for coherence, interrelationship, and comprehensive understanding. The truly liberally-educated person is professional, and no one is truly professional who is not liberally educated.

REFERENCES

1. *Achieve Learning Objectives, Become Better Learning Leaders,* Papers Prepared for a Summer Institute of Effective Teaching for Young Engineering Teachers, Pennsylvania State University, August 26–September 8, 1962, The American Society for Engineering Education and The Engineers' Council for Professional Development, project supported by The Ford Foundation, Otis E. Lancaster, Director.
2. Gordon Aldridge and Earl McGrath, *Liberal Education and Social Work,* Teachers College Press, Columbia University, 1965.
3. Eric Ashby, *Technology and the Academics,* Macmillan Company, London, 1959.
4. Turpin C. Bannister, ed., *The Architect at Midcentury: Evolution and Achievement,* Reinhold Publishing Co., New York, 1954.
5. Walter Beggs, *The Education of Teachers,* The Center of Applied Research in Education, Inc., Washington, D. C., 1965.
6. Werner W. Boehm, et al, *The Social Work Curriculum Study,* Fourteen Volumes, Council on Social Work Education, New York, 1959.

7. D. Bratchell and Morrell Heald, eds., *The Aims and Organization of Liberal Studies,* Pergamon Press, Inc., New York, 1966.

8. Bonnie and Vern L. Bullough, *The Emergence of Modern Nursing,* Macmillan Company, New York, 1964.

9. Thomas H. Carroll, ed., *Business Education for Competence and Responsibility,* North Carolina University Press, 1954.

10. D. F. Carvers, *Legal Education in the United States,* Harvard Law School, Cambridge, Mass., 1960.

11. John J. Clark and Blaise J. Opulente, *The Impact of the Foundation Reports on Business Education,* St. John's University Press, 1963.

12. John Clark and Blaise Opulente, eds., *Business and Liberal Arts,* St. John's University Press, 1962.

13. John Clark and Blaise Opulente, eds., *Professional Education for Business,* St. John's University Press, 1964.

14. Lowell T. Coggeshall, *Planning for Medical Progress Through Education,* Association of American Medical Colleges, Evanston, Ill., April, 1965.

15. Arthur W. Combs, *The Professional Education of Teachers,* Allyn and Bacon, Inc., Boston, 1965.

16. Charles R. DeCarlo and Ormsbee W. Robinson, *Education in Business and Industry,* Center for Applied Research in Education, Inc., Washington, D. C., 1966.

17. John E. Deitrick and Robert C. Berson, *Medical Schools in the United States at Mid-Century,* McGraw-Hill Book Company, Inc., New York, 1953.

18. Paul L. Dressel, *Liberal Education and Journalism*, Bureau of Publications, Teachers College, Columbia University, 1960.

19. Paul L. Dressel, et al, *The Liberal Arts as Viewed by Faculty Members in Professional Schools,* Bureau of Publications, Teachers College, Columbia University, 1959.

20. Paul L. Dressel and Margaret F. Lorimer, *Attitudes of Liberal Arts Faculty Members Toward Liberal and Professional Education,* Bureau of Publications, Teachers College, Columbia University, 1960.

21. *Education for the Public Social Services,* Report of the Study Committee of the American Association of Schools of Social Work, University of North Carolina Press, 1942.

22. "Engineering Faculty Recruitment, Development, and Utilization," Report of the Committee on the Development of Engineering Faculties, American Society for Engineering Education, *Journal of Engineering Education,* May, 1960, pp. 757–828.

23. Herman A. Estrin, ed., *Higher Education in Engineering and Science,* McGraw-Hill Book Company, Inc., 1963.

24. Lester J. Evans, *The Crisis in Medical Education,* University of Michigan Press, 1964.

25. Harrop Freeman, "Legal Education: Some Farther-Out Proposals," *Journal of Legal Education,* Vol. 17, 1965, pp. 272–284.

26. Ira Freeman and Beatrice Freeman, *Careers and Opportunities in Journalism,* E. P. Dutton and Company, Inc., New York, 1966.

27. Robert A. Gordon and James E. Howell, *Higher Education for Business,* Columbia University Press, 1959.

28. Kathleen K. Guinee, *The Aims and Methods of Nursing Education,* Macmillan Company, New York, 1966.

29. Loretta E. Heidgerken, *Teaching and Learning in Schools of Nursing,* J. B. Lippincott Company, Philadelphia, 1965.

30. Nelson B. Henry, ed., *Education for the Professions,* Sixty-First Yearbook of the National Society for the Study of Education, University of Chicago Press, 1962.

31. Ernest V. Hollis and Alice L. Taylor, *Social Work Education in the United States,* Columbia University Press, 1951.

32. Edwin Holstein and Earl McGrath, *Liberal Education and Engineering,* Bureau of Publication, Teachers College, Columbia University, 1960.

33. B. Hollinshead, *Survey of Dentistry,* Final Report of the Commission on the Survey of Dentistry in the United States, American Council on Education, Washington, D. C., 1961.

34. *Interim Report,* Committee on Goals of Engineering Education, American Society for Engineering Education, E. A. Walker Chm., Purdue University, April, 1967.

35. Walton John and H. P. Hammond, *Graduate Work in Engineering in Universities and Colleges in the United States,* U. S. Department of the Interior, U. S. Government Printing Office, Washington, D. C., 1936.

36. Ann M. Heiss, et al, *Graduate and Professional Education,* An Annotated Bibliography, The Center for Research and Development in Higher Education, University of California, Berkeley, 1967.

37. Milton J. Horowitz, *Educating Tomorrow's Doctors,* Appleton-Century-Crofts, New York, 1964.

38. Bryant Kearl, "Journalism—What Is It? A Re-definition," *Journalism Quarterly,* Vol. 20, March, 1943.

39. Charles E. Kellogg and David C. Knapp, *The College of Agriculture: Science in the Public Service,* McGraw-Hill Book Company, Inc., New York, 1966.

40. William M. Kephart, et al, *Liberal Education and Business,* Bureau of Publications, Teachers College, Columbia University, 1963.

41. Frank Kreith and Jeremiah Allen, eds., *Honors Programs in Engineering,* Report of the Conference on Honors Programs in College Engineering, University of Colorado, Boulder, Colorado, 1963, Allyn and Bacon, Boston, 1964.

42. Jeanette Lee and Paul L. Dressel, *Liberal Education and Home Economics,* Bureau of Publications, Teachers College, Columbia University, 1953.

43. Charles S. Levy, *Education for Social Group Work Practice,* School of Social Work, Yeshiva University, New York, 1959.
44. Myron Lieberman, *Education as a Profession,* Prentice-Hall, Inc., Englewood Cliffs, N. J., 1956.
45. Kenneth S. Lynn, ed., *The Professions in America,* Houghton Mifflin Company, Boston, 1965.
46. Kenneth S. Lynn and the Editors of *Daedalus,* eds., *The Professions in America,* Beacon Press, Boston, 1967.
47. Gwendoline MacDonald, *Development of Standards and Accreditation in Collegiate Nursing Education,* J. B. Lippincott Company, Philadelphia, 1965.
48. John Mayor and Willis Swartz, *Accreditation in Teacher Education—Its Influence on Higher Education,* National Commission on Accrediting, American Council on Education, Washington, D. C., 1965.
49. Earl J. McGrath, *Liberal Education in the Professions,* Bureau of Publications, Teachers College, Columbia University, 1959.
50. Earl McGrath and Charles Russell, *Are Liberal Arts Colleges Becoming Professional Schools?* Bureau of Publications, Teachers College, Columbia University, 1958.
51. George E. Miller, ed., *Teaching and Learning in Medical Schools,* Harvard University Press, 1961.
52. James Newcomer, et al, *Liberal Education and Pharmacy,* Bureau of Publications, Teachers College, Columbia University, 1960.
53. Blaise J. Opulente, ed., *Toward a Philosophy of Business Education,* St. John's University Press, 1960.
54. Frank C. Pierson, et al, *The Education of American Businessmen,* McGraw-Hill Book Company, Inc., 1959.
55. Mary K. Pillepich, *Development of General Education in Collegiate Nursing Programs: Role of Administrator,* Bureau of Publications, Teachers College, Columbia University, 1962.
56. Clarence M. Randall, *A Business Man Looks at Liberal Education,* The Adult Education Association, White Plains, New York, 1966.
57. "Report of the Panel on Pre-Professional Training in the Agricultural Sciences," *CUEBS News,* Vol. III, No. 4, April, 1967.
58. Charles H. Russell, *Liberal Education and Nursing,* Bureau of Publications, Teachers College, Columbia University, 1959.
59. Aura E. Severinghaus, et al, *Preparation for Medical Education,* McGraw-Hill Book Company, Inc., 1961.
60. Leonard S. Silk, *The Education of Businessmen,* Committee for Economic Development, New York, 1960.
61. William E. Simons, *Liberal Education in the Service Academies,* Bureau of Publications, Teachers College, Columbia University, 1965.
62. *Social Work as a Profession,* Revised Edition, American Association of Social Work, New York, 1949.

63. Symposium on Legal Education, Association of American Law Schools, *University of Miami Law Review,* Vol. 21, No. 3, Spring, 1967, pp. 505–570.
64. *University Education and Business,* Cambridge University Committee, Cambridge University Press, Cambridge, England, 1946.
65. Willis Wager and Earl McGrath, *Liberal Education and Music,* Bureau of Publications, Teachers College, Columbia University, 1962.
66. Eric A. Walker, "Report to the Society on the Goals of Engineering Education," Paper presented at the annual meeting of the American Society for Engineering Education, Washington State University June, 1966.
67. W. B. Webb, ed., *The Profession of Psychology,* Holt, Rinehart and Winston, New York, 1962.

7

Developments and Trends in Graduate Education

Although our primary concern is with curriculum, any discussion of graduate education must consider its rapid rate of growth. Doctorates have doubled in almost every decade since 1900. Approximately two hundred institutions now award doctorate degrees, and over six hundred award master's degrees. Legislatures have been generous in giving the title of university to former teachers colleges and, as soon as an institution acquires the title, it initiates plans for a graduate program. Probably another fifty or one hundred institutions will add doctorate programs to their curriculum in the next ten years. Graduate education has expanded not only in enrollment and in number of degrees and institutions, but also in the range of degrees granted. Ashton, for example, reports sixty-four doctorates, including professional degrees in medicine and dentistry (1, p. 67). Berelson reports over five hundred and fifty (3, p. 35) fields in which doctoral degrees are offered, and there are now nearly four hundred master's degree titles in use (15, p. 86).

Graduate education might be ignored in a volume primarily concerned with curriculum, for there is very little over-all institutional planning of graduate curricula. Liberal arts colleges which are planning a master's program for a particular clientele may develop some distribution requirements in various fields or at various levels. A few universities which have developed from teachers colleges have attempted to encompass the many specializations in the field of education in their doctoral programs, and have proposed some broad institutional curricular policies to maintain a balance between education and the various specializations. However, graduate education is usually characterized by departmental autonomy and flexibility in planning individual programs. One might argue that there is no such thing as a graduate curriculum, that there is only an array of graduate courses, seminars, and research opportunities from which a program is constructed for individual students.

However, graduate education does have a significant effect on undergraduate education. For many years the vast majority of undergraduates in many eastern colleges have gone on to graduate or professional school, but in midwestern institutions where, ten or fifteen years ago, only twenty to thirty percent of the entering freshmen planned to continue their education, now fifty to sixty percent are indicating an interest in higher education. Undergraduates are continually reminded of the possibility of graduate education by the large number of students enrolling in graduate school, by the widespread faculty commitment to graduate education and research, and by the requirement of graduate degrees for many positions in business, government, social work, and education. The involvement of an institution in graduate work directly influences instruction and curriculum on the undergraduate level. Although faculty members committed to research argue that faculty research guarantees improved instruction, they forget that such faculty members are primarily interested in graduate instruction and often avoid undergraduate responsibilities. Thus, too many universities assign undergraduate instruction, particularly at the freshman and sophomore levels, to a graduate assistant or a teaching fellow whose primary commitment is to the completion of his program of graduate study. The part-time graduate assistant or teaching fellow may be as capable a teacher as the professor, but he labors under two handicaps. First, the students recognize his lack of stature and, second, he himself knows he will be judged on the quality of his graduate work rather than on the quality of his teaching.

Graduate education also has a direct impact on the curriculum. In the early stages of the graduate program, this effect may be beneficial in that better-trained and more alert faculty members may be employed to develop the program. Some courses may be open to both advanced undergraduates and beginning graduate students, and able undergraduates may be challenged by their classmates to greater achievement. However, accrediting agencies and graduate education authorities generally oppose such courses and, as soon as the graduate enrollment is large enough, they are usually limited to graduate students. A graduate program also initially necessitates a reduction in courses offered and a re-examination of the content of advanced undergraduate courses in the discipline. Ultimately, however, the senior faculty may withdraw from undergraduate education because of their interest in specialized graduate courses, and those who continue to give undergraduate courses may insist that the courses be related to their specialized interests. Some universities require all professors to teach at the undergraduate level, but this does not necessarily benefit undergraduates. One department chairman, when asked what his undergraduate majors did after the A.B., responded that the good ones went on to graduate school, and he never gave any thought of what the rest of them did. The title of Earl McGrath's book, *The Graduate School and the Decline of Liberal Education* (11), is, unfortunately, an apt description of graduate study.

The impact of graduate education on the undergraduate program is not altogether bad, and the undergraduate may profit in several ways. First, an institution with a strong graduate program will usually attract an outstanding faculty. Undergraduates will be stimulated by contact with those scholars who retain some interest in undergraduates. Course content and laboratory equipment will often be more varied and modern. Opportunities for advanced study and research are more readily available to the unusually able undergraduate who may merge elements of his undergraduate and graduate programs and thereby accelerate his education. The range and value of graduate study are more apparent. Old prejudices against continuing graduate study in the institution of undergraduate study have largely dissipated and the student can often move ahead with more efficiency and continuity.

MASTER'S DEGREE

Despite attempts to salvage the master's degree, its significance can only be determined through knowledge of the institution which granted the degree, and of the field and courses studied. Some larger universities award the master's degree for a full year of credit, a practice which results from the course and credit emphasis at the baccalaureate level. In many cases, individuals can fulfill the requirement through a combination of summer school and off-campus or extension credit. The student may receive excessive credit in undergraduate courses, although most institutions require that at least half of the master's degree credits be at the graduate level. Even when such a specification exists, there is some doubt about what constitutes a graduate level course. The situation has become particularly critical in recent years, since so many state certification agencies now demand a master's degree or its equivalent for permanent certification. This demand forces institutions actively concerned with teacher education to provide a post-bacclaureate degree resulting in a teacher's certificate.

The myth that one should have at least a B average to enter graduate school is often upheld by extensive granting of conditional admissions, and by encouraging relatively easy grading in graduate courses. A problem still remains for students with a C undergraduate average who lack sufficient background in any discipline to study at the graduate level, but who are under pressure to acquire a master's degree.

Elementary teachers are a special problem, for their undergraduate major is usually in education rather than in a single discipline which they might continue to study at the graduate level. To permit them to concentrate in education is to neglect the real need for upgrading elementary education in the basic disciplines, such as mathematics and science. For such persons, a fifth-year program including both undergraduate and graduate courses appropriate to their needs should be developed. However, institutions which offer both fifth-year and master's programs have difficulty in determining to which program this student should be admitted, and must confront the fact that the master's has more prestige and is therefore more desirable. Moreover, since almost every teacher will take some graduate work in education, it is difficult to maintain an acceptable distinction between the two programs. A few institutions have attempted to define an institutional degree which involves a combination of work in education, study in one of the disciplines, and possibly a general course in literature and history. One or two institutions have required at least two courses in religion for the master's degree on the grounds that all teachers must accept some responsibility for religious education. The Master of Education degree, which aptly characterizes such composite programs, is usually rejected because it implies concentration in education. Such possibilities as a Master of Arts in Teaching and a Master of Liberal Studies have also been considered. Since there are already some six hundred different master's degrees, the addition of a few more makes little difference, and perhaps even a Master of Elementary Teaching and Master of Secondary Teaching could be developed. The Master of Arts in Teaching is not a tenable solution, for this program was designed to attract individuals who had completed a bachelor's degree in liberal arts and wished to prepare for teaching. It is, in many ways, a fifth-year program, but one at a fairly high level and directed to a rather able group of students.

The small liberal arts college faces somewhat different problems. Small colleges often dislike their students to take their graduate work in teaching elsewhere. The faculty, even though not qualified to offer graduate courses, finds the idea of teaching graduate courses very appealing and thus may prefer the master's program to the unglamorous fifth year. The program developed is often more demanding in time than that of many universities, and it often emphasizes education courses. Nevertheless, each department will add a course or two in order to be represented in the graduate program. While the graduate enrollment will be primarily in the summer, a few offerings will be provided during the year. Indeed, the faculty usually hopes that, in the course of several years, some full-time graduate students will be found. Some faculty members may also wish to add specialized degrees in some of the basic disciplines to meet needs in the immediate area. Specialized education degrees in guidance and administration are easily justified once the advance to the graduate level has been achieved. Thus a faculty, with a heavy course load and minimal qualifications to teach graduate courses, adds a graduate program and perhaps even a thesis requirement, to be directed by nonresearchers. It becomes a distinction to teach a graduate course, and the distinction may be sought even on a overload basis. Resources are strained, and the undergraduate program suffers so that mediocre postbaccalaureate study can be provided. Certification requirements are met, but teachers are rarely better qualified.

There are a number of widely known and accepted professional master's degrees which require more than one year of study. Some of these are combinations of internship experience and on-campus study. The Master of Social Work, Master of Fine Arts, Master of Business Administration, and Master of Public Health are well known degrees which require at least two years of work. Yale University has recently proposed a Master of Philosophy degree in an attempt to provide a degree for college teachers short of the Ph.D. with its heavy dissertation and research orientation. Similarly, the University of Tennessee has proposed a Master of Arts in College Teaching. While these degrees, particularly if combined with an internship in college teaching, might correspond to the professional master's degree, it is unlikely that they will be widely accepted.

CERTIFICATE, DIPLOMA, AND SPECIALIST PROGRAMS

Several special programs with a distinctive vocational purpose have been developed recently to carry the student beyond the master's but short of the doctorate degree. This development has been primarily in education where the significance of the master's degree is so questionable that some other designation seems essential for certain specialties. Thus, there has arisen the degree of Educational Specialist (Ed.S.). This program is particularly designed for teachers who wish to qualify as administrators, curriculum specialists, and counselors. Generally, the program combines formal course work with an internship or practical work experience. In some cases, the student already holds the job for which his specialist work is being completed, and his internship consists of a few visits from his professor to observe and discuss his work. The program frequently is tied in with state requirements for certification of specialties. In several states, certification for vocational guidance or counseling requires study well beyond a master's degree.

Ideally, the educational specialist program should be planned as a two-year unit. It should be oriented to a particular specialty and offer a carefully-planned sequence of courses and experiences. Too often, however, the individual acquires a master's degree and then desires to obtain the educational specialist degree. Unless the Ed.S. program builds directly on the master's study, it would be more suitable to award a second master's degree. If groups presently concerned with this problem do not produce a set of recommendations which are widely accepted by accrediting agencies, colleges, universities, and state departments of education, the Ed.S. may come to mean little more than one year of credit accumulation beyond the master's degree.

Although the Ed.S. is a terminal degree, many programs are sufficiently ambiguous that an individual acquiring the degree may return and be expected to complete a doctorate in approximately one more year of study. This threatens the integrity of the doctoral program, for it substitutes credit accumulation for demonstrated achievement of a new level of competency. One solution might be to place the specialist programs outside the degree category. However, the certificate has little prestige, either for the individual or for the institution.

One other two-year degree has been developed in recent years, the Diploma for Advanced Graduate Study. This designation usually connotes two years of graduate study beyond the baccalaureate degree and could be applied to arts and sciences as well as to education. Its use in these fields has been limited and it is competitive with the M. Phil., the M.A.C.T., and other programs which emphasize preparation for college teaching but avoid the research emphasis of the Ph.D. In a sense, all of these degrees come under the category of "A.B.D." (all but dissertation) degrees. Also in this group is the Certification of Candidacy, which is awarded by the University of Michigan to persons completing all requirements for the doctorate except the dissertation. The relation of these degrees to undergraduate education will be discussed in the next section, which comments on the relevance of the doctoral program for college teaching. Several institutions grant an intermediate degree in engineering designated as Engineer, Civil Engineer, etc. These programs usually require two years of graduate study and a thesis. Although this degree has been awarded by Stanford since 1894, it is not widely used, and the same problems arise in its relation to the master's and the doctor's degrees that have been noted for the Ed.S.

DOCTORAL DEGREES

Since there are sixty-four distinctive doctorates, it may be of interest to note several of the well-known professional degrees. The Ed.D. (Doctor of Education) was introduced for professional educators interested in administrative posts or educational research. Originally, some institutions required experience in elementary or secondary school teaching and administration. In practice, it is almost the equivalent of the Ph.D. in Education. Although research for the Ed.D. presumably emphasizes practice, there is very little difference between Ed.D. and Ph.D. research studies. Perhaps the one distinctive element is the lack of foreign language requirement although, in some institutions, candidates for the Ph.D. in Education may also avoid foreign language.

A second professional degree is the Doctor of Business Administration (D.B.A.). This degree usually is not for people going into college or university teaching but rather for individuals involved in business and industry. No dissertation is required, and the orientation is primarily vocational. The Doctor of Engineering, Doctor of Public Health, and Doctor of Social Work are also purely professional degrees. So, too, is the Doctor of Music, but this degree exists partly because of the reluctance of faculties to accept creative work as a substitute for the Ph.D. dissertation. A relatively new degree is the Doctor of Psychology, initiated at the University of Illinois. This is a professional degree oriented to the practice of clinical psychology; it involves an internship and a written report, but not a research dissertation. Once the D. Psych. is established, it will probably become the requirement for professors in clinical psychology. Of course, all professional degrees constitute relevant preparation for teaching in the appropriate professional schools.

The preceding degrees are approximately at the level of the Ph. D., but many fields also offer advanced special degrees. The J.D. (Juris Doctor) in law, which is generally replacing the Ll.B., is a professional degree, but the J.S.D. (Doctor of Juridical Science) is an advanced professional doctorate similar to professional doctorates in religion (Doctor of Theology, Doctor of Sacred Theology, Doctor of Religious Education, Doctor of Sacred Music), and in medicine (Doctor of Medical Science and Doctor of Clinical Science). The first-level and advanced professional degrees have little influence on curriculum developments, but their existence does document the increasing specialization and interest in graduate work.

It is possible to identify and characterize four types of doctorates. The first, of course, is the Ph.D., which emphasizes original research. The second is a first-level practitioner degree, which usually requires the same amount of time as the Ph.D., but often substitutes an internship and report for the dissertation. Examples are the Doctor of Business Administration, Doctor of Psychology, and Doctor of Public Health.

The third doctorate degree recognizes creative work of high quality as a substitute for the research dissertation. Many research dissertations are creative efforts of a high level, as in mathematics, but they are usually acceptable because of their relation to past research. An art work or a novel, however, cannot be considered research and rarely has an integral relation to research in the field. Curiously, dissertations on the history of music or art are acceptable for the Ph.D., but dissertations on the history of mathematics, although acceptable in some departments of mathematics, are often regarded as second-rate productions.

The fourth doctorate combines practice and research, and is exemplified by advanced professional degrees in law and medicine. Many professional schools are developing their own graduate schools so that faculty members can engage in research and graduate study.

None of the four doctorates is directly related to the preparation of the college teacher. Certainly, the college teacher must be well trained in the disciplines he teaches. However, few would maintain that the Ph.D., however well it provides competency in the field, is directly relevant to teaching or to the associated responsibilities of advising and curriculum development. Several attempts have been made to provide a substitute for the Ph.D.: the M.Phil., the M.A.C.T., the Certificate of Candidacy, and the Diploma for Advanced Graduate Study. A few institutions, such as Syracuse, Minnesota, and Iowa, have offered broad doctoral programs in the humanities, social sciences, and natural sciences which were developed twenty years ago in response to the general education movement. These programs usually provide a broad base in a group of related disciplines, focus on teaching and curriculum problems, and involve an internship in teaching. A few attempts have been made to develop a Ph.D. for college teaching by adding to the standard Ph.D. requirements two or three courses in education and a supervised teaching experience. Such degrees suffer from being regarded by departmental faculties as second-rate because candidacy for them constitutes an avowal of concern for undergraduate teaching, and by students as unreasonable because the total requirements are considerably more demanding than those of the traditional and more respected Ph.D.

Another recent proposal, the Doctor of Arts, was suggested by the University of California at Berkeley. The degree would be based on a particular discipline, as is the Ph.D., but would allow certain substitutions for the traditional Ph.D. dissertation. It would also include some exposure to the problems of teaching and of the undergraduate curriculum. Although this degree and designation seems the best solution to the preparation of college teachers, departmental reactions have been negative. Thus, we continue to face the curious fact that doctorates are being offered for almost every conceivable purpose except undergraduate instruction.

The Curriculum for the Ph.D.

The continuing debate about the relevance of the Ph.D. to college teaching raises certain questions about the nature of the doctoral program. The doctoral program is usually planned by an adviser and approved by a doctoral committee. Initially, the student often takes an examination to evaluate his competency to do graduate study in the discipline. The examination may be constructed to provide scores in the major subdivisions of the discipline. This indicates some minimal faculty concern for breadth in the discipline. The student, if accepted, may be required to take certain courses in his major or in other departments to make up identified deficiencies. If students undertake graduate work in a field different from their undergraduate specialty, they may face extensive, required course work. Because better graduate schools rarely accept students with such deficiencies, undergraduates are forced to select their graduate specialization early and acquire as many credits as possible. The social sciences and the humanities, because they are less sequential than the sciences, do allow for greater mobility. Indeed, the chairman of one of the best sociology departments in the country expressed a preference for students with majors in other fields, particularly in mathematics or statistics.

A well-planned doctoral program draws upon the total educational experience of the student. It combines course work, seminars, independent study, research, and possibly internship esperience. New graduate programs tend to overemphasize course work, whereas well-established programs concentrate on seminars, independent study, research, and the dissertation. Many programs encourage early involvement in research projects and familiarity with research techniques and methodology as preparation for the dissertation. Such a program might well be adapted to undergraduate honors work and independent study.

Some institutions apply the undergraduate emphasis on credits to graduate work, and even assign the dissertation a block of credits for which the student must pay regular fees. More mature graduate schools rarely worry about credits, although some may insist on a minimum residence requirement phrased in terms of credits.

Course work for the doctorate often includes study in several departments or disciplines, a practice appropriate to preparation for undergraduate teaching. Concern for breadth in the doctorate is also reflected in the preliminary examinations required at the close of formal course work which are used to certify that the student has attained sufficient competency in his field to engage in independent research. The examination often covers major subdivisions of the discipline and may even include questions involving closely-related disciplines. Students in education may have significant portions of their doctoral programs in psychology and sociology. Graduate students in physics and engineering usually take mathematics. Students in biochemistry often take advanced work in chemistry or in biological science. Some fields, such as African studies, offer a limited number of courses, and the student's program is planned on an interdisciplinary basis. However, individual interdisciplinary programs at the doctoral level often develop into a formal series of courses and occasionally into a full-fledged department. Such interdisciplinary developments at the doctoral level effect undergraduate instruction by providing capable instructors and sufficient substance for interdisciplinary courses.

Internships play an often concealed and somewhat ambiguous role in doctoral programs. Many independent study and seminar experiences in the social sciences become internship experiences through the conduct of surveys. In education, students often receive credit for working in administrative offices or research units on the university campus. Such practical experiences are rarely appropriate to the classical conception of the Ph.D., and are more consistent with professional doctorates. Yet field work has been a part of the degree program in the natural sciences for many years. Such field work corresponds quite closely to the undergraduate practice teaching requirement in education. Perhaps a major issue is whether such experiences should be assigned credit or whether they should be postdegree or supplemental degree experiences. Field work and internship experience in the doctoral program could provide a useful background for teaching in an undergraduate program which encourages similar experiences.

Most Ph.D. programs still require some foreign language competency, although the specification of reading competency in two foreign languages has been liberalized in several ways. Many institutions now accept English as a foreign language for those whose native tongue is not English. The student can frequently substitute for one of the languages a group of courses in a discipline or area which his committee accepts as relevant to his doctoral program. In the social sciences, mathematics or statistics are often used to waive the language requirement. A few institutions permit a high level of mastery (reading and oral proficiency) of a single language to replace reading competency in two.

The demands of course work, seminars, and research on the doctoral student, the distrust of education courses by faculty members in the arts and sciences, and the general view that anyone who knows his field can teach it have made it difficult to incorporate into the doctoral program any work in curriculum study, instructional methodology, or study of higher education. These same prejudices have led to the proliferation of specialized graduate degrees in other professional fields. Tradition decrees that the Ph.D. must be oriented toward research in the discipline rather than toward a particular profession. Even attempts to develop a substitute degree for college teaching have often maintained the Ph.D. orientation. Thus, the certificate of candidacy only recognizes that the student has completed all Ph.D. requirements except the dissertation. Chapter 8 will suggest relevant experiences which might be provided for the potential college teacher.

The foreign language requirement presents certain problems in the development of special programs for college teachers. One justification of the foreign language requirement in doctoral programs has been that the researcher must be able to read about significant developments in other countries. However, it has rarely served this purpose for many Ph.D.'s, either because they soon forget the language or because they engage in very limited research. This conception of the foreign language requirement suggests that it is irrelevant for college teachers. However, if one considers competency in one or more foreign languages to be essential for a liberal education, he might take a different view. It is pointless to require undergraduate competency in a foreign language if only foreign language faculty use foreign languages. Thus, it would seem appropriate to require all college teachers to demonstrate a fairly high level of reading ability in at least one foreign language. The college teacher should be able to encourage his students to utilize their language ability by reading and reporting on articles or books in that language. Foreign language competency should not be lightly dismissed from curricula for college teachers.

Postdoctoral Study

The rapidity of developments in several disciplines, the advent of new interdisciplinary specialties, and the limited availability of expensive, advanced research equipment have generated a rapidly growing program of postdoctoral study in most major graduate schools. The policy of extending faculty status to visiting scholars has prevented most universities from recognizing the extent of this activity, especially since stipends for postdoctoral study often do not come through university channels. The scholar who is engaged in serious postdoctoral study and is using the facilities and the faculty of the institution should be distinguished from the visiting scholar who is occupied with writing and giving an occasional lecture. At the moment, postdoctoral study probably has a limited effect on the graduate and the undergraduate curricula, but the increasing use of faculty and resources for such study may force additional curtailment of the undergraduate program. Moreover, future expansion of postdoctoral study may become essential to maintain the competency of faculty members primarily concerned with undergraduate instruction and too heavily burdened with instructional responsibilities to keep abreast of their fields.

Graduate School and the Decline of Liberal Education

Many feel that Earl McGrath was unduly pessimistic in attributing the decline of liberal education to the graduate school. Certainly one could argue that the presence of graduate students and the research involvements and discoveries of faculty have increased the stature of higher education and have made the undergraduate program more exciting and more relevant. It is extremely difficult, particularly in the sciences, to maintain an up-to-date curriculum without an alert faculty which is well informed and involved in research. Much research in the humanities, however, merely re-examines in greater detail an area of study already well surveyed, and is completely irrelevant to the undergraduate program. In the sciences, too, graduate study and research can become highly specialized and result in a proliferation of undergraduate specialized courses which may prevent the student from acquiring a broad base in his discipline or investigating related disciplines.

One can also argue convincingly that methodological emphasis, internship experience, cognate study, and interdisciplinary study and research at the doctoral level can contribute directly to undergraduate instructional competency. Mastery of a discipline is obviously beneficial, and the foreign language requirement can be made functional. The doctoral program fails in its preparation of college teachers only in its refusal to provide study or supervised experience directly related to their instructional and curricular responsibilities.

Much criticism of the effect of graduate education on undergraduate education has dealt with undergraduate education in a broad sense rather than specifically with liberal education. If liberal education means that the undergraduate must have contact with almost all fields of knowledge, the development of an undergraduate program is a meaningless and impossible task. The decline of the classical conception of liberal education is not the fault of the graduate school, but of the heavily technological society which has vastly increased our knowledge and demands a high degree of vocational specialization. If liberal education is redefined as a broad set of individual qualities, then liberal education must continue to be a major concern of all undergraduate, graduate, and professional schools. The liberally-educated person is aware of his cultural heritage, able to think critically and objectively and to make wise judgments based on his experience in depth with the structure and methodology of one or more disciplines, and capable of communicating easily and clearly with others. Finally, commitment to a set of values appropriate to our democratic society is essential for all educated persons. If graduate and professional schools cannot cultivate these, not only undergraduate education but also our whole society will suffer. We must have humane, socially conscious, and responsible specialists in all fields, not specialists who pursue their work with complete disregard for its effects on the community, the nation, and the world.

REFERENCES

1. John W. Ashton, "Other Doctorates," in *Graduate Education Today*, Everett Walters, ed., American Council on Education, Washington, D.C., 1965, pp. 62–73.
2. Joseph Axelrod, ed., *Graduate Study for Future College Teachers*, American Council on Education, Washington, D.C., 1959.
3. Bernard Berelson, *Graduate Education in the United States*, McGraw-Hill Book Company, Inc., New York, 1960.
4. Oliver C. Carmichael, *Graduate Education: A Critique and a Program*, Harper and Brothers, New York, 1961.
5. Allan M. Cartter, *An Assessment of Quality in Graduate Education*, American Council on Education, Washington, D.C., 1966.

6. Walter C. Eells, *Degrees in Higher Education*, Center for Applied Research in Education, Inc., Washington, D.C., 1963.
7. James N. Eshelman, ed., *The Graduate Student*, American Council on Education, Washington, D.C., 1966.
8. Ann M. Heiss, et al, *Graduate and Professional Education, An Annotated Bibliography*, The Center for Research and Development in Higher Education, University of California, Berkeley, 1967.
9. H. Glenn Ludlow, et al, *The Doctorate in Education*, Vol. IV, Follow-Up Study, American Association of Colleges for Teacher Education, Washington, D.C., 1964.
10. William J. McGlothlin, *The Professional Schools*, The Center for Applied Research in Education, Inc., Washington, D.C., 1964.
11. Earl J. McGrath, *The Graduate School and the Decline of Liberal Education*, Bureau of Publications, Teachers College, Columbia University, 1959.
12. John P. Miller. "The Master of Philosophy: A New Degree is Born," *Journal of Higher Education*, Vol. XXXVII, October, 1966, pp. 377–81.
13. Frederick Ness and Benjamin James, *Graduate Study in the Liberal Arts College*, American Council on Education, Washington, D.C., 1962.
14. Israel Scheffler, ed., *The Graduate Study of Education*, Harvard University Press, 1965.
15. John L. Snell, "The Master's Degree," in *Graduate Education Today*, Everett Walters, ed., American Council on Education, Washington, D.C., 1965, pp. 74–102.
16. Everett Walters, ed., *Graduate Education Today*, American Council on Education, Washington, D.C., 1965.

8

Instruction and the Curriculum

Discussions of instruction too frequently assume that instruction can be separated from other aspects of the educational experience. The assumption is partly valid, but it is also misleading. A coherent, unified educational experience does not necessarily result from good instruction. Even if every instructor is outstanding in all aspects of teaching (knows his subject, presents it effectively, is interested in students and readily available to them, is reasonable and clear in assignments, and evaluates fairly), the student who takes a miscellaneous and unrelated array of courses may not obtain a sound education.

Too often, no clear distinction is made between teaching and the broader concept of instruction. Teaching refers to the activities of the teacher in his direct contact with students. This direct contact, as practiced by Socrates, was a rich experience involving profound interaction of students and teacher, but Socrates was not only the teacher, he was also the total faculty and curriculum. There are few such teachers available, and the modern college is too large and complex to permit continuing relationships between one great teacher and a small group of students. Furthermore, Socrates could not teach all the subjects offered in a modern college and, even if he could, the faculty would not permit it. Yet many faculty members still entertain the thought that they are great teachers in the Socratic pattern. In most institutions, teaching is equated with the classroom activities of the teacher. Well-organized and precisely stated lectures, skill in evoking discussion, story telling, clowning, and insistence on carefully-defined and rigorously-applied standards have been observed as major characteristics of individuals who have been acclaimed by students and colleagues as good teachers. Although these attributes may make a course interesting and challenging, it is noteworthy that they have been accepted as indications of good teaching, without any evidence of their impact on student achievement. Only the insistence on student adherence to carefully-defined and rig-

153

orously-applied standards displays a real concern for student learning and suggests an acceptance of responsibility for promoting it.

The problem with defining teaching in this limited sense is that it focuses on teacher activities and characteristics rather than on student learning and achievement. The term "instruction" is much broader than the term "teaching" because it focuses on all the opportunities for response provided by an instructional staff. In relation to a single course, the concept of instruction extends the concept of teaching to include the teacher's preplanning and preparation and the student's contacts with the teacher or with assigned learning materials outside of class. If the course involves a team of teachers, then instruction pertains to the total effort rather than to the effort of any one teacher. In terms of the total curriculum and four-year experience of the student, instruction involves the combined efforts of the entire faculty to plan and execute a program which achieves certain objectives. Teaching tends to focus on the teacher, on the course, and on immediate goals which often are not essential steps in the achievement of long-range goals. This distinction poses a problem, but it also leads to a significant conclusion.

The problem is that evaluation and reward of good teaching always necessitate making decisions about individuals. Evaluation of teaching on the very limited grounds of classroom performance is grossly inadequate and unfair, for it ignores significant contributions made in other ways. However, if student learning results from the efforts of many individuals, including those of the students themselves, then instruction must be regarded as, in part, a team effort. Individuals must then be evaluated both for their contribution to the team and for their own direct contribution to student learning.

The significant conclusion suggested by this discussion of the relation of teaching to instruction is that both evaluation and planning of instruction must start from some agreement as to the responsibilities of instruction. The interrelation of various concepts introduced in this volume (objectives, teaching, learning, courses, grades, and competencies) is diagrammatically indicated by the model in Figure 1. At the base of this model there is a triangle whose vertices are marked instruction, grade, and course, and inside the base triangle is a point labeled objectives. Objectives are the basis for the selection of materials and for the organization of a course. They are the grounds for the teacher's selection of methods and activities and for grades or student evaluations. For simplicity, this diagram assumes only one course and one teacher, but the base could be expanded to include additional ones. As the student takes more courses and meets more teachers, these ac-

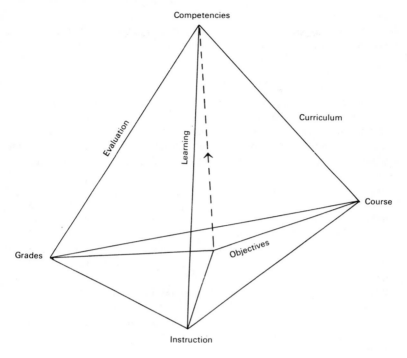

Figure 1

cumulated experiences become his curriculum, as is indicated on one
of the lateral edges of the pyramid. The accumulated work of individual
teachers becomes a pattern of instruction aimed at imparting significant
learning, and learning is indicated as a second lateral edge of the pyramid. The course grade, which constitutes an appraisal of the student's
attainment of objectives in a particular course, is replaced by long-
term cumulative evaluation which helps the student assess his progress
toward the stated competencies which spell out the ultimate meaning
of the objectives. Thus, evaluation, learning, and curriculum all focus
on the attainment of certain competencies. Although the teaching and
grading in a particular course may be oriented toward the present or the
past, good instruction, good course planning, and good evaluation focus
on the future. The significant question is not how much a student has
assimilated of his past work, but how far he has progressed toward attaining the desired competencies. In short, the evaluation should not

be of present knowledge but of present capability and additional experiences required to attain the stated competencies. Thus, it is essential to clarify the functions and obligations of instruction.

THE OBLIGATIONS OF INSTRUCTION

There are conflicting views of the functions of instruction. One is
that any learned man can teach. In this conception of instruction, the
instructor presents his wisdom, and the students absorb it. Highly
motivated individuals may learn through such procedures, but a teacher
who functions in this manner is not engaged in instruction. The following section will clarify the nature of instruction by delineating several
functions of instruction.

The first function of instruction is to motivate the student. Most
university students have a basic motivation toward self-improvement,
but this basic motivation may not extend to every course and requirement. A young man interested in engineering may fail to see how mathematics or the physical sciences relate to engineering practice. Thus, the
student must be shown the relevance of the particular course to his
ultimate goals. The student should understand what changes the course
attempts to promote, the importance of these changes, and the necessity of them for his future professional role. Until the student recognizes
the relevance of an experience, he will do very little to effect the desired
changes.

The second function of instruction is to clarify to the student what
new knowledge, behavior, and reactions are expected of him. This obligation requires supervision or guidance of the student's efforts to acquire these reactions. Laboratory instruction provides a good illustra-
tion of this function. The students, as a group, may be shown how to
use certain equipment. Some may operate effectively on the basis of
this demonstration, but others will have to be observed, helped, and perhaps even guided through the operation once or twice. In mathematics
classes, a general demonstration of a solution to a certain kind of problem is frequently followed by a request that everyone go to the board
and attempt the solution of a similar one. The instructor then helps
those who have difficulty to insure that they successfully complete the
procedure at least once. In the future, programed learning may supplement or replace this direct teacher supervision.

A third function of instruction is to provide extensive and meaningful materials for the students. A demonstration of a new experience, or
even careful guidance of the student through it, will not yield mastery.
The teacher must realize that what is done in the classroom is only

preliminary to the significant learning which occurs when the student repeatedly engages in the behavior until he understands it and can include it among his skills and abilities. Educational technology may also supply improved and self-correcting materials for this procedure.

The fourth function of instruction is to give the student satisfaction by showing him his progress. This involves pointing out to the student his accomplishments and his weaknesses. Unfortunately, grading practices usually emphasize the poor aspects of the performance rather than the good, because an A indicates the only completely adequate performance and any grade below an A suggests inadequate or bad performance. Thus, grading frequently injures or interferes with the learning process. Study and learning materials with built-in evidence of progress can be effective, but they cannot replace the personal commendation of an admired teacher. Moreover, tasks which are sufficiently complex to demonstrate progress require planning, comment, and critical review by the teacher.

The fifth function of instruction is to organize the work so that its sequential, cumulative aspect is readily apparent to the student and so that current learning is related to past and future study. The learning of isolated facts or skills must be reinforced by activities which indicate how these skills fit together. No tennis instructor would sustain the interest of his students if, for weeks or months, the students had to practice each stroke without ever being allowed to play the game. Repetitive practice of particular skills bores the student, and his loss of incentive will interfere with mastery. When the skill or understanding is related to other skills or ideas, the student may see its significance. Also, course work should be organized so that there is some novelty and increasing complication to maintain interest and concentration.

The sixth function of instruction is to provide the student with high standards of performance and with means for judging his performance in relation to these standards. If this function is to provide an incentive for continuing learning and increased mastery, it must be based on something other than the standard testing practices which emphasize completion of a phase of learning and assign a grade from A to F. Such practices encourage the student to settle for a satisfactory grade rather than to strive for high performance. The student who receives a C feels he has satisfactorily completed that particular unit of work. The emphasis is not on attaining greater mastery but on moving to the next task. This function is particularly important if the student is to assume some responsibility for planning and evaluating his own efforts.

If these six functions describe the obligations of college and university instruction, then evaluation of instruction can proceed by examining the extent to which these functions are fulfilled. It can also proceed by determining the extent to which these functions have resulted in significant learning or change in the student. One approach examines the process; the other focuses on the results.

Those functions which emphasize evidence of progress, sequential learning, and standards for evaluation of performance clearly imply a future orientation. This orientation suggests a seventh function of instruction, which is to show the student the relation of a particular course or experience to other courses and experiences in which he is involved. Each course should encourage the student to relate to it his past course work and experience, and each course should be seen as a step toward the ultimate competencies which result from a college education. The student cannot and will not do this alone, and the instructor must provide him with continuing motivation and assistance.

Although evaluation is frequently regarded as a process of judging how much learning has occurred, it also has a significant role in the learning process. In fact, each of the functions of instruction requires or utilizes certain evaluation practices for its fullest implementation.

Careful testing or evaluation of the knowledge, skills, and abilities of students at the beginning of a course may be used to show them that they have not yet mastered the objectives of the course. This indication of deficiency can provide motivation by demonstrating to students the need for and significance of the course.

Since the purpose of any evaluation instrument is to demonstrate whether the student has achieved the objectives of a course, the instrument must be based on clear definitions of these objectives. Evaluation forces the instructor to define his purposes and clarify the kind of behavior he desires of students. Thus, the evaluation instrument itself may help the student to understand what new behavior is expected of him.

Since the evaluation instrument must sample tasks which the student is expected to perform, materials developed for the purpose of evaluation also may be regarded as practice exercises. Repeatedly, evaluators working with teachers have discovered that teachers often regard materials developed for a test or evaluation device as some of the best learning materials they have seen. Even the taking of the test may be considered an opportunity for practice. However, the assignment of a grade to the test may suggest the termination of that phase of learning or behavior. An alternative practice is to use a test to provide the student with a concrete indication of his mastery of materials up to that point. The unsuccessful student can determine his deficiencies, and perhaps retake the test or a similar one to fulfill the necessary grading function. This use of tests approximates the organization of programed materials to provide practice and reinforcement.

Tests and evaluation instruments should provide evidence of the student's progress. Any review of a student's performance should emphasize those aspects in which he has excelled or displayed some originality. If his performance is weak, the student should be encouraged to restudy the principles and concepts he has misunderstood or misapplied, either by annotations on the test or by discussion.

A test or evaluation device which provides only routine tasks in which the student has been repeatedly drilled may demonstrate his mastery of skills, but it does not reveal his ability to apply principles. Every test should include some new tasks which the student can adequately handle by applying the knowledge, skills, and abilities he has mastered up to that point. Thus, the test itself helps the student to see that individual parts of the course do combine and add up to something beyond what has been fully treated in the classroom. The task of organizing course materials in a sequential, cumulative way cannot rely solely on logical analysis of content. The difficulty of any content is determined not only by its intrinsic nature, but also by human reactions to it. Sequential organization of content poses several research or evaluation problems, and one organization is preferable to another only if it increases the student's motivation and understanding.

To select an evaluation instrument, the instructor must decide what aspects of the course the student can be expected to handle adequately. In turn, the evaluation device defines for the student the behavior he is expected to master. The number of correct answers or the grade should show the student the extent to which he has achieved standards which the instructor thinks appropriate for the course. When subjective judgment is involved, as in the evaluation of a written report, the student may be encouraged to seek the judgment of his peers as well as that of his instructor. If other students find the report incomplete or incomprehensible, the writer may be forced to look at his work from a different point of view. The student's realization that he was unable to communicate his ideas to his peers is often more devastating than the professor's criticism.

Thus, evaluation can and should play a significant role in each of the six functions of instruction. If the definition of instruction implied by these functions is acceptable, evaluation of the instructional process may be based on the instructor's acceptance of obligation for these functions and on the extent to which he translates this obligation into practice. Since evaluation plays a necessary or, at least, a significant role in the accomplishment of the six functions of instruction, instruction may be assessed in part by the instructor's success in devising adequate evaluation practices.

THE ROLE OF INSTRUCTIONAL METHODOLOGY

Much has been written on the relative virtues of the lecture, seminar, discussion, and case method, and much research has attempted to ascertain which method is superior or which method is best for certain objectives. Most of the research and much of the discussion have been a waste of time and effort. Any generalizations about method, particularly at the college level, must be greatly qualified. A qualified generalization will tell us that, in certain disciplines with objectives of a particular kind, teachers with certain personalities and interests working with students of certain abilities and educational backgrounds may find this method superior to others. Such a generalization tells us very little, and may not even be true. Methods have never been clearly defined, and one teacher's lecture may be another teacher's discussion. Some professors' graduate seminars are uninterrupted lectures, and even two presentations which are clearly lectures may evoke very different reactions, depending upon the personality and the approach of the lecturer.

The findings of current research in this problem can be summarized in two generalizations:

1. If objectives stress factual knowledge and understanding, then lecture, discussion, case method, problem orientation, group dynamics, and television patterns of instruction have proved about equally effective.
2. For some students and for higher level cognitive goals or objectives in the affective domain, discussions and student-centered instructional techniques may prove more effective than teacher-dominated instruction.

McKeachie has provided an excellent and detailed summary of instructional research in Chapter 23 of his *Handbook of Research on Teaching* (11, pp. 1118–1172).

Some positive statements can be made about instructional method. First, every teacher should be aware that there are many different ways of working with students, and that some may be more efficacious than others in attaining desired results. The teacher who wants extensive student participation and desires that students formulate and express their own ideas will certainly find discussion groups or seminars preferable to lectures. Moreover, differences in teachers and in students may result in certain methods being more appropriate to some than to others. The teacher who can prepare stimulating lectures but cannot establish personal contact with students should concentrate on lectures and avoid working with discussion groups or individual students. Conversely, the teacher who works best in a tutorial relationship should not be forced to prepare and deliver poor and boring lectures. Finally, discussions of instructional methodology should confront the basic issue of what type of educational experience will best help the student achieve his and the institution's long-term goals. Thus, the problem of instructional methodology is only one aspect of the larger issue of educational technology.

THE ROLE OF EDUCATIONAL TECHNOLOGY

Advocates of programed materials, teaching machines, computer-based learning, and educational television often appear to believe that educational technological developments can replace the teacher or greatly delimit his role. If one regards teaching as nothing more than classroom activities, then educational technology does constitute a threat. The professor who teaches to satisfy his own ego rather than to motivate students to learn may disparage these new developments. History reports that the development of printing and the textbook were greeted in a similar fashion by some teachers. Now even the most traditional conception of teaching admits the necessity of reading books and articles as well as listening to a professor. In the broader concept of instruction, only two questions are essential: (1) What specific kinds of stimuli are needed to produce the type of responses and the ultimate competencies desired? (2) What method or technological aid is best adapted to presenting these stimuli and evaluating these responses?

Instruction can be evaluated only in terms of its effectiveness in producing learning, although methods of instruction can be examined in terms of their relation to the ultimate goal. For example, scientists have often argued that the many hours in the laboratory are essential for all students taking science, because it is the only way they can understand the experimental nature of science. However, the nature of the laboratory work, which too often only verifies what the student has already learned, may convey a totally erroneous conception of experiment. The tedium of some laboratory work often causes the student to lose sight of the goal and focus on details. Science is hardly exemplified by twenty students all performing an experiment, which is really an exercise, in order to verify a known conclusion. Filmed or televised presentations can be far more effective by presenting the research activity of a skilled scientist. On the other hand, there are essential skills of observation and manipulation in the relating of knowledge to substance and procedure which can only be attained in the laboratory.

Socrates taught in a way similar to the modern learning program in that he responded to the student at each point and forced him to engage in further thinking or rethinking of the matter under discussion. Thus, programed materials may provide an instructional and learning experience which the teacher cannot personally provide. Yet, teachers must assume the instructional role of developing these materials, studying their impact on students' learning, and revising them as necessary. The safest generalization about educational technology is not that it will replace the teacher but that it will redefine the role of the teacher by focusing on the impact of a particular educational experience on the learning of the individual student. Moreover, educational technology focuses on learning as a mode of inquiry. For example, a dictionary is a fine means of learning, but no program of education should foster such complete reliance on it that the student never feels secure without it. A program or an instructional system may teach the student to carry on independent analysis in depth or to master some particular ability or concept, but it should not force him to require a program whenever he needs to master some new idea. It is somewhat horrifying to envisage a time when libraries or bookstores might offer a vast range of programed materials for anyone wishing to master any new principle or skill. Many able students have always used books and resource materials in a way which closely parallels the best learning programs. They have defined issues, sought answers, verified or negated these by comparison with the views of others, and organized their final conclusions clearly and succinctly. The job of instruction, either for an individual teacher or for a complex learning system, is to provide a means of learning, but it must also provide the resources and abilities so that the student can continue his own learning without these means. A child learns to walk by clutching at every available object, but an adult does so only if he is infirm.

APPRAISAL OF FACULTY EFFORTS

The evaluation and reward of instruction are so important in effecting the concept of instruction here presented that the problem should be considered at some length. A program of evaluation of instruction can only be developed in the broader context of a complete program of faculty appraisal. This broader conception is essential when under-graduate education includes experiences in research, foreign travel and study, community service, supervised employment, and community living and governance. Moreover, decisions as to the appropriate func-tions of the faculty often dictate the range of experiences open to the undergraduate. Only by complete appraisal of faculty effectiveness in all these functions can wise decisions be made in allocating faculty re-sources to the education of undergraduates.

The task of faculty appraisal is complicated by oversimplification. The generalization that promotions and rewards are based largely on research and very little on teaching is misleading in at least two re-spects. First, faculty members engage in many activities outside of re-search and teaching. Second, faculty members and administrative officers are usually aware of their colleague's publications but they rarely have evidence of the quality of his teaching and the extent of his other activities. The task of appraisal might be simplified by requiring each faculty member who expects a promotion or salary increase to present convincing evidence of the extent and quality of his perfor-mance in all areas.

The remainder of this chapter will analyze various categories of faculty activity and will suggest certain methods of obtaining evidence on the quality of performance. The chapter will also discuss the nature of a faculty assignment and suggest certain methods of effecting a program of development, appraisal, and reward.

Professional Competence and Professional Activity

Scholarship and Advanced Study. The heading of professional competence certainly includes scholarship and advanced study. The word "scholarship" is selected because the term "research" is often restricted to the pursuit of new knowledge and to original publications. In this country, too few persons are attempting to develop new and more meaningful organizations of what we already know. Such scholar-ship is in no way inferior to research and is often more closely related to instruction. It is essential that good minds continuously examine the implications of rapidly increasing knowledge for the organization of more effective and more efficient curricula. The question of advanced study is related to that of scholarship. The existence of numerous fel-lowship programs and institutes for advanced study suggests that the doctorate is no longer regarded as the termination of formal study. In fact, with the rapid expansion of knowledge and development of new research techniques, the professor who fails to engage in continuing study is soon outmoded. For example, the faculty member who is ignorant of the capabilities of a computer has greatly limited his own productive possibilities and the character of his instruction.

Research. A second type of professional competence, research, has already been mentioned. A common complaint is that research is the *sine qua non* for recognition. In a university, research is a major function, and no faculty member should instruct at the graduate level unless he is engaged in significant research. However, much nonsense has been said about the relation between research and instruction. A person cannot remain an outstanding teacher, even in a liberal arts college, without engaging in scholarly activity. But research, in the restricted sense, is unnecessary for undergraduate instruction. Certainly there is no evidence for the contention that a person who is a good researcher is also a good teacher. Frontier research and undergraduate instruction are independent functions, although instructors must be aware of research developments.

Often, the quality of research is difficult to evaluate. Some institutions ask leading researchers in other universities to evaluate the research of persons considered for tenure. These institutions appear to doubt the competence of their own faculty to evaluate adequately the research of their colleagues. This indicates three things: (1) that bias, jealousy, and personal aspirations may interfere with an honest evaluation of the work of a competing colleague; (2) that a lengthy list of publications may be too readily accepted as evidence of research capacity because no one locally dares to say that the research lacks merit; (3) that an unusually creative individual may produce research which is disparaged by his immediate colleagues, though highly regarded by others. Evaluating research presents the same problems as evaluating instruction. If one cannot produce objective evidence that it is unsatisfactory, then one must assume that it is commendable. Thus, pointless research is encouraged, subsidized, and praised, while performance in other functions is neglected.

Professional Activity. Professional activity is classified with professional competence on the grounds that participation in many professional associations is related to research interests and capacities. An individual can become an officer in a professional organization without major research contributions. However, he usually appears on programs and panels, and ultimately is elected to an office or a committee because of his research or scholarly activities.

One responsibility of professional activity is the dissemination of the results of scholarship and research to the profession and to the community. This includes not only publications, but also speeches and consultation. Most faculty members need little encouragement to publish research or to engage in consultation in the area of their specialty, especially if they receive sizeable honorariums for their work. In many fields, however, research discoveries have immediate relevance to problems with which communities, government, business, and industry are currently concerned. The university should accept this service obligation and the university professor, as a member of a profession, should also recognize an obligation to make his competencies available for the improvement of society. He should be encouraged to do so, and he should be recognized for it. Furthermore, he should not always expect additional reimbursement for such activities. Kept within reasonable limits, such activity makes instruction more current and more practical.

Classroom Teaching and Instruction

Curriculum Planning and Evaluation. In recent years there has been a great deal of emphasis on improvement of teaching. One major obstacle to good teaching is that the average instructor knows little about the prior or subsequent educational experiences of his students. If the undergraduate program is to be a sequential, cumulative, unified experience, then certain broad objectives must influence all phases of the student's instruction. Instruction must evidence concern for these objectives and for the relation of the student's other learning experiences to those provided in the course. The exposure of a student to several outstanding professors does not insure a good education.

A professor cannot assume that his course should be organized to suit his own convenience. Everyone in the university who encourages or requires students to take his course has a legitimate concern with what is taught, how it is taught, and how it relates to other offerings. In turn, the department and the professor of the course must accept some responsibility to satisfy these concerns. The professor who relates his course to other fields will be a more inspiring teacher and a better adviser.

New knowledge is reflected rather quickly in graduate courses and seminars but rarely in undergraduate courses. Elementary and secondary school educators are sometimes well ahead of the colleges and universities in this respect. If the undergraduate curriculum is to be up-to-date, curriculum planning and evaluation must be major faculty functions. As much time must be provided for these functions as for research and instruction, and these efforts must be evaluated and rewarded.

The stature and value of a department should depend on its concern for the total undergraduate curriculum and for the relation of its offerings to that curriculum. Each department and each professor must be concerned about the competence of each graduate of the institution. Likewise, each department and professor should recognize that the cost of education depends very heavily on the curriculum. Some argue that good faculty members can be attracted only by catering to their course demands, regardless of costs and consistency with the existing curriculum. Administrators, too, have contributed to this proliferation because of their pride in diverse and unique offerings and their misunderstanding of what constitutes a sound curriculum. Few departments or professors are recognized and rewarded for restraint in proposing new courses or for reducing the existing offerings. Yet those who do so out of concern for the quality and coherence of the student experience are making a significant contribution to instruction and learning.

Planning of Instruction. Formulating objectives for a course, relating them to the broader objectives of the total educational program, and communicating them to students are important instructional functions. Another significant instructional function is the selection of those educational experiences which seem most likely to help the student achieve the stated objectives. The selection of textbooks, readings, laboratory activities, classroom activities, methods of presentation, appropriate assignments, and tests should not be based only on subject matter. The professor should consider what each of these activities will require or encourage the student to do and whether each one will contribute to the goals of the course. The average professor is more concerned with what he is doing than with what the student is doing. Few professors pay enough attention to the organization of their courses. Learning experiences may move from the simple to the complex, from the specific to the general, or from the remote to the immediate, and each of these may be reversed. In some circumstances, it is preferable to introduce a general idea first and then talk about specifics. In others, it is better to start with specifics and let the students construct their own generalizations.

Course work should be frequently and clearly related to the world beyond. Students remember and prize those teachers who assist them to see some relation between the course and real life. Such connections arouse the student's interest, increase his retention, and encourage him to relate his knowledge to his own problems.

Evaluation of Student Progress. A major element in good teaching is the construction of adequate means of evaluation. Probably the examinations given by an instructor provide the best single bit of evidence to judge the effectiveness of instruction. The objectives implicit in testing practices determine student learning much more effectively than the objectives stated to impress colleagues.

Evaluation plays many roles in teaching. Ultimately, students must assume some responsibility for evaluating and improving their own activities. If the student is graded in every aspect of his performance, he is not likely to engage in self-evaluation. He should be encouraged, at least occasionally, to use the results of evaluation for improving his own activities.

Students should not always be evaluated solely in terms of the instructor's objectives in the course. If an instructor's objective is to develop the student's interest in his discipline, he expresses a reasonable hope, but he has no right to fail the student who performs well but despises the field. A course or an instructor may be evaluated in terms of the student's response to the field, but the student himself should not be downgraded on these grounds.

The final and perhaps least significant role of evaluation is determing a grade for a student. Ideally, grades should be eliminated, but this is possible only in a few small experimental institutions. Grading evaluates only a limited number of objectives, but it should be done as honestly and fairly as possible. The objectives which are not graded may be the most important, and the student must recognize that grades cannot appraise some of the most important outcomes of education.

Effective Communication. Good classroom teaching requires effective communication. The instructor's use of the English language should be understandable and exemplary. Incomplete or poorly constructed sentences, mispronounced words, and misused words should not be tolerated in any college classroom, and the teacher who fails to improve in this respect should be released. Too many colleges and universities employ foreign-born and foreign-educated faculty members whose mastery of English is extremely rudimentary. Occasional mispronunciations, unusual accents, and odd sentence constructions may add charm to the classroom, but students should not have to cope with professors who are incomprehensible. Some universities also employ graduate teaching assistants of foreign background whose English is virtually unintelligible. The ability to use understandable English is a minimum requirement for presence in the classroom.

Good classroom teaching also requires the ability to give clear direction to students for study and performance. Too often the professor fails to analyze in detail what he expects of students. Some students demand more specificity in instruction than is consistent with their acceptance of responsibility for their own learning, but this is no excuse for vagueness and ambiguity in assignments.

Effective communication is facilitated by careful assessment of student ability, interest, and background. The teacher should specify what background he assumes of students, and he should verify that the students possess it. Some rapport with students should be established for effective communication. Some professors claim that they can assess a student's understanding by his expression. Rapport, however, is more than attentiveness, and it is certainly more than an occasional injection of humor. It involves some recognition that student viewpoints and student interests may be somewhat different from those of the professor. The professor, by showing that he recognizes this, can bridge such differences and even capitalize on them.

Evaluation of Teaching. Good classroom teaching requires that the instructor be interested in his own improvement as a teacher. Thus, he should welcome periodic evaluation of his classroom teaching. One method is student evaluation, using either a rating scale or an open-ended essay comment. Many instructors argue that student evaluation is not a valid indication of good teaching. However, good teaching is basically a facilitation of the learning process, and it is essential that the instructor have some conception of what his students think about the experience provided in the course. This includes not only an appraisal of what the teacher does but also an appraisal of the assignments, the examinations, and the textbook. Furthermore, the student should appraise himself, for he must realize that he, too, has some responsibility for his learning. He ought to know what the objectives of the course are, and he should try to see the relation of his activities to these objectives. If the student cannot define the objectives, the teacher may assume that he did not present them adequately; he may also question whether he has adequately related the course experiences to his objectives.

A high student rating does not necessarily mean that a teacher is doing a good job, nor does a low one necessarily mean that he is doing a poor job. However, if students feel the experience was inadequate, they probably will not have attained optimal benefit from it. Students will often speak more frankly to a third person than they will to the instructor or in writing. If the student is required to put his response in writing, he is often hesitant about being overly critical for fear that his response may be traced back to him. Thus, systematic interviewing of students by a third person may be a very revealing way to evaluate the instructor's efforts.

A second way to evaluate teaching is to have colleagues visit classes, and review teaching plans and tests. Every new member of a faculty should have his classroom regularly visited by the department chairman or another member of the faculty. Such visits will assist the instructor in making an adjustment to a new institution and a new group of students, point out any obvious errors or flaws in his approach, and provide first-hand information as to the quality of instruction.

A third mode of evaluation is by recording or taping a class. The instructor who can hear the recording or view the videotape without flinching must be either unusually insensitive or extraordinarily conceited. This approach is particularly useful for self-evaluation, but the presence of one or two colleagues to make comments on various phases of the playback will be revealing and humbling!

It has often been suggested that the final evaluation of the quality of teaching is the achievement of the students. In a sense this is true; yet, one can readily imagine a teacher who is so demanding and so unreasonable that students attain a high level of achievement but despise the field. In some respects, these affective outcomes are more important than cognitive ones. Nevertheless, if there are a number of sections of a course and if students are not grouped according to ability, the teacher whose students regularly excel is demonstrating some evidence of his capability. Common examinations are a less effective mode of evaluation because the teacher whose students fall below the mean usually claims that the examination did not test what he was trying to accomplish. The professor whose students score above the mean is unlikely to complain.

Academic Advising of Students

Faculty advising receives far less attention than instruction, but it is generally ineffective. Even graduate students in some major universities complain that their adviser is never available, or that he is so rushed with appointments or so concerned with his own research that he gives the student rather cavalier treatment. Only when the graduate student is doing research which requires close contact with his major professor does he have an opportunity for informal discussions of problems, courses, and career.

Academic advising to undergraduates suffers because few faculty members have any conception of what undergraduate education is all about. Few professors are familiar with educational opportunities outside their disciplines, and the proliferation of courses within the discipline impedes understanding even in their own. Many institutions still require students to select an adviser in their major field, despite the fact that the undergraduate major should be no more than a fourth to a third of the total degree requirement. The problems of the undergraduate student frequently concern not the major, but the choice of a major and the selection of courses to satisfy distribution requirements and incidental interests. Faculty advisers must regard students as individuals whose programs should be suited to their particular needs. The adviser must have enough interest in advising to acquire adequate and up-to-date knowledge of the university, its course offerings, and its regulations so that he can provide accurate and useful information to the student. A good adviser should fulfill many of the functions of a tutor in the English university.

If faculty members are to accept academic advising as an important function, they must have time to give to it. If the faculty is not interested in advising, or if faculty time is too expensive to allot to this activity, other methods must be established to assist undergraduates in planning their programs. A corps of advisers might be established apart from the deans and departments. Thus, colleges and departments would provide the resources for obtaining an education, but advisers with an overview of education would tell students how to utilize these resources. However, considering the difficulties which student personnel programs have introduced into higher education, such a step may be unwise. Perhaps the special corps of advisers could be based in colleges or even in departments. Certainly academic advising is an important and time-consuming function; it is not a task that every faculty member should be required to do; and it should be recognized and rewarded when well done.

Public Service

In the present day, practically all colleges and universities engage in public service and recognize it as a major function. Faculty members should be willing to participate in public service, with or without pay. The faculty member gains from this experience, the public benefits from it, and instruction becomes more realistic. Public service is a professional responsibility and, if it is accepted as such, time should be assigned for it and the service should be evaluated. One problem is drawing a line between personal participation as an individual and participation as a representative of the university. One conflict in land-grant institutions is between faculty members who are heavily engaged in public service without pay, and faculty members who spend a great deal of time away from the campus and receive compensation for it. Many institutions overlook excessive absence and are unwilling to admit that it creates an unnecessary and unjust burden for other members of the faculty. Institutions, professors themselves, should clarify

the public service role and provide guidelines for distinguishing between institutionally-supported public service and individual service
and consultation which require additional remuneration. Clarification
of this function and its relation to instruction is especially important in
institutions which recommend or require off-campus service experiences for students.

Faculty Statesmanship

Many faculty members have no loyalty to the institution which
employs them. At one of the Big Ten institutions, a faculty member who
had recently been imported at a high salary described his response to
the university: "They're paying me well, and they are giving me all the
time I want for research. I have no interest in further involvement in
this institution, and at any time that any other one offers me more advantages I'll leave immediately." Each faculty member should take
some interest in the effectiveness and efficiency of the total program of
the university. He should look realistically at the student body and at the
institution as it exists and is likely to exist in the future, and adapt to it.
He may feel that changes should be made but, if he cannot effect these
changes, he should not destroy his own morale and that of his colleagues
by constant carping; rather, he should seek an institution more to his
liking. Negative attitudes of faculty members are readily communicated
to students, who may seek to emulate their malcontent or may become
antagonized by or vaguely suspicious of the motivations of both the
professor and the institution.

Faculty members should re-examine and clarify the objectives
of the institution, and relate their courses and instructional patterns to
these objectives. Faculty members should also appraise the offerings of
the institution, recognizing that not all parts of an institution can be of
equal excellence and that not all institutions can offer everything. They
should try to understand the problems of the secondary schools, adjust
courses and instruction to the students admitted, and not blame every
unsatisfactory student performance on admission requirements or
secondary school preparation.

Higher education faces many problems: increasing enrollments and
costs, expanding knowledge which threatens the unity of undergraduate
education, and the lack of sequence in secondary, undergraduate, and
graduate education. We need faculty members who are aware of these
problems and who can deal with them intelligently.

Faculty statesmanship implies a willingness on the part of the
faculty to engage in continuing evaluation. This evaluation may include

institutional studies of the future of the university, of grading practices, and of university-wide requirements. It may include college and departmental reviews of curriculum, of the demands of other departments and colleges on a given department, of qualifications and supervision of teaching assistants, and of workload of regular faculty and assistants. The purpose of evaluation is to improve and, by engaging in continuing evaluation, the professors and the institution provide a model of the examined life in which the student is expected to engage.

SUMMARY AND IMPLICATIONS

All these functions are important, but few faculty members can engage in all of them. Indeed, such attempts should be discouraged, because few faculty members are able to do all of them well. Instructors should decide which functions they can perform adequately and with personal satisfaction, and their performance of these duties should be appraised and appropriately rewarded. This will permit faculty members to devote most of their time to those tasks for which they are best suited. By adjusting the total load of those who engage in several functions, they will have more time to consider how these experiences can be drawn upon to improve instruction.

It is difficult to develop a program which adequately assesses faculty efforts in these areas because the functions are not clearly defined and graduate study provides no background for them. Thus, the faculty member is unprepared for many of his assignments, and he resents appraisal of his performance in tasks he never agreed to undertake. The following recommendations suggest methods to correct these deficiencies in background and experience:

1. Every college faculty member should be familiar with the history, issues, and trends of American education so that he may have more insight as a classroom teacher and more understanding as a member of decision-making committees.

2. Every college faculty member should understand the organization and administration of a college. The problems of admission, counseling, residence halls, fund-raising, budgetary allocation, and institutional self-study are much more complex than the average faculty member realizes. Much suspicion of administrative policies could be alleviated if each instructor were to examine these issues from a broader point of view than his personal and departmental objectives. Too often faculty members are unable to relate personal and departmental interests to the needs of the institution as a whole.

3. The faculty member should study the nature of the learning process and the many alternative methods of instruction. Consideration of

the relation of different methods of instruction to various objectives provides a new conception of instruction to many teachers. They realize that it is impossible to talk intelligently about instruction without examining the principles of the learning process. Many discover that the selection of a textbook or the presentation of a lecture hardly fulfills the essential obligations and functions of instruction. They learn, too, that an effective learning program requires concentrated effort and an awareness of the technical resources available.

Audiovisual aids are available on most university and college campuses, but they are rarely used effectively. Closed circuit television allows audiovisual aids to be brought into the classroom much more effectively and efficiently. Programed learning can emphasize student activity and release the teacher from many unnecessary chores. To use this technology, teachers must understand the nature of learning and current methods of implementing instruction. Since few college teachers receive graduate training in this area, every institution should provide a program of in-service training. Such a program could provide a faculty library of literature on the history of American higher education and its continuing problems, instructional developments, and developments in the use of technological learning resources. The program might include a lecture series by authorities in these fields. Grants for individual faculty members to explore instructional problems or to study curriculum projects in other institutions can be very effective. Administrative recognition of faculty efforts in this area also encourages faculty members to confront the problems of the undergraduate curriculum.

Orientation of new faculty members should include seminar programs which discuss some of these essential problems. The novice faculty member usually appreciates such a series, and is glad to discover that the institution provides resources from which he can get continuing assistance. The greatest opposition to such ventures is usually found among senior professors or department heads who view such programs as a reflection on their capabilities or as an interference with their prerogatives. To avoid this reaction, they should be asked to help plan and carry out the program. The in-service training program might also introduce new faculty members to the unique qualities of the program and philosophy of the institution. In institutions which have already sponsored extensive curriculum planning, new staff members do not readily assimilate the rationale for it, and even older ones need to be reminded of its underlying principles.

The rapid development of technological learning resources will greatly effect the role of faculty members in the future. Current trends indicate that technical aids will be used more extensively, students will be responsible for phases of their own learning, and residence halls will be more closely related to instructional programs in an attempt to develop a total environment of learning. Thus, each professor will have to reconsider his role and develop his course to include the best combination of all available resources and possible experiences. Such planning will require a more thoughtful integration of single courses and of the total curriculum. Some programs will require the cooperation of professors, learning resources specialists, evaluators, and technicians. The institution should provide a research and service center from which faculty members can obtain specialized assistance, and should develop a continuing in-service training program to acquaint college faculty members with possibilities for improving their instructional practices. Finally, faculty members will have to know how to assist the student in integrating this extended and enriched pattern of experiences into a coherent and cumulative education.

REFERENCES

1. Arno A. Bellack, ed., *Theory and Research in Teaching*, Bureau of Publications, Teachers College, Columbia University, 1963.
2. James W. Brown and James W. Thornton, Jr., *College Teaching: Perspectives and Guidelines*, McGraw-Hill Book Company, Inc., 1963.
3. _____, eds., *New Media in Higher Education, Association* of Higher Education, National Education Association, Washington, D. C., 1963.
4. Jerome S. Bruner, *Toward a Theory of Instruction*, Harvard University Press (Belknap Press), 1966.
5. Claude E. Buxton, *College Teaching: A Psychologist's View*, Harcourt, Brace and Company, New York, 1956.
6. George W. Denemark, "Concept Learning: Some Implications for Teaching," *Liberal Education*, Vol. 51, March, 1965, pp. 54–69.
7. Helen I. Driver, et al, *Counseling and Learning Through Small Group Discussion*, Monona-Driver Book Company, Madison, 1958.
8. "Effectiveness in Teaching," *New Dimensions in Higher Education* No. 2, Office of Education, OE-50006, U. S. Department of Health, Education, and Welfare, Washington, D. C., 1960.
9. Herman A. Estrin and Delmer M. Goode, *College and University Teaching*, Wm. C. Brown Co., Dubuque, 1964.
10. Sidney J. French, ed., *Accent on Teaching*, Harper and Brothers, New York, 1954.
11. N. L. Gage, ed., *Handbook of Research on Teaching*, Rand McNally and Company, Chicago, 1963.

12. Robert M. Gagnè, *The Conditions of Learning*, Holt, Rinehart and Winston, Inc., New York, 1965.
13. Carl Gross and Roslyn Blum, eds., *College Teachers Look at College Teaching*, American Association of Colleges for Teacher Education, Washington, D. C., 1965.
14. Ralph N. Haber, ed., *Current Research in Motivation*, Holt, Rinehart and Winston, Inc., New York, 1966.
15. Melvene D. Hardee, ed., *Counseling and Guidance in General Education*, World Book Company, Yonkers, N. Y., 1955.
16. Harold D. Hauf, et al, *New Spaces for Learning: Designing College Facilities to Utilize Instructional Aids and Media*, School of Architecture, Rensselaer Polytechnic Institute, 1961.
17. Ernest R. Hilgard, ed., *Theories of Learning and Instruction*, Sixty-Third Yearbook of the National Society for the Study of Education, Part I, University of Chicago Press, 1964.
18. B. Lamar Johnson, ed., *New Directions for Instruction in the Junior College*, Junior College Leadership Program, School of Education, University of California, March, 1965.
19. Patricia B. Knapp, *College Teaching and the College Library*, American Library Association, Chicago, 1959.
20. Calvin B. T. Lee, ed., *Improving College Teaching*, American Council on Education, Washington, D. C., 1967.
21. Ralph C. Leyden and Neal Balanoff, *The Planning of Educational Media for a New Learning Center*, A Report by Stephens College, Office of Education, U. S. Department of Health, Education, and Welfare, Washington, D. C., 1963.
22. Earl J. McGrath, *The Quantity and Quality of College Teachers*, Bureau of Publications, Teachers College, Columbia University, 1961.
23. Fred B. Millett, *Professor*, Macmillan Company, New York, 1961.
24. Francis C. Rosecrance, *The American College and Its Teachers*, Macmillan Company, New York, 1962.
25. Peter Rossi and Bruce Biddle, eds., *The New Media and Education*, Aldine Publishing Company, Chicago, 1966.
26. J. G. Umstattd, *College Teaching: Background, Theory, Practice*, The University Press of Washington, D. C. and the Community College Press, 1964.

9

Evaluation and the Curriculum

The importance of evaluation has already been discussed in the chapter on instruction and the curriculum. That chapter focused on evaluation of teaching and instruction, and on appraisal of all faculty efforts which relate to instruction and the curriculum. This chapter is concerned specifically with evaluation of the curriculum. Evaluation must be involved in every stage of planning and executing an educational program. Any practice in an institution results from the belief that it is the most convenient, most appropriate, or most effective procedure. The very existence of a practice involves evaluation. The issue is not whether evaluation will occur, but rather how it will occur, how evidence will be accumulated and used to appraise the value of a program. A curriculum does not exist as an isolated entity. It must be reviewed in relation to the background, ability, and personalities of the students and to the personalities, values, and aspirations of the teachers. Presumably the curriculum reflects an accepted set of objectives and offers experiences or courses in a number of different disciplines, each of which may emphasize or interpret the objectives differently. The choice of instructional methods and practices varies not only with the objectives and the disciplines but also with the students and the teachers. Environmental factors affect all educational programs, and evaluation of the curriculum must take these into account. An institution which has overheated, poorly ventilated, and noisy classrooms cannot expect a valid appraisal of either its curriculum or its instructional program until these physical deficiencies are remedied. The total campus learning climate, which results from its physical environment, students, teachers, objectives, instruction, and curriculum, may be more significant in determining student learning than any aspect of the curriculum. Thus, the curriculum must be evaluted in terms of its impact on the campus learning climate as well as its impact on students in relation to specific objectives.

177

The process of the development of a curriculum is a major factor in the success of the curriculum. A curriculum imposed on students and faculty by the administration or by some powerful minority is unlikely to be effective, no matter how excellent the conception. The role and method of evaluation in a program have a profound impact on students and on the effectiveness of the curriculum. For example, if a new curriculum is introduced with no student involvement and no plan for assessing student reaction and achievement, the failure of the program will be blamed on the students rather than on the curriculum. Students cannot attain a spirit of continuing inquiry and evaluation if the program itself does not exhibit these qualities. An effective curriculum must specify methods for evaluating both the curriculum itself and the progress of students under it.

POSSIBLE PERSPECTIVES OF EVALUATION

Evaluation may focus on three distinctive aspects of higher education. First, evaluation may concentrate on the environment, on the characteristics of the scene in which education takes place. It may also focus on the process, the quality and organization of the learning experiences provided. Finally, it may concentrate on the results, on the progress and achievement of students.

The Environment.—Evaluation focused on environment examines instructional and library facilities, extracurricular cultural programs, residence halls, student activities centers, and the climate of learning generated by these facilities. The relations, values, and responsibilities of students, faculty, and administrative officers are also part of this environment. The nature of the college or university community, the resources and facilities available, and the ways in which its members live and work together and relate to the larger community of which the institution is a part affect both the structure of the educational program and its success. Study of environment, then, will review statements of institutional objectives and purposes, characteristics of clientele supported and served by the institution, administrative and financial organization and procedures, library facilities and holdings, faculty characteristics, admissions practices and resulting student characteristics, faculty and student personnel policies, previous and existing curricular organizations, and practices in coordinating and evaluating the instructional program and the curriculum. A full understanding of the environment requires a study which probes into all aspects of the institution's operations. Processes, particularly administrative and decision-making processes, are involved in the environmental focus, but the process focus concentrates on learning experiences rather than on the surroundings in which those experiences occur.

The Process. Focus on process involves the study of the organization and quality of the learning experiences provided. This includes an examination of the process of curriculum development, for this process has great impact on the receptivity of faculty and students to the program. Such examination should not be based only on planning committee reports, statements of rationale, syllabi or course outlines, or even statements by the students and the professors. The process should be seen as the students experience it, for reports of instructors do not necessarily accord with reality. Professors have been known to comment on the effectiveness of a discussion when an observer in the classroom verified from the stopwatch in his hand that the professor had talked all but five minutes of the period. In examining the process, it is important to look not only at daily experiences in residence halls and courses, but also at the relationship of the process. Attempts to combine off-campus work experiences, travel abroad, independent study, and honors programs often conflict with, rather than reinforce, one another. The study of the impact of the various processes on individual students is also necessary to assess their effectiveness and value.

In focusing on process, the following questions must be answered: What is the exact nature of the experience offered by each course and program? What do instructors do? What do they expect of students? What do students actually do? When? Where? How are the classroom experiences, the assignments, and the examinations related to the objectives? How are the various elements of the processes interrelated to provide and encourage sequence, coherence, and integration? Do instruction, residence hall living, student activities, and curriculum requirements reinforce or conflict with each other?

In studying the process, the number and range of possible experiences make it difficult to relate each experience to long-term objectives. Some intermediate structure may be usefully imposed. For example, all statements of educational goals encourage students to think critically and engage in inquiry. Thus, one may ask whether a given course or experience requires or encourages critical thought or inquiry by students. Are sophomores, juniors, and seniors given increasing opportunity to engage in such behavior? If ability to carry on independent study is a goal, to what extent is it permitted or required of freshmen? Does the program encourage and enable advanced students to attain greater self-sufficiency? Unless such questions can be answered positively, the process is deficient; it has not been planned to effect the desired changes in students, and will not do so.

A structure similar to the four continuums discussed earlier may also be applied. If an objective is to attain a balance of these extremes, such questions as the following may be posed: do the various disciplines recognize that the interests, motivations, and preparation of students differ greatly? Do the disciplines adjust to these differences or even capitalize upon them by flexibility in requirements and instruction? Can the student investigate practical problems and explore various perspectives and solutions which the different disciplines offer them? Is the program sufficiently structured to allow instructors and students to see the significance of the total college experience, yet sufficiently flexible to adopt to individual interests, abilities, and goals? Is the student encouraged to seek coherence and integration but also taught that knowledge and experience cannot be totally unstructured, and that meaningful and essential categories do exist?

End Results.   A third focus is on the results of a program. These results are more complex than such phrases as "achievement of students" or "changes in students" imply. Many objectives are cognitive in nature and some educators feel these are the only ones of consequence. Although knowledge and patterns of thought are important, not all knowledge is of equal worth. Critical thinking and judgment necessarily involve attitudes and values. Thus, although we may argue that institutions should not specify particular attitudes and values, we cannot avoid concern about affective outcomes. Values affect our thoughts and judgments. Psychomotor outcomes are also important. Speech involves a complex coordination of mind and body; writing involves certain physical skills. In many professional fields, physical dexterity controlled by knowledge and judgment is essential to performance. Statements of these cognitive, affective, and psychophysical outcomes constitute the objectives of a program. There may also be unanticipated outcomes. A student can have an apparently beneficial educational experience yet derive from it a highly undesirable outcome. For example, a student interested in art but with little aptitude for it may be so antagonized by his initial experience that he comes to dislike art and artists. A social scientist who emphasizes analysis and the importance of suspended judgment and who is unwilling to make value commitments, may unwittingly encourage students to avoid the uncertainties and irrationalities of community affairs and politics. Even the process of evaluation itself may influence results. Comprehensive examinations which emphasize isolated information cause students to learn isolated information. Evaluation instruments which encourage certain attitudes, beliefs, or values may force students to give a dishonest response.

Evaluation of a curriculum may appraise the changes (desired or unanticipated) in individuals or a group which result from the experiences. The rationale for this approach is that the basis for evaluating the worth of any program must be its impact on the students for whom it was designed. The implicit assumption is that, if the changes observed are not in accord with reasonable expectations or if they are unanticipated and undesirable, the program of experiences and the instructional practices must be modified to bring about a harmony between expectations and results. This approach raises many problems. First, the concern with changes in students or with student achievement may shift attention from evaluation of the curriculum to evaluation or grading of students. The responsibility of the faculty for motivating students and for informing them of their progress toward clearly-defined objectives may be ignored. Second, an evaluation program which accumulates evidence of student competencies over long intervals of time actually encourages faculty members to teach their courses without regard for students' experiences or long-term educational goals. The program does not pressure them to do otherwise, and gives no evidence of their shortsighted practices. Third, lack of congruence between anticipation and outcome may result from environmental conditions or from a disparity between actual and planned experiences.

Rather than appraise changes in students, an evaluation program may judge the effectiveness of a course or of a total curriculum. Student achievement still constitutes a major element in such an appraisal, but evaluation concentrates on the course, the practice, the curriculum as effectuating agents. The task is to find out not only what happens to the students but also why, when, and where it happens. If something undesirable occurs, can it be traced to a particular aspect of the program or to the interaction of several? Does it require the elimination of a course, the revision of a course, the introduction of new courses, or the reorganization of a sequence? While evaluation still emphasizes end results rather than daily experiences of students, it recognizes that these results are fostered by courses and other daily experiences. Lack of congruence between these experiences and the goals may become apparent. For example, unrelated courses will not form a student capable of inquiring into, making analysis of, and reaching judgments about issues that transcend the framework of a particular course or discipline. Thus, within the evaluation program for the total curriculum, smaller evaluation projects must be planned to assess the impact of particular course experiences, student activities, and residence hall living on both immediate and long-term objectives. These smaller evaluation projects are beneficial for two reasons. First, they force the faculty and staff to recognize that their individual efforts are part of a larger operation, and that their success is measured in part by their contributions to that effort. Second, they help students realize that each aspect of their educational experience is an essential part of a larger whole, and that the program under which they are studying is, in itself, a model for learning.

Evaluation may be a goal of education in its own right. There are fads in education. A few years ago any statement of educational objectives used the phrase "critical thinking." Currently, "mode of inquiry" is in vogue. Evaluation, as a process of making judgments, involves inquiry and critical thinking. The evaluation instruments we give to students constitute the most obvious evidence to them of what we believe to be important and of how we make judgments about them. Our evaluation of the curriculum or of instructional practices demonstrates to students our belief in the necessity of continual evaluation and our own concept of relevant evidence and action. Education attempts to develop in the individual the ability to make sound judgments of his own ideas, motivations, and mental processes (self-evaluation), and of the ideas of others (analysis, synthesis, criticism). Students must define their own values, and examine and select courses of action appropriate to the achievement of these ends. The model that the institution provides in its own functioning is a potent influence on student behavior. Furthermore, the involvement of students in the evaluation program of an institution provides experience in the behavior we are trying to inculcate. If evaluative behavior is a goal, then the evaluation program should encourage students to evaluate the processes and results of their own learning activities.

Need for Composite Approach

None of these perspectives of evaluation can be ignored. Each one, pursued by itself, will produce interesting information, but will not result in modification or improvement of a program because the omission of relevant considerations will be detected when proposals for change are made. Environment must be examined in relation to its influence on educational experiences and objectives. The daily process of education should be assessed, but we can become so involved in petty arguments about whether two or three hours in one laboratory should be required or whether videotape presentation might be used instead of live instruction that we fail to confront the significant issues. The results of a program should be examined, but we can become so enmeshed in the niceties of constructing instruments to appraise affective outcomes that we ignore basic question of how effective outcomes can and should be translated into daily educational experiences.

PRINCIPLES IN PLANNING AN EVALUATION PROGRAM

A number of general principles apply to evaluation programs. One is that, unless there is an *a priori* commitment to evaluation when a new curriculum is planned, much time will be wasted in arguing about details of the evaluation program, and probably evaluation will be largely ignored. The commitment of innovators to their curricula makes them suspicious of evaluation. They are often unwilling to plan their own appraisal, and they may be antagonistic to a plan prepared by someone else. The president of one large state university recently told his faculty that the institution would not support any new curricular and instructional programs unless they included a program of evaluation which specified in detail the kind of evidence which would be gathered and the way in which it would be used to evaluate the worth of the development.

A second principle is that there must be widespread involvement in planning and in accumulating evidence for evaluation. If only a small segment of the faculty is charged with the task of evaluation, friction and disagreement may destroy the worth of the evaluation and of the project itself. Students should be involved in evaluation, partly because they have distinctive points of view and concerns, and partly because their cooperation in responding to questionnaires, interviews, and other evaluation instruments will indicate their understanding of and commitment to the endeavor. Evaluation should consider the effects of the new program on faculty and their attitudes toward it. It should include evidence of changes in students both as a group and as individuals, for a group change does not guarantee corresponding changes in all individuals.

Too often evaluation is regarded as a conclusive enterprise which will result in a final decision about the abandonment, inprovement, or replacement of a program. This is unrealistic. A single comprehensive evaluation carried on for a year or even two will have little or no impact on a program. The evaluation report is rarely completed until six months or a year after the evidence is accumulated. Thus the evaluation is outdated before it appears. A third principle, then, is that an evaluation program should be continuing, comprehensive, and accumulative rather than complete as of a particular date. Findings should be repeated, and must be emphasized to faculty, who are likely to meditate at some length before taking action. When results are unpleasant, extensive confirmation may be necessary to attain acceptance and action. The evaluation program must be oriented toward the future rather than the past. It should emphasize suggestions for improvement or further investigation, rather than dwell on weaknesses and errors.

A fourth principle is that evaluation studies should be designed with specific questions and hypotheses in mind. The collection of vast amounts of data on every question someone thinks might be interesting insures an unmanageable and useless evaluation study.

To design an evaluation study which allows efficient statistical treatment of data and maximizes chances for positive statements and conclusions requires expert counsel. Chapter 5 of the *Handbook of Research on Teaching* by Campbell and Stanley deals with experimental designs for research on teaching, but the discussion is appropriate to the problem of evaluating a curriculum (2). The designs most appropriate for curriculum evaluation require annual collection of evidence for a period of years so that the observed changes can be related to program features, even though cause and effect cannot be unambiguously established. Statistical designs which indicate the over-all effect of the curriculum but do not isolate particular strengths and weaknesses are rarely helpful. Probably, no single design will assess all the issues involved in curriculum evaluation. A curriculum usually contains several objectives which are relatively independent and which require very different kinds of evidence. Thus, evaluation requires a number of simultaneous or sequential studies rather than a grand, all-embracing statistical design.

A fifth principle is that it is unwise to rely too heavily on complex designs and statistical treatments. Continuing involvement in evaluation is far more significant than attempts at precision through rigorously-planned experiments. A four-year curriculum, and perhaps even a single course, is not a precisely-defined series of learning experiences. Even a structured curriculum required of all students does not provide the same experiences for all, because differences in background and personality result in different interpretations of the same experience. In a flexible curriculum, the range of individual possibilities is so great that no curriculum evaluation design can account for all of them. Evaluation should include a wide range of studies which can be coordinated to provide useful evidence on various parts of the program but which also can offer insight into the cumulative impact of all of the parts. The whole should be greater than the sum of the parts, but some of the parts will be as important as the whole. Experimental designs and statistical tests which are not well understood may be less effective than a professor's realization that even the most careful planning of curriculum and instruction does not insure the desired results.

SOME PROBLEMS AND CAUTIONS IN
CURRICULUM EVALUATION*

The phases in curriculum development have been described as the selection and formulation of objectives, the selection and organization of experiences, and evaluation. These phases are interrelated rather than sequential. Formulation of objectives involves evaluation because it requires the application of criteria to select, define, and reduce the possible objectives to a reasonable, consistent, and attainable set. Likewise, the selection and the organization of appropriate educational experiences require many evaluative judgments. The complete cycle of the development of a curriculum, followed by a comprehensive evaluation of that curriculum, is seldom accomplished. It is a difficult task, because many factors interact in numerous and complex ways. The total curriculum includes not only courses, but also instructional patterns in the courses and relations of the courses. Course by course evaluation does not constitute an evaluation of the curriculum.

Few students or teachers are able to grasp the total program. The curriculum consists of courses offered in many different departments and taught by a large and continually-changing corps of teachers. Each teacher is most concerned with his own course, and may not know or care how it fits into the cumulative pattern of experiences called the curriculum. If he does think about it, he may decide that it is the job of the administrators or of the students to make the connections. Thus, student and faculty may be unaware of pervasive objectives and the relevance of courses and experiences unless they engage in continuing evaluation activity.

Another problem in evaluating a total curriculum is that courses, experiences, and even specific goals of a curriculum rarely remain constant for any length of time. New teachers, new textbooks, and new demands result in continuous change in the curriculum. Thus, evaluation of a curriculum through appraisal of student achievement may be impossible or ineffective. The results inevitably apply to a curriculum of the past, and the faculty can rightly claim that the findings are irrelevant to current problems. When evaluation emphasizes measurement of results over a long period of time, so many uncontrolled or unplanned factors may have promoted or destroyed progress toward the objectives

---

*Many of the ideas developed in this section came from a curriculum evaluation project carried out by Dr. Twyla Shear and reported in her dissertation. ("An Evaluation of Core Curriculum in the College of Home Economics," Thesis for the Degree of Ed.D., Michigan State University, 1964.)

that it is doubtful whether the results can be attributed to the *planned* curriculum, even though it has remained largely unchanged.

This analysis indicates that curriculum evaluation must be undertaken from several different perspectives. First, since the success of a curriculum depends heavily on the developmental process itself, the process should be examined to determine the strengths or weaknesses which will influence the effectiveness of the program. Second, the curriculum must be logical and consistent if faculty and students are to grasp its significance. Unless they understand the curriculum, they are likely to resist it. Third, evaluation must seek evidence of changes resulting from curriculum. This includes not only the students' attainment of its objectives but also the student's attitudes, changes in the characteristics of students selecting or withdrawing from the program, and the subjective appraisals of advisers and counselors who influence student selection and attitudes. Not all outcomes of curriculum revision can be anticipated. The following paragraphs will examine each of these three perspectives for evaluation of curriculum in greater detail and attempt to isolate factors and criteria which should be considered.

EVALUATION BASED ON THE CURRICULUM
DEVELOPMENT PROCESS

In revising old curricula or planning new ones, needs and desired competencies should be analyzed in detail. One of the first steps is to arrive at a set of clearly-stated behavioral objectives and to specify what kind of evidence would determine the attainment of these objectives. Objectives must be clear, consistent, and realistic. One cannot insist on specific attitudes and values as outcomes if the objectives also specify the development of critical thinking and judgment. Objectives should be based on a philosophical point of view and on generally accepted principles of learning, and should specify the desired level of accomplishment. If the level of accomplishment cannot be defined in detail then it will be impossible to develop a sequential program or to determine when students have met degree requirements.

If objectives are adequately defined and desired behavior clearly specified, the selection of appropriate learning experiences and instructional procedures will not present great difficulties. The learning experiences must be related to the objectives and to the accepted principles of learning. The developmental process should also consider principles of continuity, sequence, and integration. The learning experiences not only should be derived directly from the objectives, but also should be sufficiently related to them that students will have the objectives kept clearly before them at every stage of progress.

The process of curriculum development should include methods of achieving understanding and commitment to the program by students and faculty. This involves the role of leadership, the extent of faculty participation, the communication processes, and the development of group cohesiveness. Successful curricular change requires positive leadership by the administration, but the entire faculty should be involved in the process. Communication channels should keep everyone informed of developing ideas and encourage everyone to express his own point of view. Curriculum development takes time, and so time, facilities, and other resources conducive to greater productive effort and to increased understanding and unanimity should be provided. Finally, evaluation and modification of defects must be part of the process, for evaluation of the process after the fact can only explain failure or highlight success.

If the new or modified curriculum is to be effective, the majority of the faculty must concur with all major decisions. A few highly-critical faculty members can discourage students, new faculty members, and even faculty members who originally favored the change but abhor the continuing dissension. Thus, those involved in curriculum development must consciously strive to attain the understanding and acceptance of all students and faculty.

Although alternative curricula will rarely be introduced in order to evaluate one against the other, there may be a need for experimentation with particular phases of the curriculum to determine whether one organization, sequence, or mode of instruction is more effective than another. Indeed, this examination of alternatives may resolve certain differences of opinion among faculty members. Flexibility and continuing adaptation is the goal of curriculum change, and evaluation will play a vital role only if it is viewed as the basis for such change.

Unless the faculty has engaged in evaluation during the development of the curriculum and has formulated at least broad outlines for a comprehensive evaluation, evaluation evidence will not be seriously regarded. Nevertheless, an evaluator or evaluation committee may be asked to assess the curriculum and the developmental process after the task is completed. In such cases, major sources of information on developmental phases are to be found in the minutes of faculty meetings, in committee reports, in workshop materials or proceedings, in interviews and questionnaires given to the faculty and to students, and in the interpretative materials developed for the new curriculum and its courses. The examination of such materials will not determine the effectiveness of the curriculum, but it may reveal many reasons why the curriculum has failed to meet with wholehearted acceptance. Such evidence may convince faculty members that curriculum study must be a continuing process.

LOGIC AND INTERNAL CONSISTENCY OF THE CURRICULUM ITSELF

Even though the curriculum development process has been acceptable, the curriculum may not be logical and internally consistent. The complexity of developing a four-year curriculum often requires that a number of subcommittees deal with various segments of it. Although each may reach an acceptable set of conclusions, the sum of the component parts may not make an integrated whole. The subgroups may have somewhat different philosophies of education and may interpret the behavioral objectives differently. Incidental objectives may obscure the long-term objectives. For example, a group may be so concerned with reducing laboratory requirements that it ignores the objective of teaching the student to adapt various techniques to practical problems. Hence an examination of the logic and internal consistency of the curriculum is essential.

If the curriculum emphasizes the understanding and application of basic concepts and principles, courses outlines should identify these concepts and principles and indicate their applicability to other areas. Examination of curriculum materials should reveal that the principles of continuity, sequence, and integration have been employed in the selection of educational experiences for both the individual courses and the series of courses. The curriculum should emphasize both breadth and depth, and should provide for the interaction of liberal and vocational education.

If independent study is an objective, then the curriculum should provide possibilities and incentives for independent learning. The student should be encouraged to engage in independent projects which include several courses or fill some of the gaps between them.

The curriculum should consider and utilize the available resources. It should be based on a rational assessment of the competencies of the staff, the library holdings and accommodations, the availability and adequacy of classroom and laboratory facilities and equipment, and the level of financial support. Deficiencies in any of these areas indicate a failure in the original planning and a lack of consistency in the program.

A rigid calendar and course-credit structure may interfere with significant curricular change by causing artificial and disruptive breaks in the curricular experiences. Conversely, a major calendar change without curriculum adaptation to that change only generates additional difficulties.

A curriculum is not entirely logical unless it conforms to general university requirements and to those of national or regional accrediting agencies. Colleges or departments sometimes ignore or misinterpret general university policies in the development of a curriculum. Such practices confuse students and faculty and invite administrative criticism which will seriously undermine the effectiveness of the program. University policies may be modified, but they should not be flouted. Similarly, the requirements of accrediting associations should be met, although a college may be justified in ignoring such requirements if it has a sound rationale for doing so and is willing to accept the consequences. The alleged inflexibility of accrediting agencies is more often a faculty defense than a fact.

CHANGES RESULTING FROM THE CURRICULUM

The classic mode of evaluating a course or curriculum is to collect data on the achievement or progress of students in relation to the objectives of the program. Since absolute performance criteria are seldom available, a comparison with one or more alternative programs having the same objectives is considered desirable. However, a single institution usually cannot operate several distinctive curricula simultaneously because of the expense involved and the difficulty of isolating students and instructors in each of the curricula.

Following a curriculum change, some data on the preceding program may be available from tests, questionnaires, or other instruments. It is tempting to compare such data with current data obtained through reapplication of the same instruments. However, as definitions and emphases change, a particular instrument may no longer provide the same stimulus as it did at an earlier time. If the objectives of the new curriculum are different from those of the old, evaluative comparisons will have little significance.

In studying the attainment of objectives by students, both the short-range objectives of certain courses and the pervasive long-range objectives of the total program may be considered. Evaluation of short-range objectives usually emphasizes the content of a particular course. However, changes in critical thought or in attitudes and values cannot be measured at the end of a single course, for such changes rarely occur in short periods of time. Even when such changes in students are noted, it is difficult to relate these changes to specific aspects of a particular course. Many researchers in the area of attitudes and values have concluded that the total campus environment, and especially interaction with the peer group, have a more potent influence than the structured curriculum. Furthermore, the problem of how to measure changes in students over a period of time has no simple solution. Simple arithmetical differences between pretest and posttest scores are dubious measurements of achievement, and the assumptions upon which the tests are based often dictate the nature of the findings.

The reputation of a curriculum and a faculty is a major factor in attracting students. Changes in the curriculum may change this reputation and attract a different kind of student. For example, a new home economics curriculum which minimizes core courses in the various fields of home economics and which reduces laboratory requirements may encourage students with specialized interests in particular areas of home economics to enter the program. A change which stresses theoretical rather than technical skills may attract more intelligent students. Thus, changes noted in students may result not from particular features of the curriculum but from the nature of the student it attracts. The enthusiasm and commitment of the faculty to the curriculum are major factors in its success. If the new curriculum makes students and faculty more aware of the broad and the specific objectives of the program, more concerned with continuity, sequence, and integration, and more committed to individual instruction and independent study, the curriculum changes have been successful. Such changes in attitudes will positively affect the performance of students.

The impressions of individuals not directly involved in a curriculum will be helpful in evaluating it. Professors teaching courses which include students in several different programs may compare the achievements of students in each of the programs. In a study of journalism curricula a few years ago, several professors pointed out that students in the journalism program had developed a distinctive critical approach to analysis of social and economic issues. Individuals not directly involved in a curriculum often hear student comments on the quality of the program. If a particularly weak or unsatisfactory program has been revised, it is important to know whether the changes in the curriculum have modified the opinions of outside observers. Are they aware that changes have been made? Do these changes rectify their criticisms and doubts about the program as it formerly existed? The answers to these questions will reveal a great deal about the relation of the developmental process to the success of the final result. If the criticisms of outsiders have not been carefully assessed and investigated, and if these persons have not been able to make suggestions for the improvement of the program, probably few of the changes made will seem to rectify the inadequacies they observed. Thus evaluation of curriculum change should investigate the extent to which the total undergraduate faculty and administration of the institution is aware of why the changes were made, what they have accomplished, and upon what assumptions and expectations they were based.

Every curriculum evaluation project should also attempt to assess the extent and nature of unanticipated outcomes. Students under pressure from a teacher may achieve the objectives, but may also develop such antagonism that they avoid both the teacher and the field for the rest of their college career.

SUMMARY

Evaluation of a curriculum solely by collection of data on student achievement is inadequate. The methods of such evaluation are always inaccurate, and the approach rarely leads to constructive modification of the program unless the original curriculum development specified the relevant data and means of collecting them. Other changes resulting from the curriculum, such as changes in the attitudes and impressions of students and faculty and in the learning environment, are just as important and should be investigated. Evidence on the kinds of students who are attracted to or discouraged from the program is also relevant. Another approach to evaluation is the examination of the process of curriculum development. The curriculum should be based on an acceptable theory of curriculum development, and each aspect of the curriculum should be consistent with that theory.

A study of course materials, outlines, syllabi, and policy statements should reveal the logic and internal consistency of the curriculum. The relation of objectives and philosophy to educational experiences, evaluation practices, and resources should be clearly specified, logical, and reasonable.

These alternative methods of evaluation will affect faculty thinking about the problem of curriculum development. All these approaches to evaluation view curriculum development as a continuing process rather than as a search for an ideal curriculum. Curriculum development is too involved with people and with continuing change within and outside of the institution to expect that any program will stand still long enough to be fully evaluated or that any clear-cut answers will emerge. One of the virtues of American higher education has been its flexibility and adaptability. Evaluation concepts which seek stability must be replaced by approaches which interpret and influence changes as they occur. Evaluation must also offer students a pattern for planning and evaluating their own continuing learning. Evaluative behavior is a goal as well as a method of educational planning.

REFERENCES

1. Benjamin S. Bloom, ed., *Taxonomy of Educational Objectives:* The Classification of Educational Goals, Handbook I: Cognitive Domain, Longmans, Green and Co., New York, 1956.
2. Donald T. Campbell and Julian Stanley, "Experimental and Quasi-Experimental Designs for Research on Teaching," Chapter 5 in *Handbook of Research on Teaching,* Part II, N. L. Gage, ed., Rand McNally and Company Chicago, 1963, pp. 171–246.
3. Lee J. Cronback, "The Psychological Background for Curriculum Experimentation," Chapter 4 in *Modern Viewpoints in the Curriculum,* Paul C. Rosenbloom and Paul C. Hillestad, eds., Mcgraw-Hill Book Company, New York, 1964, pp. 19–35.
4. Richard P. Dober, *Campus Planning,* Reinhold Publishing Co., New York, 1963.
5. Paul L. Dressel and Associates, *Evaluation in Higher Education,* Houghton Mifflin Company, Boston, 1961.
6. Paul L. Dressel and Lewis B. Mayhew, *General Education: Explorations in Evaluation,* American Council on Education, Washington, D. C., 1954.
7. Edward D. Eddy, Jr., *The College Influence on Student Character,* American Council on Education, Washington, D. C., 1959.
8. *A Guide to Institutional Self-Study and Evaluation of Educational Programs Abroad,* Council on Student Travel, New York, 1965.
9. David R. Krathwohl, et al, *Taxonomy of Educational Objectives:* The Classification of Educational Goals, Handbook II: Affective Domain, David McKay Company, Inc., New York, 1964.
10. Theodore M. Newcomb, et al, *Persistence and Change—Bennington College and Its Students After 25 Years,* John Wiley and Sons, Inc., New York, 1967.
11. Nevitt Sanford, *Where Colleges Fail,* Jossey-Bass, Inc., San Francisco, 1967.
12. Ralph Tyler, et al, *Perspectives of Curriculum Evaluation,* Rand McNally and Company, Chicago, 1967.

10

Curriculum Review
and Control

The word curriculum may refer either to courses or to the total range of educational experiences. Even the limited sense of the word has two distinct usages: it may include all courses offered by an institution, or it may refer to a specific program or course of study leading to a degree, certificate, or diploma. In the discussion which follows, the word will be used in this latter sense as a synonym of "course of study." The word "course" will be used to connote a unit of instruction in a particular subject.

In the United States, a course usually has a departmental designation, a numerical designation, a title, and a specified number of credits. Whereas a curriculum emphasizes a unified experience directed toward specific ends, courses may exist as discrete units which are unrelated to other courses or to any curriculum. A curriculum should be more than an array of independent courses. A curriculum may be a *common* experience if it is required of all students, but it will not be a *unified* experience unless it is based on clearly-defined objectives, competencies, or knowledge.

Curriculum and course development are closely related. The addition of a new course, such as Canadian history or biochemistry, can lead ultimately to a major in the field or even to a new department. Thus, the addition of courses can lead to new curricula and even to new administrative units. It is equally true that new curricula may result in the addition of courses and of new administrative or coordinating units. Curriculum and course development require continuing review and control if a reasonable balance is to be maintained between enrollment, demands of society and students, costs, and number of courses or curricula.

CURRICULUM AND COURSE DEVELOPMENT

In Professional and Technical Education

In professional and technical fields, the goal of preparation for a reasonably well-defined career encourages a rigid and highly-organized curriculum. Requirements are heavy, electives rare, and course proliferation unlikely simply because units which are not required attract few students. Thus, new curricula are more likely to be added than new electives. New specialties appear which either require a new course of study or radically modify an existing one. Educational planning tends to emphasize the curriculum as a whole, and individual courses usually have a reasonably well-conceived place in that whole. Furthermore, many professional fields have attempted to reduce and consolidate professional requirements to provide for increased study of the basic and contributive arts, sciences, and social sciences.

In Liberal Education

For the disciplines included in the sciences, social sciences, arts, and humanities, the objective of producing a liberally-educated person no longer provides clear direction for planning the baccalaureate program. Vague principles, loosely defined in terms of majors, minors, and distribution requirements, do not define a unified four-year experience and many courses taught in the basic disciplines have no relation to courses in other departments or even in the same department. Courses often exist for reasons which have no relation to the requirements of a liberal undergraduate education, and the number and variety of these reasons encourage continuing proliferation.

REASONS FOR COURSE EXPANSION

New Curricula

New curricula contribute to course proliferation. Occasionally a new curriculum simply groups together existing courses to provide a clearer organization for prospective students, but usually new courses are required. Those proposing the curriculum usually overestimate student and financial support for it. Every proposal for a new curriculum should be critically examined, for a faculty group with vested interest in a new development cannot always decide objectively whether a program has sufficient substantive content, distinctiveness, and clientele to justify its addition to the institutional offerings. Screening procedures which examine these points and also consider the possibility of duplication of effort among neighboring institutions are advisable. Every institution should insist on at least a two-year interval between the proposal of a new curriculum and its initiation. This interval would provide adequate time to develop the program in detail and to study in depth its quality and implications.

Competition

Competition plays a major role in increasing the number of courses. Departmental course listings are a source of pride to faculty members, admissions officers, deans, and presidents, who like to refer to the richness and variety of their institution's offerings. Faculty members argue that limited departmental offerings cause prospective students to select other institutions which offer a greater variety. Even departments within an institution compete for majors. Departments with many majors tend to offer many courses, so the generalization is made that expansion of course offerings will increase the number of majors. The number of majors, the number of courses, the size of staff, and the degree of specialization are all related. A department which has few majors must concentrate on basic courses, and there is little outlet for the "my course" affectation which faculty members find so satisfying.

Special Adaptations

Special adaptations, primarily in introductory or fundamental courses, present another common pressure for course expansion. Mathematics, chemistry, English, economics, and other disciplines which appear in many different curricula face this problem. Faculty members responsible for a specialized curriculum request a new course because they feel the existing offering does not suit the needs of their students. This often leads to multiple introductory sequences in chemistry or mathematics which vary in credit, content, or sequence. Vocational faculties may also urge that basic courses emphasize applications to their particular field. Thus, a university may offer introductory statistics for statistics or mathematics majors, for business administration students, for psychology majors, for education majors, and for agriculture students. A further problem results from differences in the quality of students selecting various curricula. In many institutions, students in business administration or in education are less able than most other groups. Mathematics or statistics, taught with the rigor appropriate to the average undergraduate, may be too difficult for students in unselective curricula. Often a particular curriculum is so constructed that it is impossible for a student to schedule a particular course at the level at which it is usually offered. For example, beginning statistics may be offered at the freshman or sophomore level. If students in a particular curriculum must have beginning statistics but cannot take it until their junior year, the request will be made to offer the course at the junior level. Thus, one finds beginning statistics offered from the freshman through the doctoral levels.

Frequently special course adaptations are introduced by a department because another department threatens to offer a competing course. There are, of course, two sides to this. It is unreasonable to contend that there should be *no* adaptation of content material to the requirements of particular curricula, but a new course should be more than a matter of one additional credit hour, or an advanced level numbering.

The Problems and Evils of Expansion

The duplication of courses within and among departments allows students to acquire easy credits. Few institutions will deny a student credit for two similar or even identical courses because such a denial is an admission of duplication. If beginning statistics is offered in several different departments, the departments may try to conceal the fact, especially if the institution does not permit duplication. Also, many departments hesitate to accept offerings of other departments as substitutes for their own.

Salaries, instructional load, and class size can be related by the formula

$$S = \frac{B}{T} = \frac{BCL}{KN}$$

where S = average salary,
   B = total instructional salary budget,
   C = average class size,
   L = average number of classes per instructor,
   T = number of instructors,
   N = total number of students,
   K = number of classes per student.

Assuming that B (the total salary budget), N (the total number of students) and K (the number of classes per student) are fixed, it is apparent that a decrease in average class size must be balanced by an increase in faculty load or by a decrease in salary. Since increasing the number of courses almost always decreases the average section size, the implications are clear. Either costs or loads go up, or salaries go down as courses proliferate. Furthermore, small course enrollments prohibit large group instruction and the use of specially prepared videotapes, programed materials, and other expensive instructional approaches which require extensive use to be economical.

Initially, a faculty member may propose to teach a course in which he is particularly interested as an extra instructional load. However, the real issue is not whether the professor should be paid, but whether the course should be offered. If the course is worthwhile, then it should be given under the usual load pattern. The institution should not take advantage of the individual or let the individual take advantage of himself. In any case, within a few years the professor will resent his overload, and the institution will have to assume the cost of a course it has never evaluated.

Many new courses are offered for only one or two credits. Thus, students may take anywhere from five to eight courses and have no time for concentrated activity in any of them. A profusion of small credit courses allows a faculty member to develop his own particular specialty into a course. It is no accident, but a matter of clear self-interest which causes faculty members dependent upon elective audiences to decry large credit courses, despite their obvious educational benefits for students.

When the number of courses becomes large, conflicts develop in scheduling, and the result is inflexibility in institutional curricular patterns and student programs. Fewer and larger courses with multiple sections ease this situation and increase the possibility of developing meaningful relationships. Proliferation of courses also disrupts sequential organization. This is especially true in the social sciences and the humanities. To encourage elective enrollments and to ease scheduling conflicts, successive terms of a three-term sequence in Russian history or English literature are often offered independently without requiring the preceding term. Thus, the instructor must teach a segment of history without relating it to what preceded or follows it. Courses become isolated experiences, and emphasize content rather than the development of intellectual abilities or scholarly skills. Thus, one result of course proliferation is a decline in standards of achievement.

The provision of opportunities for independent study is an increasing concern in higher education. Few institutions can offer every course a faculty member would like to teach and also provide opportunity for independent study. Faculty members who are already teaching courses in all their specialized interests may have neither the time nor the desire to direct independent study. Many courses which appeal to a limited number of students might be offered as independent study experiences. Most institutions could decrease the number of courses, reduce the faculty load, and thus gain time for independent study.

CURRICULUM AND COURSE REVIEW

Without continuing review and control, university courses increase without apparent rationale. A recent examination of offerings at one university revealed that some courses added seven years ago had never been taught, that courses which had not been offered for five years were still in the catalog, and that the departments concerned had no one qualified to teach the courses. Yet faculty members refused to discard them until they were forced to do so. Although colleges and departments argue that control of course offerings and curricula is their province, it is clear that, without administrative supervision or pressure, departments seldom drop courses. Departmental bias or ineptitude occasionally hinders even the addition of new courses which are badly needed as a result of discoveries and changing emphases in the discipline. Departmental domination and course proliferation interfere with sequence and integration to such an extent that the development of certain principles to review and control course offerings is essential.

Departments and individuals often add courses or propose programs for which institutional resources are inadequate. The institution may not possess the necessary instructional, library, or laboratory facilities. Permission is sought to add the new course or program, and the required resources are demanded afterward. This procedure allows a decision to be made without full awareness of its implications. Moreover, the department may actually offer the course without taking the necessary corrective steps.

Most courses and new curricula are added without sufficient information and evaluation. Frequently the information provided obscures the relation of the course to existing courses or is so vague that the instructor can do anything he wants. Objectives are rarely defined, no selection of content and materials is made, and no text or bibliography is provided. Departments and colleges demand approval of additional courses and curricula as an act of faith, and unfortunately, usually succeed.

As an institution expands, the departmental structure limits the understanding of faculty members to offerings in their own department. This may not be detrimental at the graduate level but, at the undergraduate level, it encourages the student to concentrate on his major and to regard all other courses and requirements as nuisances or fillers. If the faculty is to maintain some concept of the total undergraduate experience, then it must be continually educated regarding course offerings, general curricular principles, and specific objectives in particular areas and courses.

The department or individual professor should not be the only or even the final authority on the content and mode of instruction in undergraduate courses. Any institution will have individuals outside of a department whose training, interests, and objectivity make them better equipped to determine what is appropriate in a given department than those whose vision is limited by departmental myopia. The original decision of the university to adopt a particular program was not made by the faculty, because there was no faculty. Likewise, the decision to abandon a particular offering will not be made by the faculty involved. These extreme cases demonstrate that individuals outside of the departments must be involved in major curricular decisions concerning departments. Every departmental decision or recommendation for course and curricular additions requires the allocation of total institutional resources. Departmental autonomy on curricular matters is unrealistic, yet it remains the major argument against central review and control of the curriculum.

Most colleges offer certain courses or curricula which reflect administrative or public pressure rather than faculty inclination. This suggests the necessity of cooperation between the administration and faculty on curricular decisions rather than complete control by either group.

Another argument against review and control of the curriculum is that too much time is lost between the presentation of a proposal for change and the effective date of that change. Departments and individuals usually want immediate authorization of new courses and curricula, while systematic review of proposals for curriculum change requires the collection of extensive data, the involvement of many persons, and a period of deliberation. However, delay is fully justified if the full implications of course and curricular additions are realized. Many hastily-adopted, regrettable additions would have faded quietly away in the several months required for study.

AN OUTLINE FOR COURSE REVIEW AND ANALYSIS

The introductory remarks emphasized the differences between a course and a curriculum. These differences are significant enough that one outline will not suffice for both purposes. However, experience suggests that the accompanying outline for course analysis includes most of the points involved in review and analysis of curricular innovations and modifications. The outline is based on four principles. First, the department or instructor must define the course coverage and the instructional patterns to be used, and must review the adequacy of available resources. Second, the proposed course must be compared with all related courses in the university, not only by those proposing the course, but also by those involved in related courses. Third, the clientele to be served by the course must be identified and the probable enrollments estimated. Finally, the financial implications of the change or addition must be analyzed. The outline demands collection of data and deliberation, and permits intelligent administrative and committee review.

Ideally, the institution should conduct a thorough review of all existing courses, and then insist that this analysis be applied to all future additions or proposals for change. Clearly, the principles which have determined this outline for course review are equally relevant to curricular review and analysis.

Comments on the Outline

The outline is divided into three sections.* The first section, entitled *Identifying and Descriptive Information*, is divided into two parts. The first part indicates information which should be included in the catalog course description. Some catalogs do not include a description of the hours and types of instruction in a course. Students who are planning their future program find it helpful to have some indication of the pattern of instruction. For example, 5(2-1-4) could be used to indicate a course offering five credits, of which there are two hours in lecture, one hour in recitation or discussion, and four hours in laboratory work. Catalog course descriptions should also indicate for what kind of students the course is designed.

The information in the second part of this section is too detailed to be included in a catalog course description. However, this information should be available to advisers or students on request. It constitutes a contract by which the department assures each student enrolling in the course that he will have an experience as indicated by the outline or syllabus. It also assures that a new course will not be just a random thought that the department might offer some previously ignored aspect of the discipline.

---

*For curriculum study and review, an additional section specifying the purposes of the program and providing justification both for its need and for adding it in this institution will be required.

The second section, entitled *Analytical Information*, requires detailed information on the type of instruction, class size, required number of staff, and scheduled hours per week. The breakdown of total credits into various types of learning experiences may carry the course-credit pattern to the point of becoming ridiculous. However, this breakdown does force a department to consider whether the number of hours required by the course is appropriate to the number of credits assigned to it. Science courses frequently require too much laboratory work for the number of credits received. In the social sciences, field work requirements are excessive. This information may also help institutions to assess total course costs by computing the cost of the different types of instruction.

This section also demands an estimate of special or additional resources and personnel required. The department is asked to submit in advance a statement of the inadequacies of existing resources and of the required additional resources. Information is also required on the relation of the course to other courses offered in the department or in other departments, both in terms of prerequisites and in terms of duplication of content. Finally, this section requests estimates on the size and source of enrollment in the course, and on the additional cost of the course.

The last section, entitled *Historical Information*, pertains only to existing courses currently under review. The enrollment in each offering, the sources of enrollment, the section size, the number and type of staff, and the cost per credit hour may already be recorded in institutions with offices of institutional research. In other cases, the information should not be difficult to obtain. Departments which carry a large service load should have a breakdown of the sources of their students. This information is particularly helpful when curriculum changes are being considered which will modify the number of hours or courses which a given group of students take in other departments. By increasing electives or requirements outside the field of specialization, the staff responsible for a particular curriculum can unload a good portion of their work on other departments without the knowledge or consent of the faculty members involved.

OUTLINE FOR COURSE ANALYSIS

1. Identifying and descriptive information
   1.1 Catalog course description including
      1.11 Departmental or generic title and number
      1.12 Descriptive title

      1.13 Prerequisites

      1.14 Terms offered

      1.15 Credits so presented as to identify hours and type of instruction provided (lecture, discussion, laboratory, independent study)

      1.16 Statement of objectives, content coverage, and students to whom directed

   1.2 Outline or syllabus including

      1.21 Detailed statement of objectives

      1.22 Text and other materials to be used

      1.23 Day-by-day or week-by-week indication of topics covered, types and amounts of work expected of students, standards to be met, and methods of evaluation to be used

      1.24 Bibliography

2. Analytical information

   2.1 Instructional model—credits, hours, and types of instruction

Type of Session	Preferred Class Size	Staff Required*	No. Hours per Week	No. of Credits
Lecture				
Recitation or discussion				
Laboratory				
Field work				
Independent study				

      *Indicate separately the numbers of senior staff (instructor or above), and junior staff (graduate assistants, assistant instructors) required.

   2.2 Special or additional resources and personnel required

    **2.21 Special facilities (classrooms, auditoriums, laboratories, etc.)

    **2.22 Library and other learning resources required (books, films, slides, prints, etc.). List with indication of whether the items are here available, can be ordered, or must be made.

      **New courses especially

     2.23 Special staff competencies required

        2.231 Number of persons now on staff qualified to teach course

2.232 New staff requirements and individual competencies needed (project for at least two years)

2.3 Relation to other courses
- 2.31 Offered by the department
  - 2.311 Course or courses replaced by this course
  - 2.312 Prerequisite courses
  - 2.313 Courses for which this course is a prerequisite
  - 2.314 Courses covering some of the same content
    - 2.3141 Safeguards against acquiring of duplicate credits by the student
- 2.32 Offered by other departments
  - 2.321 Courses in which enrollment may be reduced by the selection of this course
  - 2.322 Prerequisite courses
  - 2.323 Courses for which this course is a prerequisite
  - 2.324 Courses covering some of the same content
    - 2.3231 Extent and nature of relationships
    - 2.3232 Distinctive factors justifying existence of this course
    - 2.3233 Safeguards against acquiring of duplicate credit by the student
- 2.33 Offered by other colleges or universities
  - 2.331 In the immediate community
  - 2.332 In the state

2.4 Size and source of enrollment
- 2.41 Departmental majors (indicate whether required or elective, number involved)
  - 2.411 Sub-major within department
- 2.42 Majors in other departments, curricula, or colleges (indicate for each whether required or elective, number of students involved)
- **2.43 Anticipated enrollment in first and second year of offering

	First Year	Second Year
Summer		
Fall		
Winter		
Spring		

**New courses

2.5 Details of instructional planning

Objectives	Experiences Especially Related to Objective	Means of Evaluation of Student Achievement
1.		
2.		
3.		
4.		
5.		
6.		
7.		

**2.6 Estimated new funds required by addition of this course

Salaries
Supplies and services
Equipment
Remodeling
        **New courses

3. Historical information (for courses under review)

3.1 Enrollment during the previous two years
                        19—   19—

Summer
Fall
Winter
Spring

3.2 Sources of enrollment previous year

	Fr.	Soph.	Jr.	Sr.	M	G.P.	Ph.D.
Majors (departmental)							
Students from Department or College A							
Students from Department or College B etc.							

3.3 Section size for the past year

	Smallest Section	Mean	Largest Section
Lecture			
Recitation or discussion			
Laboratory			

3.4 Number (head count) of senior staff involved in past
year _____ FTE _____

Number (head count) of junior staff involved in past
year _____ FTE _____

3.5 Instructional salary cost per student credit hour _____

PROCEDURES FOR REVIEW AND ANALYSIS

This outline suggests the type of information which should be gathered and the way in which it should be organized. A number of questions arise as to who is responsible for gathering the data, what procedures are available for checking its accuracy, and what steps are involved in reaching a final decision about the proposed addition or change. The tendency to separate curricular matters from budgetary decisions allows administrators to assign this responsibility to curriculum committees. Curriculum committees, made up of busy and often biased members, are not usually rigorous in their review of curriculum change.

The procedure can be improved in several ways. Faculty members are greatly affected by curriculum decisions, and such decisions should not be made by administrators who are unfamiliar with the circumstances which generated the request. The faculty curriculum committee has its purpose and its place. However, the members of such a committee should be objective and committed to the welfare of the university as a whole. When recommendations which concern an individual committee member or his department are considered, he should not participate in the discussion. If continuing major curriculum decisions are required, committee members should be given some reduction in their teaching load to provide time for extensive discussion and for detailed study of the proposed changes. The curriculum committee should have the services of an individual or of an office of institutional research to provide historical data on courses and to accumulate and check current data on each proposed change. The committee should take as much time and demand as much information as it needs, and should be ruthless in denying proposals which are not in accord with its own policies or those of the university faculty. It should operate within a framework of clearly-defined principles or policies, rather than consider each individual proposal in isolation. Such policies may include: (1) limitations on small classes and automatic discontinuance of courses which fail to meet enrollment requirements; (2) restriction of study of a particular discipline to a single department; (3) limitations on duplication or overlapping content materials; (4) reasonable relationships between time and credit requirements; (5) limitations on over-all departmental, college, and university offerings in relation to the number of students served. In short, the suggested outline implies certain rules and principles upon which the curriculum committee can base its decisions.

This rigorous approach is very likely to reduce the number of proposals for change. If an individual or department must provide such detailed information, it may be decided that the proposal is neither important nor justified. Moreover, department chairmen and deans, who commonly screen such requests, are likely to be more careful in their examination when they realize that approval is not automatic. No one likes to be a party to a proposal which is denied. On major curriculum decisions, the vice president for academic affairs or the president should have a veto privilege based on budgetary restrictions. The faculty may not like the administrative decision, but each member must recognize that the decision represents a choice between his pet course and his salary. Over-expansion results in mediocrity and, if faculty members recognize that they obtain their courses at the expense of excellence, they may limit their requests. Decisions do have implications; curriculum review and control are essential to insure that those implications will be anticipated and beneficial.

REFERENCES

1. William T. Foster, *Administration of the College Curriculum*, Houghton Mifflin Company, Boston, 1911.
2. John W. Gould, *The Academic Deanship*, Bureau of Publications, Teachers College, Columbia University, 1964.
3. Thad L. Hungate, *Management in Higher Education*, Bureau of Publications, Teachers College, Columbia University, 1964.
4. Thad L. Hungate and Earl J. McGrath, *A New Trimester Three-Year Degree Program*, Bureau of Publications, Teachers College, Columbia University, 1963.
5. Earl J. McGrath, "The College Curriculum—An Academic Wasteland?" *Liberal Education*, Vol. XLIX, No. 11, May, 1963, pp. 235–246.
6. _____, *Memo to a College Faculty Member*, Bureau of Publications, Teachers College, Columbia University, 1961.
7. _____, ed., *Cooperative Long-Range Planning in Liberal Arts Colleges*, Bureau of Publications, Teachers College, Columbia University, 1964.
8. Francis Rourke and Glenn Brooks, *The Managerial Revolution in Higher Education*, Johns Hopkins Press, Baltimore, 1966.

9. Beardsley Ruml and Donald H. Morrison, *Memo to a College Trustee*, A Report on Financial and Structural Problems of the Liberal Arts College, McGraw-Hill Book Company, Inc., New York, 1959.

10. Harold W. Stoke, "The Flowering Curricula of American Higher Education," in *Annals of the American Academy of Political and Social Sciences*, September, 1955, pp. 58–64.

11

Competencies and Their Attainment

The four continuums, the five essential elements, the list of facilitating agents provide a structure for curriculum consideration but, since this structure is process-oriented, its application requires a commitment to anticipated results of the educational program. Otherwise, the program will lack clear objectives and will be dominated by personal preference or tradition. For example, an interim term experience might permit experiences relevant to any of the continuums and any of the five essential elements. A statement of objectives could help to determine the desirability and use of an interim term, but statements of objectives rarely provide clear direction. In this volume, the end results of education have been defined as competencies to be acquired by students. Although these competencies are objectives, to define them as student competencies clarifies their operational role. A precise statement of what the student must be able to do clearly indicates what experiences are necessary to provide practice in it. The remainder of this chapter will specify seven competencies and suggest essential related experiences. Both the competencies and the experiences are closely related to the continuums and essential elements. The role of certain facilitating agents will also be clarified, although any program oriented to the development of the individual must allow flexibility in the selection and utilization of these agents.

Seven Competencies

A philosophical commitment is implicit in any statement of competencies, but it is often very difficult to make the implicit explicit. A justification for starting with competencies is precisely that this point of departure avoids philosophical disagreements which impede progress. A faculty may or may not accept each of the seven competencies. The number in itself is not important, but seven is probably the maximum number toward which an entire staff and student body can work. The definition of each competency is followed by a brief discussion of its significance.

1. *The recipient of the baccalaureate degree should be qualified for some type of work. He should be aware of what it is and he should have confidence in his ability to perform adequately.*

One recurring complaint of students and prospective employers is that a liberal education does not prepare the student to work or to make a specific contribution to society. A college education should prepare a student for his future. Students should set definite vocational and life goals, and plan their education in relation to them. Upon graduation the student should have some salable skills and knowledge and have confidence that his college education has adequately prepared him either to continue in these or to move in other directions. Even if the student is going immediately to graduate school, his undergraduate program should provide competencies suitable to one or more occupations should it become necessary for him to work. The student need not define a specific job, but he should interpret the significance of his study in terms of competencies useful in several occupations.

2. *The student should know how to acquire knowledge and how to use it.*

This competency is consistent with the current emphasis on understanding the nature of inquiry and on developing the ability to engage in inquiry. Although the student should acquire some knowledge during his college training, he also should acquire the abilities, motivations, and insights to enable him to expand and apply his knowledge. He must be able not only to master new concepts and new patterns of thought, but also to inquire into and utilize new modes of inquiry.

3. *The student should have a high level of mastery of the skills of communication.*

The ability to read, listen, and acquire additional information and skills is a corollary of the second competency. The student should be able to express his thoughts orally or in writing so that he may better organize and assimilate them and so that they may be understood, judged, and utilized by others. Although the student will display the greatest versatility in the use of communication skills in those areas of concentration in his college study, he should be able to communicate intelligently on any problem that arises in his role as worker, citizen, and parent.

4. *The student should be aware of his own values and value commitments and he should be aware that other individuals and cultures hold contrasting values which must be understood and, to some extent, accepted in interaction with them.*

This competency may be revealed in several ways. In his conversation and in his analysis of issues, the student will demonstrate his awareness of the values and conflicts of our democratic society. He will recognize value differences among individuals, nations, and cultures, and will accept that these value differences cannot always be resolved in his favor. He should recognize that values underlie every action, and should support his own convictions through advocacy and action.

5. *The graduate should be able to cooperate and collaborate with others in study, analysis, and formulation of solutions to problems, and in action on them.*

In research and instruction within the college or university, in the involvement of citizens in community, state, national, and international affairs, and in the activities of individuals in business, industry, government, or the home, the consideration and solution of problems require close collaboration among individuals and extensive cooperation in larger groups. The college experience should train a person to operate effectively as both a participant and a leader.

6. *The college graduate should have an awareness, concern, and sense of responsibility for contemporary events, issues, and problems.*

Today, few colleges and universities are "ivory tower." Administrators and faculty members are usually involved in community, state, and national affairs. They serve as consultants to government, business, and industry, as well as teach and do research on the campus. Much of this activity, however, is not evident in the classroom, and the student's college experience concentrates on acquiring of additional knowledge without relating it to current events. Many students are disturbed by this lack of relevancy and feel that education should generate concern and obligation for constructive action. Moreover, the student who is encouraged for four years to ignore what is going on in the world and to refrain from involvement in it may continue to do so. Those students who are aware of issues and problems off and on campus are often regarded as activists, dissidents, or troublemakers by other students, as well as by the faculty and the administration. A college education should make a difference in individuals, and one essential difference is the increased ability to understand, accept responsibility for, and take action on contemporary problems. Civic responsibility is an important goal of college education and must be incorporated into the college experience.

7. *The college graduate should see his total college experience as coherent, cumulative, and unified by the development of broad competencies and by the realization that these competencies are relevant to his further development as an individual and to the fulfillment of his obligations as a responsible citizen in a democratic society.*

The student's college program should be structured in relation to these seven competencies, and he should continually try to relate his experiences to these competencies. Living and learning must be related within the college experience if continuing learning is to be a part of the student's life after college. The student's passive fulfillment of rules and requirements to attain a degree must be replaced by his active involvement in planning a cumulative experience climaxed by tangible evidence of accomplishment. These competencies can determine the type and pattern of experiences to be provided in college. Before examining these, however, a brief review of the continuums, the essential elements, and the facilitating agents mentioned in Chapter 2 may be helpful.

Continuums, Essential Elements, and Facilitating Agents

Figure 1 in Chapter 2 suggested four continuums: (1) the individual student—the disciplines; (2) problems, policies, and actions—abstractions, ideas, and theories; (3) flexibility and autonomy—rigidity and conformity; (4) integration, coherence, and unity—compartmentalization, inconsistency, and discord. Five essential elements were indicated: (1) liberal and vocational education; (2) breadth and depth; (3) continuity and sequence; (4) a concept of learning and teaching; (5) continuing planning and evaluation. Following this, ten facilitating agents were presented. These may be briefly defined as (1) requirements; (2) organization of learning and teaching; (3) noncourse experiences; (4) schedules; (5) calendars; (6) evaluation; (7) student load and faculty load; (8) selection, orientation, and advising of students; (9) selection, orientation, and evaluation of faculty; (10) administrative organization. As suggested earlier, these continuums pose real alternatives in the selection of experiences. The essential elements are not diametrically opposed but rather must be interwoven or balanced in a curriculum. Finally, the facilitating agents are specific experiences which should be selected and planned to provide the emphasis desired in relation to the four continuums and the five essential elements.

The seven competencies affect the position of a program on the four continuums. The ability to engage in productive activity, the mastery of techniques for acquiring and utilizing knowledge, the competency in communication skills, the awareness of values, the ability to cooperate with others, the concern with contemporary events, issues and problems, and the demand for a cumulative, coherent, and unified college experience suggest the importance of educational experiences which (a) relate to the development of the individual, (b) provide experience with practical problems, (c) provide for and encourage flexibility in the individual, and (d) facilitate and encourage coherence and integration. These competencies do not deny the validity of the organization of knowledge in the disciplines and the importance of student contact with these categories of organized knowledge. They do not deny the significance of ideas and theories, for these help to understand and deal with practical problems and to relate discrete facts and events. These competencies require some structure in the program, and even some element of rigidity. The seven competencies themselves provide a structure and a degree of rigidity by insisting that *all* graduates demonstrate a certain level of achievement in them. The four continuums also imply a structure of the institution that insists that experiences range over these continuums and that a set of requirements be met by both the program and the students.

The seven competencies do not deny the necessity of meaningful compartmentalization. The four continuums set up dichotomies, but only to make meaningful distinctions in educational planning. The disciplines constitute significant compartments of knowledge. The competencies do not imply specific positions on any of the continuums, but they do require that educational experiences range over these continuums. Educational experiences should merge the extremes of the continuums rather than perpetuate and emphasize the differences. Thus, the particular interests and problems of an individual might be accommodated by experiences outside of the formal academic program or by flexibility and adaptations within the disciplinary-based course offerings.

In relation to the five essential elements, these competencies require a merging of vocational and liberal education. Their phrasing rejects the dichotomy between breadth and depth by demanding both breadth and depth in dealing with knowledge, in acquiring new knowledge, and in relating to people and to society.

Finally the competencies do not prescribe specific facilitating agents. All of the ten agents may be useful if they can be related to the competencies which are to be developed. It may be helpful, then, to examine how several different curricular models might be developed by application of these continuums, essentials, and facilitating agents.

Some Curriculum Models

Few innovative ventures have described a curriculum model in detail. The models which have been suggested tend to be heavily structured by requirements of specific courses and course sequences. A few have been structured by requirements of certain types of experiences or comprehensive examinations at various stages of progress. Flexible models structured in terms of the competencies to be developed are difficult to define but, by reference to the four continuums, the essential elements, and the facilitating agents, a number of distinctive models can be presented. The models should demonstrate that curriculum development requires the recognition of many factors which can be related in several different ways. Following the discussion of these rather unusual models, we shall suggest a broader, more flexible curriculum model.

Model No. 1—A "Dewy-Eyed" Program. This model starts with the following assumptions: (1) all learning is individual and problem-based; (2) knowledge is worthwhile only if it can be used to solve problems; (3) education is life and must be a multifaceted experience as similar to life as possible; (4) sequence and integration are individual problems and cannot be planned for groups. In such a program, courses, grades, and requirements are inappropriate. Disciplines, as organized but changing bodies of knowledge, are significant but a general requirement of an interdisciplinary core or of introductory courses in the disciplines would be inappropriate because it places too much restraint on the individual. Work experience, community service, participation in campus governance, and human interaction are as important as academic learning. Such a program selects educational experiences which place it well to the left of each of the four continuums. It emphasizes people, problems, flexibility, and integration. There is no distinction between vocational and liberal education; the primary concern is the development of the individual and self-realization. Breadth and depth are not significant, because the program assumes a high level of student motivation which will result in a depth experience over a wide range of knowledge and problems. Continuity, sequence, and integration are inevitable in such a program because the student has complete autonomy in planning his program, and the only requirement is that he have a plan and a rationale for it. Learning and methods of facilitating and evaluating it are central concerns.

Such a program avoids rules and regulations. Status differences among administrative officers, students, personnel officers, and faculty are also avoided. Students are expected to be responsible participants in the governance of the institution as well as in the planning of their own programs. Although the faculty may advise, students must make their own decisions. A program of this type must select its students carefully, for not all students can accept this much freedom and responsibility. Furthermore, students who are discontent with the policies and regulations of other institutions may be attracted to the program and strive to convert freedom into irresponsibility and license. The program must find faculty members who are more concerned with students than with research and who can supply the motivation and excitement of learning so essential to the program's success. The institution must remain small, for close contact and interaction between students and faculty is crucial.

Model No. 2—A "Saintly" Conception. This model is based on the following assumptions: (1) significant truth and value have been discovered by the great minds of bygone ages; (2) education consists of bringing students into contact with these ideas; (3) development of the mind through dialectic and mastery of the existing integrations of scholars constitutes the goal of education; (4) education is for an intellectual elite. In such a program, the curriculum consists of a limited number of courses required of all students. Departmental organization and the associated sequences of courses in the several disciplines are inconsistent with this approach. The program is oriented toward the individual rather than toward the discipline; each student, by means of discussion groups, seminars, and individual conferences, must master the ideas around which the program revolves. The program focuses on the past and rarely considers current problems. Such a program focuses on ideas rather than on problems, and is likely to be rigid in its requirements, even though it concentrates on the individual. Integration rather than compartmentalization is characteristic of the model, but the integration is predetermined and is assimilated rather than developed by the student. This model has some elements in common with the first model, but it concentrates much more on content and intellect. Students and faculty must be carefully selected because of the uniqueness of the model. Interaction between students and faculty outside the formal program is not considered an essential phase of the educational program. The program offers a liberal education in the classical sense, and preparation for a vocation or confrontation with current problems is avoided on two grounds: (1) that these would confuse and dilute the essential quality of the program, and (2) that a classical education prepares the student to deal with many tasks rather than a few specific ones. The importance of the formal program and the distrust of practical and vocational education make off-campus experiences irrelevant and inappropriate. Evaluation emphasizes fluency in dealing with ideas. Students develop a high level of verbal competency, are familiar with great ideas and with the classics, but are aloof from the current scene and may be impractical in their analysis and approach to it.

Model No. 3—A "Pedantic" Pattern.   This model assumes that: (1) the major disciplines represent the best effort of man to date to organize knowledge and to systematize the task of seeking new knowledge; (2) since no one can master all knowledge, one or two disciplines should be chosen for intensive study, with appropriate attention to related or supporting fields which may be useful in mastering the chosen ones; (3) in deference to the liberal arts tradition, some contact with most or all of the broad groupings of disciplines should be required, but real understanding of other disciplines can occur only when a single discipline is pursued to the point where it impinges upon others; (4) only after a discipline has been mastered should one consider the practical implications of that discipline or explore its individual and personal implications; (5) since professors are the masters of the disciplines, they are best equipped to determine the college curriculum.

Model 3, unlike Models 1 and 2, has widespread support among college and university faculties. In such a program, the major is the most significant educational experience. Courses outside the major are chosen because they contribute to the major, although grudging consent may be given to a general distribution requirement or to a few electives. The discipline determines whether work experience, service, or participation in noncourse experiences are desirable. Generally, the social sciences are more receptive to such experiences than the natural sciences or the humanities. Concern for the individual, for problem analysis, and for practical experience is not as important as the mastery of an organized body of knowledge. Coherence, unity, and integration are achieved within the discipline, and any broader concept is regarded either as the student's responsibility or as impossible in view of the obvious compartmentalization of knowledge. In such a pattern, the liberal-vocational consideration is insignificant. The program is oriented toward graduate school and a professional career in the discipline, which is often interpreted as liberal education even though it is highly specialized and vocational. Likewise, breadth and depth are not important. The force of the liberal arts tradition elicits verbal assent to the concept of breadth, but there is no real commitment to it. Concern with learning and teaching is apt to be negated by the concept of the discipline as an organized body of knowledge which the student is to assimilate through contact with its masters. The function of the professor is to disseminate knowledge; the function of the student is to absorb it. Evaluation within this model focuses on cognitive outcomes, and usually employs course examinations. Courses are the preferred mode of educational experience, and professors generally encourage the student to remain in continuing course sequences rather than to disrupt his program with off-campus experiences. Atypical schedules and calendars have no merit in this kind of program which is best served by a pattern which divides the year into two or three equal units, each of which provides the same number of class sessions so that no adjustment need be made for courses offered in different terms. However, atypical calendars may be introduced in such a model to accommodate an entirely different pattern of learning.

Model No. 4—A Narrowly Vocational Model. This model assumes that (1) vocational education should focus on the development of knowledge and skills necessary for specific tasks or to solve specific problems; (2) any vocational area includes a number of subspecialties, so that the vocational program should encourage students to achieve some core experience as well as a high level of vocational competency in one subfield; (3) the various disciplines of the arts and sciences are relevant only if they provide knowledge and skills which are required in performing vocational responsibilities. Such a program develops a curriculum by selecting groups or sequences of courses which correspond to the several specialties within the vocational field and by defining some common core experience for all. Specific courses are chosen from the arts and science disciplines to provide knowledge and skills which are essential to or supplement the vocational field. Compartmentalization is accepted both in the disciplines and in the subspecialties within the immediate vocational field. Vocations are distinct and clearly defined, and the student is encouraged to choose a specific vocation as early as possible. Such programs emphasize skills, tasks, and problems, and frequently neglect broad ideas and principles which might be useful in dealing with an array of problems. The individual is prepared for specific tasks which may not exist by the time he actually enters the field. Such programs may appear to be flexible because of their range of choice within the vocational field, but the student's choice is often quite limited by requirements and advising practices. Such a program encourages the integration of knowledge relevant to the specific vocation, but forces the student to regard his education from a very restricted point of view. Thus, the student in home economics who is required to take work in chemistry may see relatively little direct application to her vocational field. In these circumstances, the vocational field compartmentalizes and isolates knowledge.

Each of these four models has weaknesses which result from its extreme positions on the continuums. The dewy-eyed model fails to give adequate attention to the disciplines. In its emphasis on problems, on flexibility enforced by a lack of rules, and on integration of all aspects of life into a unified experience, the program seems poorly adapted to the realities of life in the late twentieth century.

The saintly conception also fails to prepare students in the disciplines, especially in mathematics and the sciences. Science and mathematics are taught only from an historical and philosophical point of view and thus become part of a concentration in the humanities. A required, inflexible program, an imposed integration, and an orientation to the past make this model, like the first, inappropriate for contemporary undergraduate education.

The third model, the pedantic pattern, approximates existing programs in the arts and sciences in many institutions. This model is not receptive to vocational and professional education, and assigns an inferior status to it. This distinction eliminates the possibility of a general resolution of the problems of undergraduate education, and the isolation of vocational programs encourages their tendencies toward overspecialization and emphasis on skills. This third model is appropriate only if undergraduate specialization and preparation for graduate study are the primary goals of education. It is not appropriate if a college education is to develop a broader set of competencies such as the seven presented earlier in this chapter.

The fourth model, a narrowly vocational model, is determined in part by the third model. It is unsatisfactory in relation to both the seven competencies and vocational preparation. Such a program fails to stress methods of acquiring knowledge, values and value commitments, and an awareness of and concern for current events. Qualification for a job tends to outweigh all other competencies. This narrow emphasis leads to preoccupation with skills and details, and fails to provide the broader knowledge and competency required for adaptability and advancement.

The inadequacies of these four models suggest that any program based on continuum extremes will be unbalanced and will fail to develop certain competencies. Faculties may argue that certain of these competencies are not legitimate concerns of higher education. In this case, the issue is one of educational philosophy, a difference of opinion about the ends of education. Faculties also may accept all these competencies but insist that their model best develops them. Here the disagreement is with means. These two issues become one when the relevance of means to ends is established. In the four models discussed, the means do not embrace all of the seven competencies. No competency is likely to be fostered to any significant degree without overt attention being given to it. Even if the competency should appear in some or all students, this does not guarantee that it is the result of the educational program. This contention implies an obligation to propose a program of experiences which will help students to attain these seven competencies.

Experiential Elements Essential to a Balanced Undergraduate Program

The nature of each of the seven competencies suggests relevant educational experiences but their specific nature must be indicated. Twelve different, although not independent, experiences will contribute to the attainment of these competencies. Each experience is listed here with some remarks on its significance and relevance.

1. *The student should have sustained contact with at least two different disciplines or areas of study.*

The phrase, "sustained contact," is used rather than major because an interdisciplinary or problem-oriented concentration can be as demanding as the usual departmental major. Sustained contact should be distinguished from supportive study of a discipline. Limited work in a number of related disciplines is often necessary for full understanding of any discipline. Any extended study of the physical sciences or certain of the social sciences requires work in mathematics. In this case, mathematics is supportive or contributory unless the study is expanded into sustained contact. Allowing for such supportive work, sustained contact with two disciplines would seem sufficiently demanding, although certain combinations might justify a third. A student interested in Russian studies might maintain sustained contact throughout his four years with the history, literature, and language of Russia.

Sustained contact attempts to replace the superficiality of the breadth requirement and the narrowness of the departmental major with a composite experience in two or more disciplines which contributes to a central theme or concern.

This requirement encourages the student to define a pervasive theme which justifies his choice. He must plan his own program rather than select from ready-made departmental majors. The adviser or tutor must concentrate on the student's individual interests and concerns rather than on the department's disciplinary demands and convenience. Finally, it forces both student and adviser to relate the disciplines to each other and to some central theme or problem.

The two or three disciplines of sustained contact should represent different divisions of knowledge, but this may not always be possible. Disciplines such as history (which combines the humanities and social sciences) and psychology (which is both a science and a social science) lend themselves to such inter-divisional combinations. Mathematics or statistics are related to almost every other discipline. History or philosophy can apply to science or mathematics. Such combinations encourage breadth, and discourage overspecialization at the undergraduate level.

2. *The student should have an opportunity to explore the historical, philosophical, and cultural backgrounds and implications of the disciplines studied.*

Courses in these areas might be offered in the history, philosophy, sociology, or anthropology departments, if the departmental professors are sufficiently competent in other disciplines to develop the courses in a meaningful way. However, especially in the sciences, these elements would probably be best developed by scientists who are familiar with the history of philosophy of their field or by scientists in collaboration with professors from the social science or humanities departments. Students whose concentrations are in the humanities or social sciences will also benefit from study of the ways in which scientific methodology or technology contributes to these disciplines.

These experiences will add an element of breadth to the student's program. They will allow the student to recognize the inherent relationships among the humanities, the social sciences, and the sciences. These experiences will also provide deeper insight into the nature and methods of inquiry of the individual disciplines.

3. *The student should confront several current problems to which the disciplines he is studying have direct relevance.*

Such an experience might be provided in courses but, since problems tend to be interdisciplinary, probably a seminar or special interterm program which includes a heterogeneous group of students and faculty would be required. If the problems have scientific, social, and political implications, they might help the student both to explore the relations of the disciplines and to understand the interdisciplinary approach to the study of problems. From this one experience, the student might obtain a practical, problem-solving experience, collaborate in team investigation, and derive insight into contemporary events, issues, or problems. He will utilize the knowledge and methodological skills gained from his study of the disciplines and, through communicating with others, he will demonstrate and consolidate his mastery of that knowledge and skill.

4. *The student should confront a distinctively different culture and value system.*

Study or travel, such as the year abroad, or work or service in an underdeveloped country or with a deprived group in our own country might effect such a confrontation. It might also be accomplished to some extent through literature and contact with foreign students. Such an experience should span the four years rather than be limited to one particular semester or year. It should also be related to work in the student's major disciplines. For example, a science student who has his cultural confrontation with a Spanish speaking group might comment on some science textbooks used in Mexico, Spain, or South America. He might also read current Spanish newspaper or periodical articles on scientific developments. Ideally, the program would be organized so that the student develops competency in the language, works with people who speak the language, studies or travels in a country where the language is utilized, and then on his return continues to use the language in his particular areas of concentration. If this extended use of the language cannot be arranged, it may be wiser to concentrate on reading knowledge and appropriate related experiences or to discard the language requirement in favor of an experience with a deprived English-speaking group. For some students, the college experience itself is a confrontation with a new culture and a new set of values.

5. *The student should be introduced early to independent study and continue this in increasing scope throughout his four years.*

In the junior and senior years, the student's independent study work should culminate in two experiences: (1) a study in depth in one or both of the disciplines with which he maintains sustained contact, *and* (2) a study of a problem which involves all of his prior study and additional reading in fields not studied. The former would be an experience in depth. The latter, an experience in breadth and in depth. Independent study can be related to experience with current problems or with a different culture, as well as to sustained contact with specific disciplines.

6. *The student should have a practical experience which has a significant relationship to the disciplines which he has chosen to emphasize.*

For some students, this practical experience might require one or several regular semesters. Others might have a series of summer work experiences. The experience might be on the campus and involve working with a professor on a research project, preparing instructional materials, tutoring individuals, or teaching a freshman course. In any case, that student should achieve a true work experience and should not see himself as a full-time student picking up pin money by part-time employment.

For some, this experience may have direct vocational implications, such as service in a social work agency or a community program, or a job in business or industry. For those in teaching or in medical technology, the intern experience would meet this requirement. This practical experience would allow the student to apply his knowledge, help him to effect the transition from college to the world of work, develop his awareness of contemporary problems, issues, and events, and provide some experience in adjusting to and working with people who are not members of an academic community. This experience, too, should teach the student the practical value of the disciplines studied.

7. *The student should have team experiences in learning and problem-solving.*

Much current research requires the cooperation of people with various talents and knowledge. The solution of community problems brings together people with diverse interests and talents. Most problems are so complex that no one person has the time or the capacity to explore all the relevant factors and possible solutions. By working with a team, possibly under the guidance of a faculty member, the student can examine his own methods of problem-solving and approaches to learning, and can compare and contrast these with others. He learns not only how to work with others in analyzing and solving a problem but also how to improve his own learning procedures and problem-solving competencies.

This experience should occur at various levels, and might be combined with several of the other experiences. For example, the third experience (confrontation in depth with several current problems) could readily involve a team approach. Confrontation with a different culture, independent study, or practical work could also involve a team approach. If these experiences are closely related, they will reinforce one another and unify the student's total college program.

8. *The student should have the experience of living and working in a community of educated people, an experience which provides a model for the kind of living pattern which we hope to encourage by higher education.*

A community of scholars involves more than respect for knowledge and pursuit of knowledge. It involves living with a group of people who share common experiences, concerns, and goals. It includes experience in self-government, in resolving the problems of daily living, and in developing policies and regulations which encourage scholarly pursuits. Thus, students should be members of a small community for an extended period of time so that discussions of policies and problems have real significance for the future. There should be no imposed compartmentalization of responsibility, such as the distinction between student personnel, residence hall management, and academic programs. Community living will not provide the experience and responsibility desired if the compartments are predetermined and the policies imposed by external authorities. The student himself should solve the problems of developing a congenial environment appropriate to an institution of learning.

9. *The student should have continuing experiences in studying and discussing current events.*

This should be done in all courses, including the natural sciences. An alert instructor can often refer to current developments and demonstrate his own awareness of the current scene, while encouraging his students to do likewise. He will also encourage interest in his discipline by demonstrating its relevancy to life. Students can be asked to read and report on current articles after interest is aroused. The role of science in our culture or the implications of natural science policies are issues which will increase student interest at the expense of only a slight sacrifice of content coverage. Students should follow current developments, examine the implications of these developments for their field of study, and consider what solutions to current problems their field of study offers. Foreign language may be used to include in the study of current events the points of view of other nations and cultures. This area of experience is closely related to the confrontation in depth with current problems, and it can be related to several other areas of experience.

10. *The student should have continuing experiences in organizing and presenting ideas in speech and in writing.*

The attempt to express one's own point of view in speech or in writing is one of the best learning experiences possible. It is easy to mistake casual familiarity with words and phrases for real mastery. Until the student tries to work out his ideas succinctly and clearly in order to convey them to others, his inaccurate knowledge, incoherent expression, and fuzzy thinking will not become fully apparent. Collaborative experiences with other students, independent study reports, and conferences with faculty members provide situations where clear and precise communication can be required and fostered.

11. *The student should have a continuing relationship with one or more faculty members who know him well and are interested in his long-term development as a person.*

This faculty member might help the student to structure his program of studies in relation to goals which they, together, will continually define and refine. The possibility of relating these experiences sequentially and cumulatively to the desired competencies will depend, to some degree, on the student but, to a greater degree, on the faculty member's familiarity with the student's needs and problems. This individuality of planning is essential, for any attempt to structure all of the experiences in such detail as to provide unity and integration for all individuals would almost certainly substitute rigidity and compartmentalization for flexibility and unity.

12. *The individual should have containuing experience with a broad evaluation program which is future-oriented and provides detailed information about his progress toward the desired competencies.*

This evaluation program should include some culminating experience in which the student is asked to demonstrate his competency. This experience must be so clearly related to prior experiences that the student cannot doubt the relevance of or appropriateness of the final evaluation. The adviser or tutor should contribute to both the continuing and the culminating evaluation.

SUMMARY

This list of essential experiences clearly relates to the seven competencies and involves the four continuums. If independent study and study of problems which involve values relate the discipline to the student's own goals and future plans, the student will view experience with the discipline as part of his total development. A combination of problems, practical experiences, theories, and ideas will enhance the college experience and ease the transition from college to the world of work. The statement of competencies and the statement of experiences or elements underlying continuums provide a structure within which flexible planning can be done by the individual. While adherence to this framework would require changes in the attitudes and practices of many faculty members and departments, the framework provides a great deal of freedom for the faculty in planning their courses and educational activities. The program of essential experiences recognizes the existence of categories of experience and of knowledge, but it provides for a number of experiences, which relate, combine, and unify these categories.

The competencies and the experiences are both liberal and vocational in nature. Although the prejudices of faculty members or students could force the program to become predominantly liberal or vocational, the intent of the program is to give education a broad interpretation which includes cognitive, affective, and psychophysical outcomes, and to provide the student with both broad and specific competencies which will enable him to live a satisfying life and to earn a living. The traditional applications of breadth in terms of acquaintance with all branches of knowledge, distribution requirements, and core programs are discarded in favor of a concept of breadth which requires significant contact with more than one discipline, with a different culture, with current problems, and with methods of communication and cooperation. Continuity and sequence are implied rather than specified, and the student, with the help of a tutor or adviser, must plan within this framework of required experiences a sequence which at each point utilizes his highest attained competencies and promises to move him toward further achievement.

Within the framework of these experiences, faculty members would have to give more attention to planning their activities in relation to student learning. The emphasis on group or team experience and on independent study would make the student aware of his own learning and help him recognize the value of his experiences in relation to his own goals. The evaluation program would help the student assess his own progress and enable him finally to set his own standards of performance and evaluate his progress toward them. Within such a framework, the number of specific requirements would be very limited. Students *would not* be permitted to take all of their work in a single discipline. They *would not* be required to take a third or more of their work in a large number of disciplines to satisfy breadth requirements. They *would* be required to take a variety of learning experiences, such as seminars, independent study, and team experiences. These requirements would not be arbitrary, but would be closely related to the development of certain essential competencies. The flexibility might be great enough to excuse a mathematical or scientific genius from certain of these experiences so that he could emphasize others. Such a decision, however, should be made only after considerable discussion by the student and the adviser and review by an individual who is responsible for maintaining the broad approach to undergraduate education.

An annual calendar and a schedule which permit flexibility in individual programs would be appropriate, although there is nothing within the framework of the essential experiences which could not be accommodated in traditional calendars and schedules. The program clearly indicates what kind of faculty members are required. Most faculty members would have to be committed to students, interested in the relation of their discipline to other disciplines, and willing to work with students in problem-solving and team-learning enterprises. Students, also, would have to be selected with care. Students who want to specialize in a single area, who demand a high degree of vocational specialization, or who are able to work only under a specific set of requirements would be unlikely to select such a program, but many other students might find new meaning in a college education planned along these lines. Administrative organizations which compartmentalize various aspects of student education and welfare are hardly appropriate to this pattern. College and departmental units which exist primarily to foster the disciplines and insure the welfare of the faculty would have to be supplemented or modified to provide more direct focus on student experience and on methods to achieve the specified competencies. The residence hall college pattern developed in recent years in a number of universities seems particularly appropriate, but not essential, to this model. Any organization which permits the primary concern of the institution to be centered on the development of the individual will allow this model to flourish.

12

Retrospect and Prospect

This volume has stressed the importance of unity, coherence, and integration in any curriculum. Thus, this chapter attempts to organize, summarize, and integrate the major ideas which have been examined and discussed in the work. This particular integration may be unacceptable to many people. The challenge to them is obvious—develop another and more satisfactory one. However, they must remember that each student is an individual whose self-reliance, acceptance of responsibility, and competency to carry on and evaluate his own educational efforts are the fundamental concerns of undergraduate education. Each student must achieve unity, coherence, and integration on his own terms, but he must be aware that others have made this effort and have provided useful models for him. No educational program should attempt to mold students in the faculty's image; rather, the program must assist each student to the fullest realization of himself and his role in a democratic society.

Chapter 1 discussed the many integrating and disintegrating forces which affect the curriculum. Our culture values education and demands a great deal from higher education. Higher eduation too often responds to these demands by haphazard proliferation of courses and expansion of facilities. Although administrators and faculty complain that they are not given adequate resources to perform their tasks, a tour of college and university campuses forces even educators to doubt the validity of such complaints. Most institutions are building new facilities and offering new programs. Administrators report that both faculty and students are increasing in number and in quality. These are the "mores" of higher education. Perhaps higher education is asked to do too much with too little, but there is no attempt to force institutions to limit themselves to those things they can do well and for which they are adequately supported. Expediency, opportunism, and competition, rather than educational statesmanship, determine institutional programs. Our society is in flux, and higher education should respond to changing needs and should try to influence the course of future events. Undergraduate education is a central phase of that responsibility and the resources devoted to it must not be continually depleted to provide support for new ventures. Every new program or service should be scrutinized for its appropriateness both to higher education and to the particular institution. Unless these additions are essential and additional resources are available for their support, the only wise action is a polite but firm denial. However, as a result of institutional competition, this response is seldom heard.

The major obstacles to the improvement of undergraduate education exist within the institutions themselves and are a result of the over-compartmentalization of functions and responsibility. Many universities are fragmented into relatively independent colleges. The inability of such units to deal with instructional and curricular problems on an institutional basis is indicated by the statement of the president of a large private university. When asked how frequently the deans of the colleges met with him, he replied that he could not recall the last time they had all been together. Colleges, in turn, are divided into departments, each of which concentrates on developing its own discipline and increasing the stature of the department. Too many departments, even in the smallest colleges, feel that graduate study is the only meaningful goal for undergraduate specialization in a discipline. In their preoccupation with course proliferation, research, and professionally related travel and consultation, the faculty, department chairmen, and academic deans tend to neglect the student. The dean makes sure that the student has met the university requirements, and the department checks for major requirements. These isolated units, which often contradict one another, present severe difficulties to any attempt to rethink education in terms of the student.

Research is regarded as more prestigious than instruction. Instruction is preferred to learning as a topic of discussion, and evaluation is largely ignored. Educational objectives are discussed at length, but educational experiences are planned according to departmental organizations and faculty interests, and have little relevance to stated objectives. The formal curriculum of courses is distinguished from the educational environment though the latter, composed of residence halls, student activities, culture programs, and bull sessions, may have a more profound influence on attitudes and values. Student personnel administrators, counselors, and residence hall personnel are allotted the responsibility of recognizing that students are human beings with human problems. These workers are distinct from and, at best, tolerated by the academic faculty, who regard them as either baby-sitters or policemen and feel they constitute a needless drain on institutional resources. On the other hand, the student personnel workers feel their job is to alleviate the tensions and right the injustices caused by irrational and unfeeling actions of faculty and academic deans.

Great efforts are made to preserve the distinction between undergraduate and graduate instruction. Faculty members feel graduate instruction is more demanding and more prestigious. This dichotomy is maintained even though outstanding undergraduates in honors work and independent study often do graduate level work, and even though the work of many first year graduate students is often at the undergraduate level.

The practical is differentiated from the theoretical without any apparent realization that good practice is based on theory and that no theory is significant unless it has some practical implications. The liberal is viewed as essentially different from the vocational, even when the liberal arts and science departments are the most specialized and most vocationally-oriented units in the university.

These compartments and conflicts result from diverse conditions, philosophies and traditions. They also result from a struggle for power and status. Dichotomies, such as the liberal-vocational, seem to be maintained because of the need of certain groups to assign a position of low prestige to other groups. Attempts at curriculum reform which begin with such distinctions are destined to evoke endless discussion and argument, and result in compromises which preserve rather than resolve the distinctions.

Because of the entrenched strength of units and individuals who are concerned with maintaining the *status quo*, much curriculum revision consists of one or two gimmicks rather than a thorough re-evaluation of the existing program. The gimmick approach, whether the device is a new system of grading, independent study, freshman seminars, off-campus experience, or an interim term, too often adds to a program without revising either departmental offerings or faculty attitudes. Such additions to an already compartmentalized and often chaotic program may arouse some temporary enthusiasm and interest. However, unless they are related to other aspects of the program, the additions will lead to greater disunity.

Eloquent statements of rationale indicate a more thorough analysis of the total program, but even these too often provide only a broad framework within which faculty members may do as they please. Thus, the rationale may only delude the public, the administration, and the faculty into believing that something new and different is being offered.

The emperor's new clothes are but the illusion of men too timid to face reality and too traditional to be imaginative.

These difficulties impede widespread curricular reform and the general acceptance of any one structure or pattern for thinking about curricular change. However, certain things are clear. No approach to curriculum revision which eliminates the department or the disciplinary orientation can succeed except in small institutions. Even small colleges which have attempted this approach face continuing pressures to recognize some departmental unit both in organization and in curriculum. Any approach which attempts to eliminate the course as the basis of the curriculum structure also will have only a limited appeal. Finally, undergraduate education cannot be revitalized and unified without the enthusiastic participation of a significant segment of the faculty. These assumptions do not represent an acceptance of the *status quo*; they are logical conclusions based upon the preceding chapters and upon extensive observation and evidence.

One suggested solution is to develop a statement of competencies required of all graduates of the college. These competencies, defined in meaningful and attainable terms, directly imply relevant educational experiences accompanied by continuing evaluation of the student's progress toward specific goals.

Although the departmental and disciplinary organization is both inevitable and desirable, it is inadequate to achieve the seven competencies outlined in the previous chapter. Traditional distinctions between breadth and depth and between vocational and liberal education are not consistent with contemporary needs. Instead of a composite of departmental major and distribution requirements, a plan has been proposed which recommends sustained contact with two or more disciplines, combined theoretical and practical experiences, team experiences in learning, and confrontation with a different culture. The possibility of organizing a program of required experiences for all students has been rejected as both impossible and undesirable. The seven compentencies are to be attained by all students, but students differing in backgrounds and interests will attain them in different ways. Advisers or tutors, who are familiar with several disciplines and who are committed to the development and success of students, are essential in such a program. Within the framework of the required competencies and essential experiences, each student can plan his program and evaluate his progress with his adviser. By becoming a responsible participant in the planning of his own program, the student will realize the relevance of his experiences to each other and to his long-term goals. Faculty members who are helping students plan a sequential, cumulative, unified program based on competency attainment will realize that the undergraduate student is more than a possible recruit for a vocation or for graduate school. Yet, the approach is sufficiently flexible that all specialties now offered in undergraduate education can be adapted to it.

McGrath is right in arguing that the decline of liberal undergraduate education is related to the increasing influence of graduate education. A new graduate degree or revised Ph.D. which concentrates on preparation for undergraduate teaching is essential if the present trend toward hallowing research and graduate instruction is to be checked. A large percentage of the faculty in most colleges and universities will continue to participate in undergraduate instruction. Those faculty members who wish to devote themselves to improving undergraduate instruction should not be deterred by demands for research and publication. Continuing scholarship is essential, but required research is as irrelevant as it is likely to be inconsequential. If faculty members concerned with undergraduate instruction are second-class citizens, the fault lies only with the values of those who so label them.

The demands of curriculum study, undergraduate course revision, and instructional planning require more time than is ordinarily allotted. If the broader conception of undergraduate education as defined by the seven competencies is accepted, then the undergraduate faculty must be given time to fulfill its special responsibilities in curriculum planning, instruction, supervision of off-campus activities, and advising with students. The faculty also must be given time to explore relationships among the disciplines and to broaden its own knowledge and experience. If the seven competencies are to be demanded of students, the faculty must demonstrate that it too, has attained these competencies.

The role of the faculty member in undergraduate education is essential and irreplaceable, although it can be supported and enhanced by educational technology. Unfortunately, this role has been neither sought nor rewarded in recent years, and there is no reason to be optimistic about the future. Nonetheless, this volume maintains that undergraduate education can be improved and encourages rethinking of the undergraduate curriculum by

(a) outlining a more appropriate systematic approach to study of the curriculum;
(b) presenting a flexible model which negates many of the traditional conflicts, dichotomies, and contradictions, and allows undergraduate education to be regarded as a single entity

rather than a number of parallel programs related only by the common requirement of English composition and physical education, and by the ultimate award of some form of a baccalaureate degree;

(c) reasserting the importance and the possibility of an undergraduate experience which is sequential, cumulative, coherent, and which possesses a unity apparent to the student and the teacher;

(d) and by maintaining that, if the importance of undergraduate education is to be recognized and supported, faculty must be recruited, educated, supported, and rewarded for meritorious performance in undergraduate assignments.